Brickwork

A Practical Approach Level 2

Dr Joseph Durkin

Nelson Thornes
a Wolters Kluwer business

Published in 2005 by:
Nelson Thornes Ltd
Delta Place
27 Bath Road
CHELTENHAM
GL53 7TH
United Kingdom

06 07 08 09 / 10 9 8 7 6 5 4 3 2

A catalogue record for this book is available from the British Library

ISBN 0 7487 9258 9

Illustrations by Peters and Zabransky
Page make-up by Florence Production Ltd, Stoodleigh, Devon

Printed and bound in Slovenia by Delo tiskarna by arrangement with
Korotan Ljubljana

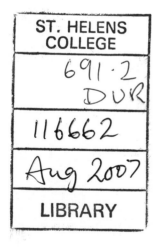

Contents

Introduction

This book has been written with the objective of assisting those students who, having gained the Level 1 National Vocational Qualification in brickwork are now studying to obtain the Level 2 certificate, or those coming straight in at Level 2. The contents are based on the new Magenta Scheme syllabus in brickwork, and should prove useful to both students and tutors alike.

Having felt the need of such a publication in my own apprenticeship days, I hope that this book will do much to help and guide all those who wish to study and maintain the genuine craft of brickwork.

Work-based Evidence

Each chapter will from time to time give you instructions on what type of evidence to gather from work. Remember, that if you are undertaking NVQ training, it is your responsibility to collect and record evidence of the tasks carried out in the workplace, then to map and record it against the syllabus.

Quick Quiz

There will usually be a Quick Quiz after each section. The quizzes are designed to test your knowledge of the work recently undertaken. They can be attempted at any time after reading the relevant section. If you do not do well first time, try again later.

Try This Out

Try This Out activities will be of a more demanding nature than the quick quizzes and are designed to assist students who have achieved Level 1, and are preparing for exams at Level 2. The contents of the questions and tasks are based on examinations of recent years and should prove useful for revision purposes.

Note: Some of the tasks are to test practical ability and need to be carried out in a workshop or on site. It would be useful therefore if you liaise with your tutor about these.

Qualification Structure

The NVQ qualification structure for Trowel Occupations (Construction) Level 2 (Magenta Scheme) is as follows.

Mandatory units

Unit No. VR 01	Conform to General Workplace Safety
Unit No. VR 02	Conform to Efficient Work Practices
Unit No. VR 03	Move and Handle Resources
Unit No. VR 40	Erect Masonry Structures
Unit No. VR 41	Set Out Masonry Structures

Plus
Optional Units (any one unit from the following)

Unit No. VR 42	Erect Masonry Cladding
Unit No. VR 43	Lay Domestic Drainage
Unit No. VR 44	Erect Thin Joint Masonry Structures
Unit No. VR 45	Place and Finish Non-Specialist Concrete
Unit No. VR 46	Plaster and Render Surfaces
Unit No. VR 47	Maintain Slate and Tile Roofing

Note. This book only covers the mandatory units.

National Vocational Qualifications

Construction National Vocational Qualifications (NVQs) are qualifications designed to reflect accurately what is expected of people working in the construction industry. An NVQ reflects a typical kind of job, in your case bricklaying. Therefore, the best place to be assessed to see whether you have reached the standard required for an NVQ, is at work. Only at work can it be seen that you carry out your job competently – to the national standard.

NVQs are not like traditional courses of study, where you sit an exam paper and never meet the examiner. With an NVQ the learner or candidate has responsibility for proving they have the necessary skills and competence to carry out the work expected of them.

Awarding Bodies

CITB-ConstructionSkills, formerly the Construction Industry Training Board and City & Guilds are the joint awarding body for the construction industry. CITB-ConstructionSkills is responsible for the setting of standards for the craft and operative routes into gaining an NVQ. In order to do this effectively it works closely with representatives from the industry to ensure that the NVQ reflects the needs of the workplace and the requirement for training a competent, numerate and literate workforce.

What makes up an NVQ?

An NVQ is made up of a number of individual units of competence; the number of units depends on the breadth of the occupation. To make units easier to assess, they are divided into elements.

Unit Title

This relates back to outcomes contained within the Functional Map of the Industry, but expressed in industry language.

Performance Criteria

These define the acceptable level of performance required for employment, expressed in outcome terms.

Scope of Performance

This details the evidence necessary to meet the requirements of each performance criterion, this is usually work based; simulation is only allowed where indicated in the standards.

Knowledge and Understanding

This links in 'generic terms' the knowledge and understanding requirement directly to the performance criteria.

Scope of Knowledge and Understanding

This takes key words contained in the knowledge and understanding (identified in bold type) and expands them to cover the scope of knowledge required by industry for competence in the workplace.

The NVQ Process

A number of people work closely together in order to see that the NVQ process works effectively. They are:

- Candidates
- Assessors
- Work-based recorders
- Internal verifiers
- External verifiers

Key Terms

Assessor – Person appointed to carry out judgement of a candidates evidence of competence.

Candidate – The person undertaking an NVQ.

Competence – The proven ability to work to the national standard for brickwork.

Evidence – Proof of competence.

Knowledge and Understanding – Links in 'generic terms' the knowledge and understanding to the performance criteria.

Level – Degree of difficulty.

National Vocational Qualification (NVQ) – Competence based qualification focused on the workplace.

Performance Criteria – Define the acceptable level of performance required for employment expressed in outcome terms.

Scope of Knowledge and Understanding – Expands key words contained in the knowledge and understanding to cover the scope of knowledge required for competence in the workplace.

Scope of Performance – Details the evidence needed to meet the requirements of each performance criterion, it is usually work based, unless indicated in the standards.

Standards – The entire collection of units and elements developed for an NVQ in brickwork.

Transferable – May be applied in circumstances additional to those in which assessed.

Unit Title – Relates to outcomes contained within the Functional Map of the Industry, expressed in industry language.

Essential Skills

It is important to make the distinction between essential skills and basic skills. The term essential skills is used to define those generic skills which individuals need in order to be effective members of a flexible, adaptive and competitive workforce and for lifelong learning. Basic skills can be defined as the ability to read and write and speak English and use mathematics at a level necessary to function and work in society and in general.

Essential skills build on basic skills in two ways. They embrace a wider range of predominantly, work-related skills. They require the application of these skills in a wider range of contexts plus the ability to transfer skills learnt in one environment to a completely different one. It is for these reasons that such emphasis has been placed on ensuring that there are essential skills tasks in the syllabus.

Work-based Evidence

The main source of evidence needed by a candidate is work-based and confirms that practical skills meet the appropriate performance criteria and range statements. Work-based evidence covers the carrying out of naturally occurring activities – with all the attendant relationships, constraints, time and other pressures, within the total working environment of a construction company.

Work-based evidence is of activities frequently carried out. Where the evidence is considered insufficient in quality or quantity by an assessor the candidate can be asked to demonstrate competence by means of simulated activities. Activities that are infrequently carried out in the workplace can also be simulated to provide evidence of a candidate's skill.

Without evidence from the workplace, a candidate will be unable to obtain a NVQ. The NVQ demands that candidates prove they can carry out tasks in a real work environment.

Gathering Evidence

Work-based evidence as has already been stated, is an extremely important part of an NVQ course. You are required to provide this evidence in order to gain an NVQ. If you think that you will be unable to gather any part of the work-based evidence required, it is important that you speak to your course tutor at the first possible opportunity. Your tutor will then speak to your employer in order to resolve the problem.

Suitable Evidence

A time sheet would provide evidence for most of the units in this NVQ, provided it was presented in the correct manner. For the time sheet to count as evidence it would need to be signed by yourself and countersigned by your work-based recorder. He could substantiate it further, by noting on the time sheet any relevant conversations that you have had, such as seeking advice or help from another member of the site team.

Photographs are also an important form of evidence. The main good practice principles are:
1 Candidate's should ideally be in the photograph for identification.
2 Photographs should:
    (a) be accompanied by a brief description of work activity
    (b) include the job/site address and the date of the work carried out
    (c) be signed by the candidate and work-based recorder or site foreman
    (d) be referenced by the assessor/candidate to the occupational unit/s performance criteria.

Photographic evidence as used above can be strong and credible supporting evidence, but observation by an assessor of some aspects of a candidates work performance is still required to be sure of competence.

Remember VACS!

Valid – Is the work/evidence relevant to the NVQ unit content?

Authentic – Can you be sure the work shown in the photograph is the candidate's?

Current – How old is the evidence and is it still relevant?

Sufficient – Is it sufficient on its own, or is some other evidence required?

Therefore, photographic evidence must meet the VACS rule as explained above.

Copies of drawings, specifications or job sheets that you have used during the dates on the timesheet can also be cross-referenced in order to provide evidence.

Besides the evidence already mentioned, other items can also be used, such as holiday forms, employment contracts, delivery notes, invoices, receipts, requisitions, company procedures or policies, for such things as health and safety, training procedures, acceptable behaviour and so on.

Note: Always get permission to take away any paperwork from site, as certain documents are confidential.

Witness Testimonies

Witness testimonies are an essential part of your work-based evidence. They can take several forms, from a simple statement confirming that you have undertaken all the work in your portfolio, to complex descriptions of work that you have carried out on site. Witness testimonies should be written by a person in a responsible position, examples of these are:

- Work-based recorder
- Skilled tradesperson
- Manager or supervisor
- Your employer
- The client.

Witness testimonies should be signed and dated by any of the above, with the relevant contact details such as address and telephone number, whenever possible, it should be on letter headed paper, it should also include the position of the person writing the testimony.

Witness Testimony Example

To whom it may concern

I would like to confirm that between the 1st September 2004 and the 20th October 2004 Ravi Singh was employed by Chorlton Building Contractors on a short term contract as a bricklayer. During this time he completed several jobs for us, I have signed and dated any relevant photographs of his work, along with copies of the original documentation that he was given (drawings, specifications, job sheets and so on) I have also signed and dated these.

During his time with us, Ravi was always punctual, his work-station was always kept tidy, and he followed company policies in all areas, including health and safety. The work that he carried out for us was to a high standard and was competed in the allocated time span. We would have no problem in employing Ravi again in the future.

Yours faithfully
Darren Howells (site supervisor)

As you can see in the example, the person writing the witness testimony has not put a detailed description of the work carried out, this is not necessary in this particular case, as the photographs and the other documentation provides a very clear picture of the work that Ravi has carried out. The important point is that the documentation has all been authenticated by the site supervisor.

The Role of the Candidate

The role of the candidate in studying for an NVQ in brickwork is as follows:

Agree an assessment plan with your assessor, ensuring that you have the following:

- Details of the relevant NVQ
- Understand what units you are to be assessed on
- Understand what type of evidence you need to produce
- Agree on how the units are going to be assessed
- Agree on the review process.

Carry out the following:

- Ensure that all the work-based evidence that you produce is recorded and mapped in a form agreed with your assessor.
- Ensure that you work closely with the work-based recorder if different from the assessor to decide if you are collecting and recording the correct evidence.
- Gather as much supplementary supporting evidence as possible.
- Always obtain signatures and dates from the work-based recorder to authenticate your evidence.

■ Present your work-based evidence to your assessor for guidance and answer any job knowledge questions asked or set by the assessor.

Supplementary Evidence

Supplementary evidence can be any of the following:

■ Photographs of the task and possibly you carrying it out

■ Site drawing you might be using

■ Time sheets and day worksheets

■ Details of the jobs worked on

■ A video of you carrying out various tasks

■ Witness testimony sheets signed and dated by your supervisor, client architect site manager and so on

■ Your contract of employment and job description

■ Reports from colleges or training providers

■ Details of your experience to date in the form of a c.v.

Work-based Recorders

Work-based recorders have the role of:

■ Observing you and the work you carry out at the workplace

■ Ensure that you carry out all work in a safe manner and that the tasks meet the industrial standard required

■ Authenticating your work-based evidence by signing and dating it as necessary

■ Meet with the assessor as required to monitor your performance

■ Ensures, whenever possible, that you are being given every opportunity to gain the relevant work experience

■ Provide support and guidance to you on the gathering and recording of evidence.

The Assessment Process

The joint awarding body CITB and City & Guilds approves organizations to carry out assessment of candidates or learners for the granting of NVQs. Usually these organizations are:

■ Further education colleges

■ Private training centres

■ Construction companies.

Once approval has been granted they are known as assessment organizations. These organizations employ staff to carry out assessment and verification. These people are known as assessors and internal verifiers.

Assessors

Assessors are occupationally competent in that they will have been a bricklayer and are qualified in the assessment process. They are responsible for deciding whether you are competent in the tasks which you are set.

Internal Verifiers

Internal verifiers are people responsible for ensuring that the quality of the assessment carried out by the assessor is to an acceptable standard. They fulfil the same role as quality control in your own organization.

The joint awarding body for Construction of CITB and City & Guilds employs a number of people to monitor the whole assessment process and to ensure that all aspects of it are carried out correctly. These people are known as external verifiers.

External Verifiers

External verifiers are there to ensure that all assessment centres are working to the standards set by the awarding bodies.

The Assessment Process and Work-based Recorders

How does the work-based recorder fit into this process? It should be understood that work-based recorders cannot carry out assessment themselves only an accredited assessor can do that. However, they are the important link between the assessor and the candidate. Usually they are given the task by their employer in order to authenticate the evidence that a candidate is gathering from the workplace and to ensure that it is valid and to the standard and quality required. Assessors and work-based recorders are usually known to each other and will be confident of each other's ability to decide whether a candidate is competent in the work he/she is set.

The Assessor's Role

It is for the assessor to:

- Direct and advise a candidate on the correct NVQ for him/her usually in agreement with the employer.
- Carry out an assessment plan for the candidate.
- Observe the candidate on a regular basis at the workplace to ensure he/she is carrying out a full range of necessary activities to create an evidence portfolio.

- Carry out regular reviews with the candidate relating to the assessment plan and adjust it if required.
- Decide on whether the candidate has the necessary knowledge and understanding required to complete an NVQ programme of study. It should be understood that candidates can take internal exams and tests either orally or in written form.
- Make a decision on all the evidence that the candidate provides to support their claim of competence.

Role of the Company

The majority of companies unless they have their own training division will use an assessment organization, for example a college of further education. In this case the assessor will visit the company usually on an eight-week cycle to see the candidate. In this situation, the work-based recorder carries out the majority of the observations of the candidate and confirms to the assessor whether he/she has carried out the work to the industrial standard.

Source: CITB-ConstructionSkills.

Acknowledgements

Many thanks to all those involved with the production, editing and publication of this book, particular thanks to my Commissioning Editor Carolyn Lee and the Nelson Thornes Team, Jess Ward, Eve Thould and Chris Wortley. Steve Tush for the photos of students involved in work-based evidence. All the brickwork team at Hopwood Hall College, Darren Whatmough, Paul Howell, Frank Watson and Phil Chadwick. Special thanks as always to my daughter Katie for filing and organising, but most of all to my wife Caroline for all her support and positive affirmation of my work.

The authors and publishers gratefully acknowledge the owners of any copyright material reproduced herein. Material reproduced from HSE on pages 4, 5, 36 and 98 and other quotes are © Crown copyright.

Thank you to the Brick Development Association for kindly allowing us to use selected material from their publications. For more information about the BDA visit their website www.brick.org.uk

Every effort has been made to reach the copyright holders, but the publisher would be grateful to hear from any source whose copyright they have unwittingly infringed.

1

Chapter One

Conform to General Workplace Safety

NVQ Level 2   Unit No. VR 01   Conform to General Workplace Safety

This unit, in the context of brickwork and the construction industry work environment, is about:

- **Awareness of relevant current statutory requirements and official guidance**
- **Personal responsibilities relating to workplace safety, wearing appropriate personal protective equipment (PPE) and compliance with warning and safety signs**
- **Personal behaviour in the workplace**
- **Security in the workplace.**

There are seven sections in this chapter, emergency procedures, fire extinguishers, hazards, notices, personal protective equipment, reporting and security.

This chapter will now cover methods that conform to general workplace safety.

Emergency procedures   1.1

In this section you will learn about emergency procedures in accordance with organizational requirements.

When you have completed this section you will be able to:

- Comply with all emergency procedures in accordance with organizational policy.

Know and understand:

- What the organizational emergency procedures are
- Accidents and emergencies associated with the type of work being undertaken and the work environment.

This section will now cover emergency procedures in accordance with organizational requirements.

Emergencies

Emergencies require immediate action. Some examples of emergencies are fire, uncontained spillage or leakage of chemicals or other hazardous substances, scaffold failure, bodily damage and health problems.

Procedures

If an evacuation alarm sounds, it must be assumed that it is a genuine alarm, unless prior notice of a test of the system has been given. In the event of an alarm sounding, all personnel should be aware of:

■ The location of the assembly point at which to report

■ The name of the person to whom they report

■ The procedure to be followed after reporting at the assembly point.

Under no circumstances should you re-enter the site or work area until authorized to by the emergency services or your supervisor.

Roles and Responsibilities of Personnel

The operatives role in dealing with incidents and emergencies is limited to:

■ Recognizing and reporting details of the incident or emergency to the person in charge

■ Following all evacuation procedures as instructed

■ Obtaining help from trained staff in situations requiring first-aid

■ Recording details of accidents in the accident book.

Common Types of Accident and Emergency

In the European Union construction is the sector most at risk from accidents, with more than 1300 people being killed in construction accidents every year.

> Figures for the UK record 71 fatalities in the year 2002/3.
> A breakdown of the 71 fatal injuries that occurred indicates that falls from height remain the biggest cause of death (47%), followed by struck by an object other than a vehicle (15%), electricity (10%), transport (7%), collapse (7%) and other kinds (10%).
>
> Source: HSE.

Risks and Procedures

Common accident risks are:

■ Slipping on uneven, slippery surfaces

■ Trapping limbs

■ Injuries caused by falling objects

■ Inhalation of toxic fumes

■ Burns/skin problems from chemical substances

■ Electrical faults

■ Strains from faulty lifting.

The law requires employers to provide:

- Adequate first-aid equipment and facilities
- A trained and qualified person to give first aid (dependent on the size of the workforce).

The role of site personnel at the scene of an accident/emergency is to:

- Ensure that own safety is not at risk
- Remove the hazard if safe to do so
- Call for help, for example, a first-aider
- Call for an ambulance if necessary.

While awaiting the arrival of the first-aider or ambulance the operative should:

- Not move the casualty, unless in immediate danger
- Not give food or drink to the casualty
- Not allow the casualty to smoke
- Remain with the casualty and give reassurance
- Make the casualty as comfortable as possible
- Keep the casualty warm.

Reporting Accidents and Near Misses

All accidents and near misses must be reported by site personnel to their supervisor and recorded. It is a legal requirement for details of an accident to be recorded in an Accident Book, which must be kept on each construction site for that purpose.

Accident Book

There is no set place to keep an Accident Book. However, it needs to be readily available to all site personnel. It is an employer's duty to inform all site personnel where the Accident Book is kept, usually by displaying the location on a site notice board. The company safety policy may also say where it is kept.

A site operative who has sustained an injury or taken part in dealing with an accident involving other people must enter relevant details in the Accident Book. These details will include:

- The date and time of the accident
- Where the accident took place and how it happened
- The cause of the accident
- The method of treating the accident
- Other people involved
- Own signature and date of entry.

The Health and Safety Executive will also need to be informed if a major injury or dangerous occurrence takes place, or if the employee is off work for more than three days – see Figure. 1.1.

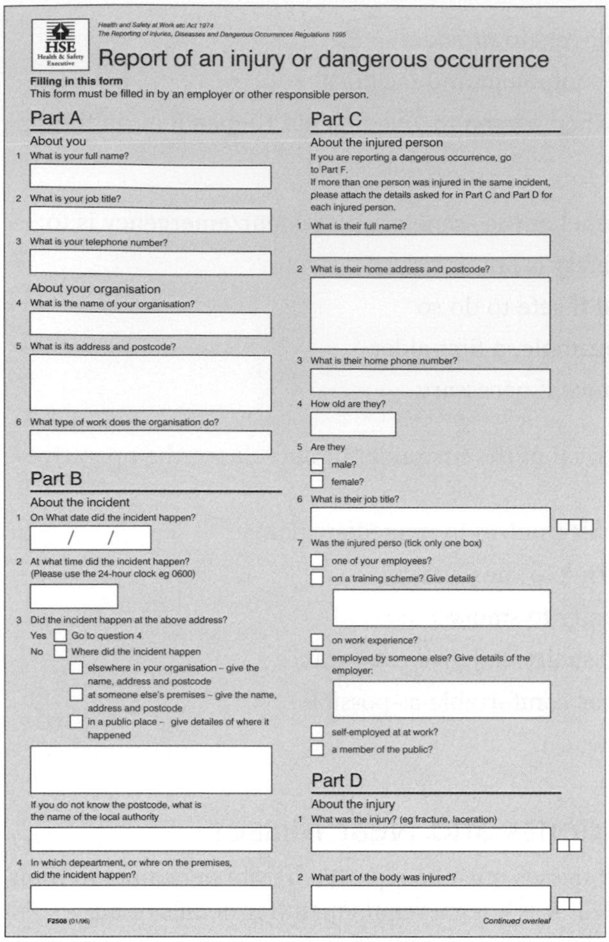

Health and Safety at Work etc Act 1974
The Reporting of Injuries, Diseases and Dangerous Occurrences Regulations 1995

HSE Health & Safety Executive

Report of an injury or dangerous occurrence

Filling in this form
This form must be filled in by an employer or other responsible person.

Part A

About you

1 What is your full name?

2 What is your job title?

3 What is your telephone number?

About your organisation

4 What is the name of your organisation?

5 What is its address and postcode?

6 What type of work does the organisation do?

Part B

About the incident

1 On What date did the incident happen?
/ /

2 At what time did the incident happen?
(Please use the 24-hour clock eg 0600)

3 Did the incident happen at the above address?
Yes ☐ Go to question 4
No ☐ Where did the incident happen
☐ elsewhere in your organisation – give the name, address and postcode
☐ at someone else's premises – give the name, address and postcode
☐ in a public place – give detailes of where it happened

If you do not know the postcode, what is the name of the local authority

4 In which depeartment, or whre on the premises, did the incident happen?

Part C

About the injured person

If you are reporting a dangerous occurrence, go to Part F.
If more than one person was injured in the same incident, please attach the details asked for in Part C and Part D for each injured person.

1 What is their full name?

2 What is their home address and postcode?

3 What is their home phone number?

4 How old are they?

5 Are they
☐ male?
☐ female?

6 What is their job title?

7 Was the injured perso (tick only one box)
☐ one of your employees?
☐ on a training scheme? Give details
☐ on work experience?
☐ employed by someone else? Give details of the employer:
☐ self-employed at at work?
☐ a member of the public?

Part D

About the injury

1 What was the injury? (eg fracture, laceration)

2 What part of the body was injured?

F2508 (01/96) Continued overleaf

Fig 1.1 **Official HSE report form**
Source: HSE

Note: The Health and Safety Executive introduced a new accident record book in May 2003. The new publication ensures companies comply with legal requirements to record accidents at work, and it has been revised to take into account the requirements of the Data Protection Act 1998.

Emergency Procedures

A common emergency on construction sites is fire, described below are the procedures for dealing with such an occurrence.

If you discover a fire:

- Raise the alarm and then call the Fire Brigade
- Close doors and windows to prevent the spread of fire
- Evacuate the building or area where you are working
- Fight the fire, if you have been trained to do so, but avoid endangering life
- Fight the fire with an appropriate fire extinguisher, fire blankets, water or sand, but do not put yourself at risk.

In order to save lives and reduce the risk of injury occurring, all site personnel must be informed of the current safety and emergency procedures. All site personnel must be aware of what to do in the event of a fire or accident.

Fig 1.1 continued

3 Was the injury (tick the one box that applies)
- [ ] a fatality?
- [ ] a major injury or condition? (see accompanying notes)
- [ ] an injury to an employee or self-employed person which prevented them doing their normal work for more than 3 days?
- [ ] an injury to a member of the public which meant they had to be taken from the scene of the accident to a hospital for treatment?

4 Did the injured person (tick all the boxes that apply)
- [ ] become unconscious?
- [ ] need resuscitation?
- [ ] remain in hospital for more than 24 hours?
- [ ] none of the above.

Part E

About the kind of accident
Please tick the one box that best describes what happened, then go to Part G.

- [ ] Contact with moving machinery or material being machined
- [ ] Hit by a moving, flying or falling object
- [ ] Hit by a moving vehicle
- [ ] Hit something fixed or stationary

- [ ] Injured while handling, lifting or carrying
- [ ] Slipped, tripped or fell on the same level
- [ ] Fell from a height
  How high was the fall?
  [ ] metres
- [ ] Trapped by something collapsing

- [ ] Drowned or asphyxiated
- [ ] Exposed to, or in contact with, a harmful substance
- [ ] Exposed to fire
- [ ] Exposed to an explosion

- [ ] Contact with electricity or an electrical discharge
- [ ] Injured by an animal
- [ ] Physically assaulted by a person

- [ ] Another kind of accident (describe it in Part G)

Part F

Dangerous occurrences
Enter the number of the dangerous occurrence you are reporting. (The numbers are given in the Regulations and in the notes which accompany this form.)

Part C

Describing what happened
Give as much detail as you can. For instance
- the name of any substance involved
- the name and type of any machine involved
- the events that led to the incident
- the part played by any people.

If it was a personal injury, give details of what the person was doing. Describe any action that has since been taken to prevent a similar incident. Use a separate piece of paper if you need to.

Part H

Your signature
Signature

Date
[/ /]

Where to send the form
Please send it to the Enforcing Authority the place where it happened. If you do not know the Enforcing Authority, send it to the nearest HSE office.

For official use
Client number   Location number   Event number

[ ] INV REP [ ] Y [ ] N

What Fires Need

In order for a fire to start the following must be present:

Fuel – This can be anything that will burn, for example wood, furniture, flammable liquid, gas and so on.

Oxygen – Or air in normal circumstances will allow a fire to burn.

Heat – A minimum temperature is required but a naked flame, match or spark is enough to start a fire especially if in contact with something flammable.

Prevention of Fires

Some actions that can be taken to prevent the risk of fire occurring are listed below:

- Not smoking at work
- Maintaining all electrical appliances in a safe manner
- Removing combustible materials to a safe place
- Storing flammable materials in metal cupboards
- Putting up signs and notices so personnel know what to do
- Training all personnel in health and safety.

Source: Department for Education and Skills.

Management Systems

The Health and Safety Executive recommend that a good management system will help you to identify problem areas, decide what to do, act on decisions made and check that the steps taken have been effective. A good system should involve:

Planning – Identify key areas of risk and set goals for improvement. Carefully select equipment and work practices that prevent or contain hazards. This helps to remove or minimize risks.

Organization – Workers need to be involved and committed to reducing risks. Give people responsibilities to ensure areas of the workplace are kept safe. Keep a record of who is responsible for which arrangements. Make these details clear to everyone.

Control – Check to ensure that working practices and processes are being carried out properly. Keep a record of cleaning, maintenance work and so on and encourage good health and safety.

Monitor and review – re-examine your approach in the light of experience. Look at accident investigation reports. Do they show any improvement? Talk to any safety representatives about hazards.

Source: HSE

TRY THIS OUT

- Prepare a list of at least eight common types of accident or health emergency that could be encountered on a building site or in the workplace.
- Describe three things you should do in carrying out your role and responsibilities in dealing with incidents or emergencies.
- Get your tutor to check if your work is accurate and fulfils the requirements of the task.

Quick quiz Quick quiz Quick quiz Quick quiz Quick quiz

❶ Give the three elements that are required to start a fire.
❷ Name three specific types of emergency.
❸ Name three common accident risks.
❹ What is an Accident Book used for?
❺ What are the procedures to follow if you discover a fire?

Fire Extinguishers   1.2

In this section you will learn about the following types of fire extinguishers, water, carbon dioxide, foam, powder, vaporizing liquid and their uses.

When you have completed this section you will be able to:

- Comply with all workplace safety legislation requirements at all times.

Know and understand:

- What types of fire extinguishers are available and how they are used.

This section will now cover fire extinguishers.

Fire Extinguishers

There are five different types of fire extinguisher for use in the fighting of fires. You will need to learn to choose the correct one. Each type of fire extinguisher is designed to put out fires that are caused by specific circumstances. It can be extremely dangerous to use the wrong type of extinguisher.

The standard colour for fire extinguishers is red, with the contents indicated by a contrasting colour band or panel on the extinguisher. There are also pictograms showing what type of fire it can be used on.

Colour Codes for Fire Extinguishers

Type of extinguisher – Water
  Colour code – Red
  For use on – Solid fuels, e.g. wood, paper and textiles
  Do not use on – Flammable liquids or live electric equipment
  (see Figure 1.2)

Type of extinguisher – Foam
  Colour Code – Cream
  For use on – Wood, paper, textiles and flammable liquids
  Do not use on – Live electrical equipment (see Figure 1.2).

Type of extinguisher – Dry powder
  Colour Code – Blue
  For use on – Wood, paper and textiles, flammable liquids, gaseous fires and live electrical equipment (see Figure 1.2).

Type of extinguisher – Carbon dioxide
  Colour Code – Black
  For use on – Flammable liquids and live electrical equipment. Do not use this type of extinguisher in a confined space (see Figure 1.2).

Type of extinguisher – Halon
  Colour Code – Green
  For use on – Flammable and liquefied gases and electrical hazards.
  Note: Halon extinguishers are being phased out for environmental reasons.

Fire Blankets

In addition to the various types of fire extinguisher, there are fire blankets. These, as their name implies, are fireproof blankets which, when laid on a fire, cut off the oxygen supply and prevent further burning of the substance. They can be used on all types of fires.

Using a Fire Extinguisher

Every fire extinguisher has brief instructions on how it should be used. The method of use varies across the range of types and makes of extinguisher.

Fire extinguishers, apart from fire blankets, are pressurized so that by operating a trigger, the contents will be forced out of the extinguisher, at

Fig 1.2 **Know your fire extinguisher colour codes**

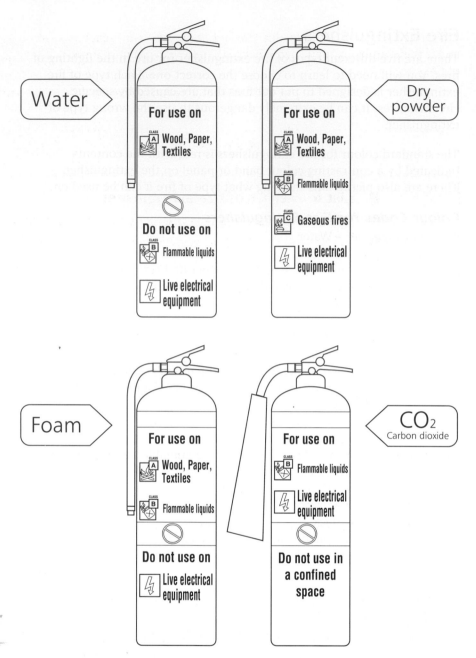

TRY THIS OUT

- Locate fire extinguishers on the college premises and prepare a chart, using information technology, i.e. a computer, if it is available, of the types of fire extinguishers found and where each was located. For example: three in the brick workshop, two in the main corridor and so on.

- Get your tutor to check your findings to see if they are accurate.

high speed, towards the source of the fire. The contents and pressure of the extinguisher should be checked regularly and each extinguisher should have a label certifying that it has been inspected and meets the requirements.

The jet from a fire extinguisher should only be directed at the centre of the fire because of the pressure at which the contents are ejected. The pressure could cause burning debris to spread and create a wider hazard. Instead, the jet should be aimed around and over the fire, gradually containing it to the point where it is extinguished totally.

Fire extinguishers should only be used when it is safe to do so and the user is properly trained. Smoke and toxic fumes are as dangerous as the fire itself and, in general, the fighting of fires is best left to the fire service. Small fires can be dealt with if there are clear escape routes and if they can be extinguished quickly, thereby preventing the spread of fire.

Source: Department for Education and Skills.

Quick quiz Quick quiz Quick quiz Quick quiz Quick quiz

❶ List four types of fire extinguisher.
❷ What is the standard colour code for a fire extinguisher?
❸ What are the colour codes for the contents of a fire extinguisher?
❹ What type of fire extinguisher is being phased out, and why?
❺ How many different types of fire extinguisher are there for use in the fighting of fires

Hazards 1.3

Definition – A hazard is something with the potential to cause harm.

In this section you will learn about hazards associated with the occupational area that include:

■ Resources, workplace, environment, substances, equipment, obstructions, storage, services and work activities.

When you have completed this section you will be able to:

■ Identify hazards associated with the workplace and record and report in accordance with organizational procedure
■ Recognize potentially hazardous situations in the workshop or work area
■ Plan, organize and maintain a safe working environment for site personnel.

Know and understand:

■ The hazards associated with the occupational area.

This chapter will now cover hazards associated with the occupational area.

Hazards in the Workplace

On the majority of construction sites in the UK today, there is great emphasis on protecting construction personnel and the general public from hazards associated with the occupational area and certain types of work practice.

Fig 1.3 **Worker wearing a hard hat**

Head Protection

Falling materials or tools on building sites can cause injury to the head and other parts of the body. It is not only essential but also the law that dictates protective headgear be worn at all times by all site personnel and visitors in order to minimize this hazard (see Figure 1.3).

Noise

Excessive noise levels from site machinery can cause hearing impairment if exposed to it continually. Therefore ear defenders must be worn to protect the eardrums. Young people can be damaged as easily as the old and premature deafness is even worse. Sufferers often first start to notice hearing loss when they cannot keep up with conversations in a group, or for example, when the rest of their family complains they have the television on too loud. Deafness can make people feel isolated from their family, friends and colleagues (see Figure 1.4).

Manual Handling

Manual handling is transporting or supporting loads by hand or using bodily force. Many people hurt their back, arms, hands or feet lifting everyday loads, not just when the load is too heavy. More than a third of all over-three-day injuries reported each year to the Health and Safety Executive and to local authorities are the results of manual handling. These can result in those injured taking an average of 11 working days off each year.

Most cases of injury can be avoided by providing suitable lifting equipment that is regularly maintained, together with relevant training on both manual handling techniques and using the equipment safely.

EAR DEFENDERS
BS 6344 EN 352-2

A wide range of equipment on site can be harmful to your ears. Even if you are not using the equipment, you can still be affected when someone is using it close by.

If you have to shout to be heard then ear defenders should be worn

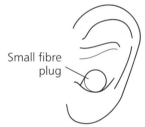

Small fibre earplugs can be used where noise is not too severe

Hands should be clean before inserting plugs and plugs should be disposed of after one use.

Where excessive noise is encountered full earmuffs should be used.

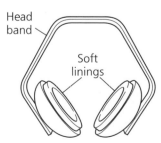

Fig 1.4 **Ear defenders**

Fig 1.5 **Bricklayer using a brick cutting saw, wearing ear muffs**

Electricity

Electricity can kill. Most deaths are caused by contact with overhead or underground power cables. Even non-fatal shocks can cause severe and permanent injury. Shocks from faulty equipment may lead to falls from ladders, scaffolds or other work platforms. Those using electricity may not be the only ones at risk. Poor electrical installations and faulty electrical appliances can lead to fires that can also result in death or injury to others.

Work Equipment

Work equipment covers an enormous range, spanning process machinery, machine tools, office machines, lifting equipment, hand tools and ladders. Important points include:

- Selecting the right equipment for the job
- Making sure equipment is safe to use and keeping it safe through regular maintenance
- Inspection and, if appropriate, thorough examination
- Training of personnel to use equipment safely and following manufacturers or suppliers' instructions.

Accidents involving work equipment happens all the time – many serious, some fatal (see Figure 1.6).

Fig 1.6 **Worker using power tools**

Workplace Transport

Every year about 70 people are killed and about 2500 seriously injured in accidents involving vehicles at the workplace. Being struck or run over by moving vehicles, falling from vehicles or vehicles over-turning, are the most common causes. Vehicles operating in the workplace include cars and vans, lift trucks, heavy goods vehicles, dumpers, specialized vehicles or plant. Often there is significantly more danger from vehicles in the workplace than on the public highway since the operating conditions are different.

Slipping and Tripping

The most common cause of injuries at work is the slip or trip. Resulting falls can be serious. They happen in all kinds of business, with sectors such as construction reporting higher than average numbers. These cost employers over £300 million a year in lost production and other costs.

Risk Assessment

The Health and Safety Executive define risk assessment as nothing more than a careful examination of what, in your work, could cause harm to people, so that you can weigh up whether you have taken enough precautions or should do more to prevent harm. The aim is to make sure that no one gets hurt or becomes ill. Accidents and ill health can ruin lives and affect business if output is lost, machinery is damaged, insurance costs increase, and so on.

Remember – You are legally required to assess the risks in the workplace.

The important things you need to decide are whether a hazard is significant, and whether you have it covered by satisfactory precautions so that the risk is small. You need to check this when you assess the risks.

Assessment of Risks

In order to assess risks in the workplace you need to follow five simple steps:

Step 1 – Look for the hazards

Step 2 – Decide who might be harmed and how

Step 3 – Evaluate the risks and decide whether the existing precautions are adequate or whether more should be done

Step 4 – Record your findings

Step 5 – Review your assessment and revise it if necessary

Anyone at work, but particularly employers, can help to reduce slip and trip hazards through good health and safety arrangements. The Health and Safety Executive recommend a five step approach to risk assessment, which is as follows:

Step 1 – Look for slip and trip hazards around the workplace, such as uneven floors, trailing cables, areas that are sometimes slippery due to spillages.

Step 2 – Decide who might be harmed and how. Who comes into the workplace? Are they at risk?

Step 3 – Consider the risks. Are the precautions already taken enough to deal with the risks?

Step 4 – Record your findings.

Step 5 – Regularly review the assessment. If any significant changes take place, make sure that precautions are still adequate to deal with the risks.

In most firms in the construction industry the hazards are many and complex. Checking them is common sense, but necessary.

Reducing Risk

There are many simple steps that can be taken to reduce risks. Here are a few examples.

Lighting – should enable people to see obstructions, potentially slippery areas and so on, so they can work safely. Replace, repair or clean lights before levels become too low for safe work.

Floors – need to be checked for loose finishes, holes and cracks. Take care in the choice of floor if it is likely to become wet or dusty due to work processes.

Obstructions – objects left lying around can easily go unnoticed and cause a trip. Try to keep work areas tidy and if obstructions cannot be removed warn people using signs or barriers.

Footwear – can play an important part in preventing slips and trips. Employers need to provide footwear if it is necessary to protect the safety of site personnel (see Table 1.1 for suggested action against hazards).

Fire Protection

Each year many people suffer burns caused by the flammable materials they work with. The wide variety of flammable substances found in the

Table 1.1 Hazards and suggested actions

Hazard	Suggested action
Spillage of wet and dry substances	Clean spills up immediately, if a liquid is greasy ensure a suitable cleaning agent is used. After cleaning the floor may be wet for some time. Use appropriate signs to tell people the floor is still wet and arrange alternative bypass routes.
Trailing cables	Position equipment to avoid cables crossing pedestrian routes, use cable covers to securely fix to surfaces, restrict access to prevent contact.
Miscellaneous rubbish, for example plastic bags	Keep areas clear, remove rubbish and do not allow to build up.
Rugs/mats	Ensure mats are securely fixed and do not have curling edges.
Slippery surfaces	Assess the cause and treat accordingly, for example treat chemically, appropriate cleaning method, etc.
Change from wet to dry floor surface	Suitable footwear, warn of risks by using signs, locate doormats where these changes are likely.
Poor lighting	Improve lighting levels and placement of light fittings to ensure more even lighting of all floor areas.
Change of level	Improve lighting, add apparent tread nosings.
Slopes	Improve visibility, provide hand rails, use floor markings.
Smoke/steam obscuring view	Eliminate or control by redirecting it away from risk areas; improve ventilation and warn of it.
Unsuitable footwear	Ensure workers choose suitable footwear, particularly with the correct type of sole. If the type of work requires special protective footwear, the employer is required by law to provide it free of charge

workplace ranges from the obvious, for example, heating fuel, petrol, paint thinners and welding gases to the less obvious, for example, packaging materials, dusts from wood, flour and sugar.

Fire protection methods should be included in the organization of any induction training or construction site safety programme. If you would like information on fire exits, alarms or extinguishers, contact your local fire authority (see Figure 1.7).

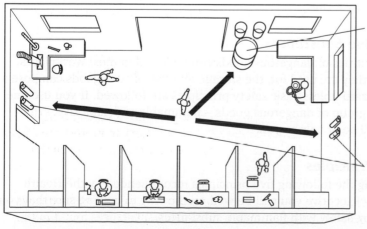

Fire barrel and buckets, easily accessible for immediate use

Fire extinguishers, suitably placed, distinctly marked and easily accessible

Fig 1.7 Example of fire protection methods

Fig 1.8 **Examples of fire fighting equipment**

Fire Protection Equipment

The most common type of fire protection equipment is the fire extinguisher. Fire extinguishers should be suitably placed, distinctly marked and be easily accessible.

Fire buckets should be painted red, marked 'Fire only' and kept full at all times. They should be clearly marked 'Fire only' and should be located at strategic points easily accessible for immediate use.

Sand is commonly used for isolating and preventing the spread of fires on floors.

Fire hoses, nozzles, connections, taps and pumps should be checked and maintained on a regular basis (see Figure 1.8 for illustrations of above).

Enclosed Workshops

All workshops that are enclosed must have ample exits and all other adjoining workshops must be separated by a fire-wall or fire doors. Fire doors and walls provide a means of containing and preventing the spread of fires (see Figure 1.9).

Hazardous Substances

Thousands of people are exposed to all kinds of hazardous substances at work. These can include chemicals that people make or work with directly, and also dust, fumes and bacteria that can be present in the workplace. Exposure can happen by breathing them in, contact with the skin, splashing them into the eyes or swallowing them. If exposure is not prevented or properly controlled, it can trigger serious illness, including cancer, asthma and dermatitis and sometimes even death.

Asbestos

Asbestos is the largest single cause of work-related fatal disease and ill health in Great Britain. Almost all asbestos-related deaths and ill health are from exposure several decades ago, but if you work with asbestos or come into contact with it during repair and maintenance work, you are at risk. You should avoid working with asbestos if possible, but if not you must do it safely. Asbestos can be found in buildings built from 1950 to 1985 in many forms.

Flammable Substances

Small quantities of dangerous goods can be found in most workplaces. Whatever they are used for, the storage and use of such goods can pose a serious hazard unless basic safety principles are followed. If you use one particular group of dangerous goods – flammable and explosive – this section will be of help to you.

Safety Principles

By applying the following five principles recommended by the Health and Safety Executive you will be well on the way to making sure that you are working safely with flammable substances.

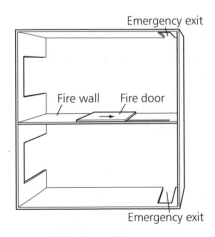

Emergency exit

Fire wall   Fire door

Emergency exit

Fig 1.9 **Example of exits**

Ventilation

Is there plenty of fresh air where flammable liquids or gases are stored and used? Good ventilation will mean that any vapours given off from a spill, leak, or released from any process, will be rapidly dispersed.

Ignition

Have all the obvious ignition sources been removed from the storage and handling areas? Ignition sources can be very varied and they include sparks from electrical equipment or welding and cutting tools, hot surfaces, open flames from heating equipment, smoking materials and so on.

Containment

Are your flammable substances kept in suitable containers? If you have a spill, will it be contained and prevented from spreading to other parts of the working area? Use of lidded containers and spillage catchment trays, for example, can help to prevent spillages spreading.

Exchange

Can you exchange a flammable substance for a less flammable one? Can you eliminate flammable substances from the process altogether? You may be able to think of other ways of carrying out the job more safely.

Separation

Are flammable substances stored and used well away from other processes and general storage areas? Can a physical barrier, wall or partition separate them? Separating your hazards in this manner will contribute to a safer workplace.

The Health and Safety Executive advise you to think about the flammable substances you have in the workplace and apply these five principles wherever possible.

Emergencies

You need to think about possible problems and make sure everyone knows what to do in an emergency. Instructing staff in emergency procedures is an important part of their job training, and should be ongoing. Examples of things to think about are:

- Make sure personnel know enough to prevent the mixing of incompatible chemicals
- Lay down the procedures to be followed if there is a leak or spill of flammable material and make sure people know and understand them
- If special first-aid facilities or equipment are required, then personnel need to be trained in their use.

REMEMBER
Keep a check on your workplace safety.

Work at Height

Falls from a height account for around 70 fatalities and 4000 major injuries every year. One of the main causes is falls from ladders. To prevent falls from height you should consider the risks to all personnel, ensure adequate training and have suitable and safe equipment for tasks, which should be properly managed and supervised. You should also ensure that sufficient protection measures, for example, suitable and sufficient personal protective equipment, are in place while personnel are working at height.

Control of Substances Hazardous to Health Regulations 2002 (COSHH)

Using chemicals or other hazardous substances at work can put people's health at risk. So the law requires employers to control exposure to hazardous substances to prevent ill health. Employers have to protect both site personnel and others who may be exposed, by complying with COSHH.

To comply with COSHH, site managers and personnel need to follow eight steps, which are:

Step One – Assess the risks to health arising from hazardous substances used in or created by workplace activities.

Step Two – Decide what precautions are needed. An employer must not carry out work which could expose site personnel to hazardous substances without first considering the risks and the necessary precautions.

Step Three – Prevent or adequately control exposure. An employer must prevent his employees from being exposed to hazardous substances. Where this is not reasonably practicable, then the hazard must be adequately controlled.

Step Four – Ensure that control measures are used and maintained properly and that safety procedures are followed.

Step Five – Monitor the exposure of site personnel to hazardous substances, if necessary.

Step Six – Carry out appropriate health surveillance where an assessment has shown this is necessary or where COSHH sets specific requirements.

Step Seven – Prepare plans and procedures to deal with accidents, incidents and emergencies involving hazardous substances where necessary.

Step Eight – Ensure all site personnel are properly informed, trained and supervised.

Hazardous Substances

Hazardous substances include:

- Substances used directly in work activities, for example, adhesives, paints, cleaning agents
- Substances generated during work activities, for example, fumes from soldering and welding
- Naturally occurring substances, for example, grain dust
- Biological agents such as bacteria and other micro-organisms.

Where are hazardous substances found? In nearly all work environments, for example:

- Factories
- Shops
- Mines
- Farms
- Construction sites.

Examples of the effects of hazardous substances include:

■ Skin irritation or dermatitis as a result of skin contact

■ Asthma as a result of developing allergies to substances used at work

■ Losing consciousness as a result of being overcome by toxic fumes

■ Cancer, which may appear long after the exposure to the chemical that caused it

■ Infection from bacteria and other micro-organisms (biological agents).

Substances Hazardous to Health

What is a substance hazardous to health under the COSHH regulations? Under COSHH there are a range of substances that are regarded as hazardous to health.

■ Substances or mixtures of substances classified as dangerous to health under the Chemicals Regulations 2002.

A warning label can identify these substances. The supplier must provide a safety data sheet for them. Many commonly used dangerous substances are listed in the Health and Safety Executives publication *Approved Supply List*. Suppliers must decide if preparations and substances that are not in the Approved Supply List are dangerous, and, if so, label them accordingly.

Substances with occupational exposure limits are listed in the HSE publication, *Occupational Exposure Limits*.

■ Biological agents (bacteria and other micro-organisms), if they are directly connected with the work, such as with farming, sewage treatment, or healthcare, or if the exposure is incidental to the work, for example, exposure to bacteria from an air-conditioning system that is not properly maintained.

■ Any kind of dust if its average concentration in the air exceeds the levels specified in COSHH.

For the vast majority of commercial chemicals, the presence (or not) of a warning label will indicate whether COSHH is relevant.

Advice and Information

If in doubt, contact your local HSE office (the address is in the phone book). The staff there can refer you to the appropriate inspector or the environmental health officer at your local authority.

First Aid

First aid arrangements will vary with the degree of risk on the site but should usually include as a minimum:

■ First aid facilities placed in a convenient location (see Figure 1.10)

■ A trained first aider, though for small sites it is sufficient to appoint a person to take charge of the first aid box and any situation where serious injury or major illnesses occurs

■ Information for site personnel about first aid arrangements, including the location of the nearest telephone.

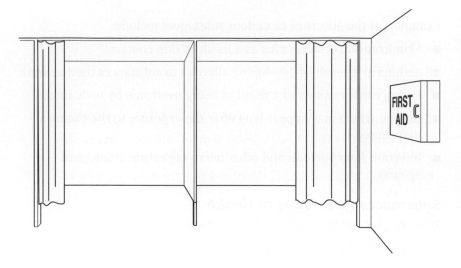

Fig 1.10 Example of a first aid box
location

Through the initial management of injury or illness suffered at work,
lives can be saved and minor injuries prevented from becoming major
ones.

The objectives of first aid are to:

■ Save life

■ Prevent the casualty's conditions from getting worse

■ Evacuate to medical help as soon as possible.

Before first aid is required:

■ Ensure you know where the first aid box is kept

■ Know who the first-aider and appointed persons are

■ If you use anything from the first aid box get it replaced

■ If you are working in a small group away from the main site you
   should have a small travelling first aid kit available

■ Always know where the nearest telephone is and understand the
   procedure for calling the emergency services.

When first aid is required

■ Call for help from someone knowledgeable, preferably the first-aider

■ Send someone to telephone for an ambulance if necessary

■ Do not move the casualty, unless in immediate danger

■ Remain with the casualty and give reassurance

■ Make the casualty as comfortable as possible

■ Do not give drinks or food to the casualty, moisten lips only

■ Do not allow the casualty to smoke.

Source: HSE

> Points to note
Reporting accidents and ill health at
work is a legal requirement.

Safety Organization

Large construction sites should have a safety officer employed by the
contractor to ensure that all work areas are safe. On smaller building
sites where there is no safety officer, the foreman or supervisor is usually
responsible for the implementation of site safety.

Safety programmes and laws are only effective if:

- They are enforced on site
- They are legally enforceable
- All members of staff are aware of safety.

The Health and Safety at Work Act 1974 (HASWA)

The HASWA covers the health and safety of almost everyone in the workplace. The main objectives of the HASWA are:

- To secure the health and safety and welfare of all persons at work
- To protect the general public from risk to health and safety arising out of work activities
- To control the use, handling, storage and transporting of explosives and highly flammable substances
- To control the release of noxious or offensive substances into the atmosphere.

HASWA is enforced by inspectors, employed by the Health and Safety Executive (HSE). Their authority permits them to:

- Enter premises to carry out investigations involving taking photographs, recordings and samples
- Take statements
- Check records
- Give advice and information
- Seize, dismantle, neutralize or destroy material, equipment or substances that are likely to cause immediate serious personal injury
- Issue prohibition notices – ban all activity until the situation is corrected
- Issue improvement notices – put right within a specified period of time any minor hazard or infringement of legislation
- Prosecute all persons who fail to comply with their duty under the HASWA.

REMEMBER
Safety is everyone's responsibility.

Points to note
Conviction in a Magistrates' Court can lead to a fine up to £20 000 and six months in prison and in the Crown Court to an unlimited fine and two years in prison.

TRY THIS OUT

- Analyse the reasons why accidents occur. Think about the reasons and draw conclusions about the ways in which accidents can be prevented. Present your findings in report form.
- On completion get your tutor to check the scope of your ideas and the validity of your findings.

Work-based Evidence Required

- **Hazards associated with the workplace and occupations at work, are recorded and/or reported**

To meet this requirement, obtain a witness testimony sheet from your supervisor stating that you recorded and reported a hazard at work. Place the evidence in your work based evidence portfolio when next in college and map and record it against the syllabus.

> ## Quick quiz Quick quiz Quick quiz Quick quiz Quick quiz
>
> ❶ Define the term hazardous substance.
> ❷ Explain the term manual handling.
> ❸ What is the most common cause of injuries at work?
> ❹ Define risk assessment.
> ❺ List three types of fire protection equipment.

Notices   1.4

In this section you will learn about notices, statutory requirements and official guidance for construction and the work area.

When you have completed this section you will be able to:

■ Comply with all workplace safety requirements at all times.

Know and understand:

■ What safety legislation notices are relevant to the occupational area.

This chapter will now cover notices used in the construction industry.

The Health and Safety (Safety Signs and Signals) Regulations 1996

These regulations bring into force the European Community Safety Signs Directive on the provision and use of safety signs at work. The purpose of the Directive is to encourage the standardization of safety signs throughout the member states of the European Union so that safety signs, wherever they are seen, have the same meaning.

Identification of Safety Signs and Notices

All employers have to provide safety signs in a variety of different situations that do, or may, affect health and safety.

Safety signs and notices give warnings of possible danger and must always be obeyed. To be safe on a construction site you will need to recognize, understand and respond to a lot of different safety signs.

Safety signs fall into five separate categories. These can be recognized by their shape and colour. This is to make sure that everyone understands health and safety information in a simple, bold and effective way, with little or no use of words.

The five categories for basic safety signs are as follows:

Prohibition Signs

Shape – They are circular

Colour – They have a red border and cross bar with a black symbol on a white background.

Meaning – They are there to show people what must not be done. For example, no smoking in college (see Figure 1.11).

Mandatory Signs
Shape – They are circular.

Colour – They have a white symbol on a blue background.

Meaning – They are there to show you what must be done. For example, wear your safety helmet (see Figure 1.12).

Warning Signs
Shape – They are triangular.

Colour – They have a yellow background with a black border and symbol.

Meaning – They are there to warn you of hazard or danger. For example: Caution, there is a risk of an electric shock (see Figure 1.13).

Information Signs
Shape – They are square or oblong

Colour – They have white symbols on a green background.

Meaning – They are there to indicate or give information about safety provision. For example, location of the first aid point (see Figure 1.14).

Fire Safety Signs
Shape – They are square or rectangular.

Colour – They have white symbols on a red background.

Meaning – They are there to give the location of fire information, fire alarms or fire – fighting equipment. For example, location of a fire extinguisher or fire hose reel (see Figure 1.15).

Fig 1.11 **Prohibition sign**

Fig 1.12 **Mandatory sign**

Fig 1.13 **Warning sign**

Fig 1.14 **Information sign**   Fig 1.15 **Fire safety sign**

Fig 1.16 Safety signs

TRY THIS OUT

There are more signs in Figures 1.17 and 1.18. Look up where they are used and write the type and meaning under each sign.

Get your tutor to check your answers.

Source; Department for Education and Skills.

Examples of Safety Signs

To be safe at work you will need to recognize, understand and respond to a lot of different safety signs. The signs in Figure 1.16 help you to recognize the types of safety signs and their meaning and to understand how and where to use the signs.

Fig 1.17 Signs with meanings left out 1

Fig 1.18 Signs with meanings left out 2

Signs With Supplementary Text

Any information signs may be supplemented by text. A number of examples of supplementary signs are illustrated in Figures 1.19 and 1.20.

Common Abbreviations and Meanings

HASWA – Health and Safety at Work Act 1974.

These are the main rules which govern health and safety in the construction industry and elsewhere in the workplace.

They are there to provide health and safety in the workplace

They protect visitors and members of the public on construction sites and elsewhere.

HSE – Health and Safety Executive

The HSE enforces the law in the workplace.

It has the powers to inspect premises and construction sites to ensure employers and employees are not breaking the law.

PUWER – Provision and Use of Work Equipment Regulations

PUWER helps to provide guidance to protect people's health and safety from equipment that they use at work.

This equipment might include, ladders, lifting equipment, earth moving machinery, powered hand tools, cutting and drilling machines and so on.

COSHH – Control of Substances Hazardous to Health

COSHH covers dangerous solids, liquids or gases and gives guidelines on how they should be used and stored.

It gives details of actions the employer and the employee must take to protect the health of the individual and others.

CDM – Construction (Design and Management) Regulations

These are rules laid down by the main contractor on a construction site that must be observed by all sub-contractors and employees on site.

Points to note

Remember always look out for and obey safety signs, they are there for your protection.

Eye protection must be worn

Ear protectors must be worn in this area

Safety helmets must be worn in this area

Caution Fork lift trucks

DANGER

No smoking

No pedestrians

Fig 1.19 Signs with supplementary text 1

Protective footwear must be worn

Danger
Men working overhead

All visitors and drivers must report to site office

This is a safety helmet area

Danger
Deep excavations

No Smoking

CAUTION Pedestrians

Sound horn

No unauthorised persons allowed beyond this point

10mph Speed limit

Fig 1.20 Signs with supplementary text 2

ACoP – Approved Codes of Practice

These rules provide general guidance for employers and employees on the most suitable and safest way to carry out activities on site.

RIDDOR – Reporting of Injuries, Diseases and Dangerous Occurrences Regulations

Certain events must be reported to the HSE: for example, major injuries and deaths that occur on a construction site, or accidents in which employees are unable to work for more than three days as well as diseases and dangerous occurrences.

RPE – Respiratory Protective Equipment

This type of equipment must be worn over the mouth and nose when working with strong smelling substances, excessive dust and so on.

PPE – Personal Protective Equipment

This might include, hard hats, safety footwear, ear defenders, protective gloves, safety goggles and so on.

MEWP – Mobile Elevating Working Platform

Used for working at height when it is not possible to erect a scaffold.

TRY THIS OUT

- Prepare a list of safety considerations that site personnel need to observe when erecting, taking down and dismantling access equipment. Present the list to your supervisor and ask him to compare it with the official procedures in order to ascertain the validity of your findings.

Work-based Evidence Required

- **Adherence to statutory requirements and/or safety notices and warning signs displayed in the workplace.**

To meet this requirement, obtain a witness testimony sheet from your supervisor stating that you have adhered to statutory requirements, safety notices and warning signs on site. Place the evidence in your work-based evidence portfolio when next in college and map and record it against the syllabus.

Quick quiz Quick quiz Quick quiz Quick quiz Quick quiz

1. What colours are used on an information sign?
2. What shape is a prohibition sign?
3. Name the categories of safety sign.
4. Draw four types of safety sign, each from a different category using the correct colours.
5. What instruction does a mandatory sign give?

Personal Protective Equipment (PPE)

1.5

Operative wearing PPE

Gloves – protective apron – protective footwear – goggles – protective mask

Fig 1.21 **Items of PPE**

In this section you will learn about PPE as required for the general work environment that includes:

■ Helmets, ear defenders, overalls, safety footwear and high visibility vests and jackets.

When you have completed this section you will be able to:

■ Comply with all workplace safety legislation requirements at all times

■ Identify building site or work conditions which require special safety precautions

■ Identify, select and use protective clothing correctly

■ Identify, select and use safety equipment correctly.

Know and understand:

■ Why and where personal protective equipment should be used.

This section will now cover personal protective equipment.

Introduction

The use of personal protective equipment (PPE) is not the solution for preventing accidents, it is used as a last resort. It is important that the primary protection against accidents is to identify possible hazards and take the necessary steps to eliminate the hazards.

Safety footwear will for example, protect against nails penetrating the foot. Ordinary shoes will probably not do so. However, the initial problem is the nail hazard, not the lack of safety footwear. The wearing of PPE is therefore a back-up for an effective site safety programme (see Figure 1.21).

Safety Provisions

■ All personnel must be provided with protective clothing and other PPE

■ National standards regarding PPE must be observed

■ All personnel must be instructed in the use of the PPE provided

■ Personnel should make proper use of and take proper care of the PPE provided

■ All PPE should be kept fit for immediate use

■ All necessary measures should be taken by the employer to ensure that protective clothing and the PPE are effectively worn (see Figure 1.22).

Personal Protective Equipment

A wide range of safety clothing and equipment is available to safeguard the health and safety of people at work. It is therefore important when working to know the different types of protective clothing and PPE required for separate tasks.

Head and Neck Protection

Safety helmets – must be worn at all times when working on a construction site.

Hazards – Helmets are worn to protect the head and neck from falling objects and from knocks against obstructions and where necessary to protect the head from possible electric shocks. The protective helmets should be insulated or made of insulating material (see Figure 1.23).

If necessary, workers should be instructed in the use of the personal protective equipment provided.

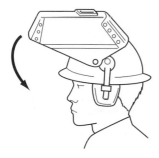

Operative wearing PPE

Workers should make proper use of and take proper care of the personal protective equipment provided.

Hard hat – ear defenders

Fig 1.22 **Further examples of PPE**

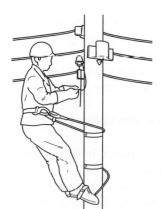 

Fig 1.23 **Examples of head protection**

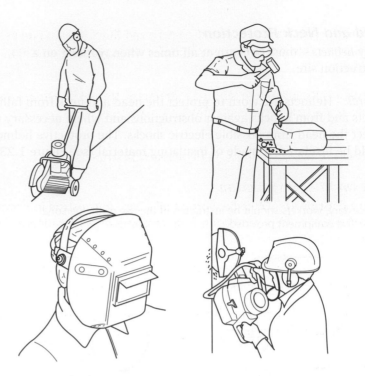

Fig 1.24 Examples of eye protection

Personnel working in the sun in hot weather should wear a suitable head covering.

Choices – helmets, bump caps, hats, caps and cape hoods.

Eye Protection

Eye protection must be worn when carrying out operations that are likely to produce dust, chips or sparks: for example cutting bricks and blocks (see Figure 1.24).

Hazards – chemical or metal splash, dust, projectiles, gas and vapour, radiation.

Choices – spectacles, goggles, face-screens.

Breathing

Dust masks – These must be worn when carrying out operations that produce dust, for example, sweeping up after the day's work. The dust masks used on a construction site are lightweight and reasonably comfortable. They should under no circumstances be shared between workers and should be disposed of after use (see Figure 1.25).

Hazards – dust, vapour, gas, oxygen deficient atmospheres.

Choices – disposable filtering face piece or respirator, half/full face respirators, air-fed helmets, breathing apparatus.

Hand and Arm Protection

Gloves – Different types of gloves are available for a variety of operations. Leather gloves are worn for general protection such as when

**DUST MASKS
BS 2091**

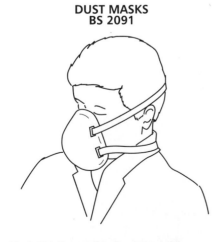

Fig 1.25 Example of a dust mask

handling timber, bricks or bags of cement and lime. Rubber gloves should be worn when using chemicals, for example brick cleaning acid (see Figure 1.26).

Hazards – abrasion, temperature extremes, cuts and punctures, impact, chemicals, electric shock, skin infection, disease or contamination, vibration.

Choices – gloves, gauntlets, mitts, wristcuffs, armlets.

Foot and Leg Protection

Safety footwear – Must be worn at all times on construction sites. Safety footwear offers protection from crushing or penetration injuries (see Figure 1.27).

Hazards – wet, electrostatic build-up, slipping, cuts and punctures, falling objects, metal and chemical splash, abrasion.

Choices – safety boots and shoes with steel toe caps (and steel mid sole), gaiters, leggings, spats.

Foot protection

Workers should wear footwear of an appropriate type when employed at places where they might be exposed to injury from:
• falling objects
• hot, corrosive or poisonous substances;
• sharp-edged tools (axes, etc.);
• nails;
• abnormally wet surface;
• slippery or ice-covered surfaces

Operative wearing protective footwear whilst cutting blocks

Operative wearing protective footwear whilst working in wet concrete

Fig 1.27 **Example of foot protection**

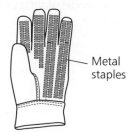

GLOVES ARMOURED WITH STAPLES
Use when handling heavy blocks, concrete and steel lintels

LIGHTWEIGHT TWILL GLOVES
Use when handling cement and timber

Protection for wrists
CHROME LEATHER GAUNTLET
Use when handling glass to give protection to the hand and wrist

Fig 1.26 **Example of gloves**

Protecting the Body

Overalls and protective clothing should be worn at all times on construction sites. They are designed to protect you from dust and spillages and other hazards, and keep your daily clothes clean (see Figure 1.28).

Fig 1.28 **Example of safety clothing**
Source: Beaver

Hazards – temperature extremes, adverse weather, chemical or metal splash, spray from pressure leaks or spray guns, impact or penetration, contaminated dust, excessive wear or entanglement of own clothing.

Choices – conventional or disposable overalls, boiler suits, donkey jackets, specialist protective clothing, e.g. chain-mail aprons, high visibility clothing.

Source: HSE

Catch Nets, Safety Belts and Harnesses
Where site personnel cannot be protected against falls from heights by any other means they should be protected by catch nets or safety harnesses or a combination of both.

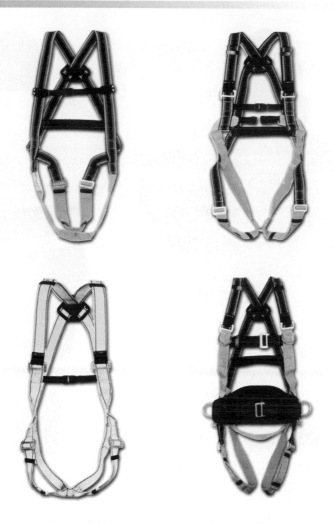

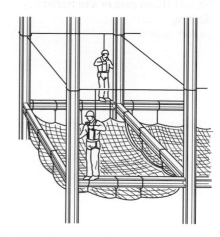

Fig 1.29 Example of a catch net

Fig 1.30 Examples of harnesses
Source: Beaver

When an operative's safety depends on a safety belt they should not work on their own. Where necessary, when working with a safety harness, there should be in addition an independently secured lifeline.

The lifeline should be attached above the work to a secure fixing and the free end should extend to ground level or the working platform. Safety harnesses, belts, straps and lifelines should be so fitted as to limit the free fall of the wearer to 1 metre (see Figures 1.29 and 1.30).

No more than one operative should be attached to any lifeline.

Protection Against Site Traffic

Operatives who are regularly exposed to danger from moving site vehicles should wear:

- Distinguishing clothing, preferably bright yellow or orange in colour; or
- Clothing of reflecting or otherwise conspicuously visible material (see Figure 1.31).

Vehicles such as earth moving equipment, fork lifts, trucks, ready mixed concrete lorries and so on, should have a distinct warning signal which activates automatically when the vehicle reverses (see Figure 1.32).

Source: International Labour Office, Geneva

Fig 1.31 **Examples of site traffic clothing**
Source: Beaver

TRY THIS OUT

- Practical exercise – cutting bricks and blocks.
- Your supervisor has asked you to sort through the PPE he has provided and to choose the following to suit your size: overalls, safety helmet, gloves, safety footwear and goggles.
- Adjust the PPE accordingly in order to fit you correctly.
- Get your supervisor to check that you have selected and adjusted the PPE correctly.

Fig 1.32 **Truck reversing**

Equipment Checks

Frequent safety checks of workshop equipment, construction sites, scaffolding and safety equipment such as fire extinguishers and so on, are mandatory on all building sites.

Work-based Evidence Required

- **Safe use of personal protective equipment (PPE) when in the work environment, in accordance with legislation and/or organizational requirements.**

To meet this requirement, obtain photographs of yourself wearing personal protective equipment whilst carrying out bricklaying activities. The PPE might include the following: safety helmet, safety boots, high visibility vest, goggles, ear defenders, gloves and so on.

When the photographs have been developed place them on a photographic evidence sheet, and get your supervisor to authenticate them by signing and dating them. Place the evidence in your work based evidence portfolio, when next in college and map and record it against the syllabus. Figure 1.33 shows a bricklayer carrying out the actions mentioned above as an example of the type of evidence required.

Fig 1.33 **A bricklayer working while wearing appropriate PPE**

Quick quiz Quick quiz Quick quiz Quick quiz Quick quiz

❶ Name the PPE that would be worn when cutting bricks
❷ List four items of PPE that should be worn when lifting heavy and sharp objects on to a platform.
❸ What does the abbreviation HSE stand for?
❹ List three safety provisions relating to the use of PPE.
❺ How would you safeguard site personnel against site traffic?

Reporting

1.6

In this section you will learn about organizational recording procedures and statutory requirements.

When you have completed this section you will be able to:

- Identify hazards associated with the workplace and record and report in accordance with organizational procedure.

Know and understand:

- The method of reporting hazards in the workplace.

This section will now cover reporting.

Reporting Hazards and Injuries

Reporting accidents and ill health at work is a legal requirement. The information enables the Health and Safety Executive (HSE) and local authorities, referred to as the enforcing authority, to identify where and how risks arise and to investigate serious accidents.

RIDDOR

RIDDOR stands for the Reporting of Injuries, Diseases and Dangerous Occurrences Regulations 1995, usually referred to as RIDDOR 95, these Regulations came into force in April 1996.

RIDDOR requires the employer to report some work-related accidents, diseases and dangerous occurrences. It applies to all construction work activities.

Reporting to the Enforcing Authority

Death or Major Injury

Reports have to be sent to the enforcing authority if there is an accident connected with work and:

- An employee, working on site is killed or suffers a major injury, or
- A member of the public is killed or taken to hospital
- You must notify the HSE without delay usually by telephone. The HSE will ask for brief details about the injured person and the accident
- Within ten days you must follow this up with a completed accident report form F2508.

Over-Three-Day-Injury

If there is an accident connected with work and an employee working on site, suffers an over-three-day injury you must send a completed accident report form (F2508) to the HSE within ten days.

An over-three-day injury is one which is not major but results in the injured person being away from work or unable to do the full range of their normal duties for more than three days.

Disease

If a doctor notifies you that an employee suffers from a reportable work-related disease you must send a completed disease report form (F2508A) to the enforcing authority. Reportable diseases include:

- Certain poisonings
- Some skin diseases such as occupational dermatitis, skin cancer, chrome ulcer, oil follicutis
- Lung diseases including occupational asthma, farmers lung, pneumoconiosis, asbestosis, mesothelioma

- Infections such as leptospirosis, hepatitis, tuberculosis, anthrax, legionellosis and tetanus
- Other conditions such as: occupational cancer, certain musculoskeletal disorders, decompression illness and hand-arm vibration syndrome.

The full list of reportable diseases, and the work activities they are related to, can be found in the detailed guide to the Regulations obtainable from the Health and Safety Executive.

Dangerous Occurrence

If something happens which does not result in a reportable injury, but which clearly could have done, it may be a dangerous occurrence which must be reported immediately by telephone to the enforcing authority. Within ten days you must follow this up with a completed accident report form (F2508). Dangerous occurrences include:

- Plant or equipment coming into contact with overhead power lines
- Electrical short circuit or overload causing fire or explosion
- Collapse or partial collapse of a scaffold over 5 metres high, or erected near water where there could be a risk of drowning after a fall
- Malfunction of breathing apparatus while in use or during testing immediately before us
- Accidental release of any substance which may damage health.

The full list of dangerous occurrences, and the work activities they are related to, can be found in the detailed guide to the Regulations obtainable from the Health and Safety Executive.

Methods of Reporting

You can report to the Incident Contact Center via a number of methods:

- By phone 0845 300 9923
- By fax 0845 300 9924
- By Internet www.riddor.gov.uk
- By email riddor@natbrit.com
- By post: Incident Contact Centre, Caerphilly Business Park, Caerphilly CF83 3GG.

Alternatively, you may contact the environmental health department of your local authority. The address and telephone number will be in the telephone book under the authority's name.

Record Keeping

You must keep a record of any reportable injury, disease or dangerous occurrence for three years after the date on which it happened. This must include:

- The date and method of reporting
- The date, time and place of the event

HSE Health & Safety Executive

Health and Safety at Work etc Act 1974
The Reporting of Injuries, Diseases and Dangerous Occurrences Regulations 1995

Report of an injury or dangerous occurrence

Filling in this form
This form must be filled in by an employer or other responsible person.

Part A

About you

1 What is your full name?

2 What is your job title?

3 What is your telephone number?

About your organisation

4 What is the name of your organisation?

5 What is the address and postcode?

6 What type of work does the organisation do?

Part B

About the incident

1 On what date did the incident happen?

/ /

2 At what time did the incident happen?
(Please use the 24-hour clock e.g. 0600)

3 Did the incident happen at the above address?
Yes ☐ Go to question 4
No ☐ Where did the incident happen?
☐ elsewhere in your organisation – give the name, address and postcode
☐ at someone else's premises – give the name, address and postcode
☐ in a public place – give details of where it happened

If you do not know the postcode, what is the name of the local authority?

4 In which department, or where on the premises, did the incident happen?

F2508 (01/96)

Part C

About the injured person

If you are reporting a dangerous occurrence, go to Part F.
If more than one person was injured in the same incident, please attach the details asked for in Part C and Part D for each injured person.

1 What is their full name?

2 What is their home address and postcode?

3 What is their home phone number?

4 How old are they?

5 Are they
☐ male?
☐ female?

6 What is their job title?

7 Was the injured person (tick only one box)
☐ one of your employees?
☐ on a training scheme? Give details:

☐ on work experience?
☐ employed by someone else? Give details of this employer:

3 Was the injury (tick the one box that applies)
☐ a fatality?
☐ a major injury or condition? (see accompanying notes)
☐ an injury to an employee or self-employed person which prevented them doing their normal work for more than 3 days?
☐ an injury to a member of the public which meant they had to be taken from the scene of the accident to a hospital for treatment?

4 Did the injured person (tick the boxes that apply)
☐ become unconscious?
☐ need resuscitation?
☐ remain in hospital for more than 24 hours?
☐ none of the above?

Part E

About the kind of accident

Please tick the one box that best describes what happened, then go to Part G.

☐ Contact with moving machinery or material being machined
☐ Hit by a moving flying or falling object
☐ Hit by a moving vehicle
☐ Hit something fixed or stationary

☐ Injured while handling, lifting or carrying
☐ Slipped, tripped or fell on the same level
☐ Fell from a height
How high was the fall
____ metres
☐ Trapped by something collapsing

☐ Drowned or asphyxiated
☐ Exposed to, or in contact with , a harmful substance
☐ Exposed to fire
☐ Exposed to an explosion

☐ Contact with electricity or an electrical discharge
☐ Injured by an animal
☐ Physically assaulted by a person

☐ Another kind of accident (describe it in Part G)

Part F

Dangerous occurrences

Enter the number of the dangerous occurrence you are reporting. (The numbers are given in the Regulations and in the notes which accompany this form)

Part G

Describing what happened

Give as much detail as you can. For instance;
• the name of any substance involved
• the name and type of any machine involved
• the events that led to the incident
• the part played by any people

If it was a personal injury, give details of what the person was doing. Describe any action that has since been taken to prevent a similar incident. Use a separate piece of paper if you need to.

Part H

Your signature

Signature

Date
/ /

Where to send the form

Please send it to the Enforcing Authority for the place where it happened. If you do not know the Enforcing Authority, send it to the nearest HSE office.

For official use
Client number   Location number   Event number

☐ INV REP ☐ Y ☐

Fig 1.34 **HSE accident report form**
Source: HSE

- Personal details of those involved
- A brief description of the nature of the event or disease.

Guidance on Record Keeping

You could, for example, choose to keep your records by:

- Keeping copies of report forms in a file
- Recording the details on a computer
- Maintaining a written log.

You can keep the record in any form you wish.

Source: HSE.

Quick quiz Quick quiz Quick quiz Quick quiz Quick quiz

❶ What does the abbreviation RIDDOR stand for?
❷ What is the role of the enforcing authority?
❸ What is meant by the term dangerous occurrence?
❹ List three methods of reporting an accident to the HSE.
❺ Which type of accidents should be recorded in the Accident Book?

Security

1.7

In this section you will learn about organizational procedures relating to the general public, site personnel and resources.

When you have completed this section you will be able to:

- Comply with and maintain all organizational security arrangements and approved procedures.

Know and understand:

- How security arrangements are implemented in the workplace.

This section will now cover security.

Security Controls

It is very important that adequate security controls are established at the start of a contract. Materials and components stored on site are valuable items, as are the plant and equipment. Loss of equipment can involve the contractor in delays both in obtaining replacements and dealing with insurance enquiries, and the extra paperwork involved.

It is no point having a complex security system on site if it is not adhered to or treated casually by site personnel.

Protection of General Public

The main contractor is solely responsible for the safety of the general public either on the site or on land or workings immediately adjoining the site. Precautions taken to protect the general public from harm are as follows.

Hoardings

To prevent unauthorized access to the site, hoardings must be in place. They should be of suitably substantial construction and properly erected. Where a hoarding approaches a public footpath adjoining a road the contractor must ensure the safety of pedestrians by constructing a walkway with a suitable barrier preventing road accidents. If there is overhead work within that area the walkway has to be covered. Adequate lighting must be installed for both day and night (see Figure 1.35).

Compounds

The site compound is vulnerable during working hours, particularly during breaks, and when hired vans and private vehicles are allowed to gain access to the site. The problem is worse outside working hours and during holidays.

There are two basic types of site storage to consider :

- Accommodation in site huts, where a storeman or -woman issues materials to authorized personnel
- Covered storage which contains bulk materials which cannot be left exposed to the weather or site personnel.

The former must be sited within the perimeter fence of the compound and provided with separate access through the fence, although the store itself must be sealed off from the compound. The store should have as few windows as possible, and they must be protected by a suitable grille or shutters secured from within the building (see Figure 1.35).

Access

Access on to and exit from the site varies according to the nature of the site, that is, the levels of any existing buildings and of those to be constructed. Exit from the site is preferable on a quiet side road free from traffic and pedestrians. Access around the site is made on temporary roads of consolidated hardcore and steel mats. The position of access roads depends upon sitings for storage, mixing points and so on (see Figure 1.35).

All lorries and private vehicles and vans must be controlled from the time they enter the site until they leave. The services of a person to man the access and egress to the site will provide more cost effective in the long term than the replacement of stolen materials.

Security of Resources

Security of materials generally poses a problem to site managers. A suitable system of materials control should be adopted to show: present stock, deliveries, amounts used and so on. Controls are required to

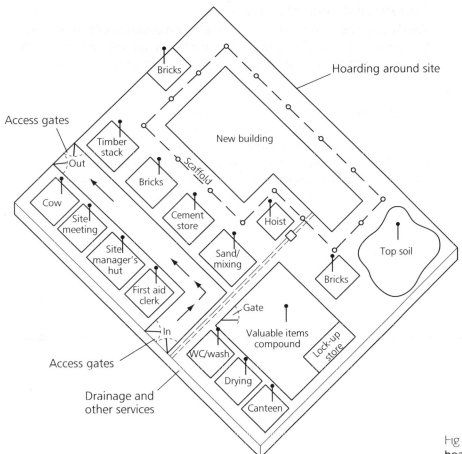

Fig 1.35 Site compound showing exits, hoardings, compounds, etc.

prevent theft from within the workplace as well as potential outside risks. These controls will monitor the materials used and hence, materials wastage. Site cleanliness and layout also gives some indication of how well a site is being run.

Large amounts of materials and components should not be left unprotected on delivery vehicles overnight, and when offloaded should be evenly distributed between various points on the site to discourage thieves. Materials should always be stored in an orderly manner and covered with protective sheeting.

Security Lighting

Good lighting of the site will help to reduce theft, vandalism and other intrusion, particularly by children. Lighting the stores and compound areas will deter intruders at night and help security patrols.

A purpose-designed security lighting system should cover the perimeter, access routes, vehicle compounds, materials compounds and open areas. The degree of risk will determine the required standard of lighting, after allowing for the brightness of the surrounding area. Lighting costs depend on the shape and contours of the area to be lit, the level of illumination required, and the hours the system will be in use.

Corrosive

Risk of explosion

Flammable

Toxic

Fig 1.36 Hazard signs

TRY THIS OUT

- Using your knowledge of safety information sources, mention organizations that could provide information on, for example, asbestos precautions, inflammable substances, fire prevention, scaffolding safety or guards for machines.

- Get your tutor to check your results.

Fire Precautions

Despite the high costs of materials and components stored in site compounds, precautions against damage by fire are very limited on the average construction site, and in some cases, non-existent.

To reduce the risk of the spread of fire, site stores, site offices and other temporary buildings should be sited at least 6 metres away from main buildings, and temporary offices should be built with a reasonable distance between them of at least 3 metres. All areas around site offices and stores should be kept free from combustible materials, which includes grass or weeds. Similar precautions should be taken at the perimeter of compounds and next to site hoardings.

Fire Fighting Equipment

Water supplies and other fire fighting equipment should be convenient for use in case of fire. All fire fighting equipment should be located and marked with a prominent notice close to the site entrance and other high risk areas and must be kept free from obstructions at all times. Notices should also be displayed in prominent places around the site drawing the attention of all site personnel to the dangers of fire, quoting the telephone number of the nearest fire station.

Flammable Substances

Small supplies of flammable substances should be kept in clearly marked cans or drums with securely fastened caps or lids, in a well-ventilated store built with brick walls, concrete floor and non-combustible roof. This store should be sited well away from other buildings, and marked with a prominent notice, stating that the contents are highly inflammable (see Figure 1.36).

Points to note Three ingredients are needed for a fire: a fuel at the right concentration, a good supply of air, and a source of ignition. If you control these ingredients, fires can be prevented (see Figure 1.37).

Work-based Evidence Required

- **Organizational procedures for maintaining the security of the workplace:**

  - During the working day
  - On completion of the day's work
  - From unauthorized personnel (other operatives and/or the general public)
  - From theft.

To meet this requirement, obtain a witness testimony sheet from your supervisor stating that you carried out organizational procedures for maintaining the security of the workplace, as described above.

When you have received the signed and dated witness testimony sheet from your supervisor, place them in your work-based evidence portfolio when next in college and map and record it against the syllabus.

Quick quiz Quick quiz Quick quiz Quick quiz Quick quiz

1. Why is it important to have security controls?
2. What is the purpose of a hoarding?
3. Where should flammable substances be kept?
4. Name two types of site storage.
5. What does good lighting of the site help to reduce?

Information on Emergency Procedures

For more information about emergency procedures why not visit the following websites.

HSE

www.hsebooks.co.uk

European Agency for Safety and Health at Work

http://osha.eu.int/

Good safety management practice is available from the Agency's website. All Agency publications can be downloaded free of charge. The Agency site links to member state sites where national legislation and guidance on construction may be found.

United Kingdom

http://uk.osha.eu.int/

Information on Fire Extinguishers

For more information about fire extinguishers why not visit the following websites or visit your local fire station.

HSE

www.hse.gov.uk

Information about Hazards

For more information about hazards in the construction industry why not visit the following websites.

Health and Safety Executive

www.hse.gov.uk

Of great help in the writing of this section was the booklet, *An Introduction to Health and Safety*, published by the HSE from which all sources have been taken.

HSE priced and free publications are available by mail order from HSE Books,

PO Box 1999, Sudbury, Suffolk CO10 2WA. Tel: 01787 881165. Fax: 01787 313995. Website: www.hsebooks.co.uk

HSE priced publications are also available from bookshops and free leaflets can be downloaded from the HSE website: www.hse.gov.uk

Information about notices

For a full range of safety signs contact the Health and Safety Executive, who will be only too happy to send you details, usually free of charge.

HSE

www.hsebooks.co.uk

Information about PPE

For more information about PPE why not visit the following website.

HSE

www.hse.gov.uk

Alternatively, product information may be found on the websites of the many commercial companies who produce PPE products.

Information about Reporting

For the majority of people with duties under the Regulations, this section of the book contains all you need to know.

However, if you have any questions, for example on reportable dangerous occurrences or diseases, just ring HSEs Info Line. If you would like to have more information to hand, a guide to the Regulations is available. It contains the full text of the Regulations and notes on interpretation. It also includes the lists of reportable diseases and dangerous occurrences.

HSE Info Line. 08701 545500
Website: www.hse.gov.uk

Information about Site Security

For more information about site security, visit the website of an appropriate commercial company

2

Chapter Two

Conform to Efficient Work Practices

NVQ Level 2   Unit No. VR 02   Conform to Efficient Work Practices

This unit, in the context of brickwork and the work environment, is about:
- ℘ **Interpreting information**
- ℘ **Planning, organizing and adopting safe and healthy working practices**
- ℘ **Planning and carrying out productive, efficient working practices**
- ℘ **Working with others or as an individual**

There are four sections in this chapter, communication, documentation, procedures and programmes, and relationships.

This chapter will now cover conforming to efficient work practices.

Communication ▬▬▬▬▬▬▬▬▬▬▬▬▬▬▬ 2.1

In this section you will learn about written, oral and electronic communication.

When you have completed this section you will be able to:
- ■ Communicate with others to establish productive work relationships.

Know and understand:
- ■ The methods of communication with other workplace personnel and clients.

This section will now cover communication.

Methods of Communication

There are three main methods of communication:

Direct speech – People talking and listening, on site this could include:
- ■ Briefings, training sessions, site meetings, interviews, conversations, telephone.

Written or printed – People writing and reading, on site this could include:

■ Specifications, instructions, notices, posters, memos, reports, forms, letters, agendas, emails, faxes and minutes.

Visual and graphic – People using pictures and symbols, on site this could include:

■ Plans, drawings, bar charts, diagrams, models, photographs, tables, graphs.

Direct Speech

We probably spend more time talking and listening to people than using any other method of communication. If it is done effectively, it is usually the most successful method to use.

It gives you direct, personal contact. You can raise questions, answer them, discuss and settle misunderstandings as they arise.

However, there are disadvantages to spoken communication, some of which are:

■ No written record, so it could lead to dispute over what was said

■ Not always enough time to think clearly

■ Harder to voice criticism

■ Hard to carry out with large numbers of people.

Written and Printed Method

The majority of site managers complain about the quantities of paperwork they have to deal with. However, as long as it is useful and relevant to work procedures, then it clearly has advantages over other methods of communication.

Some of the factors that make written communication particularly useful are:

■ Good for complicated ideas and details

■ Useful for confirming earlier spoken communication

■ Provides evidence of action taken

■ Valuable in cases of query or dispute.

Visual and Graphic

The construction industry makes great use of visual and graphic communication through drawings, plans, diagrams, models, progress bar charts, photographs and video, especially in training. In general, we find visual communication effective because:

■ It can clearly show techniques, methods and whole processes

■ It is often easier to understand than the same information given in written or spoken terms

■ You can use it to support writing or speech with visual aids and illustrations

■ It is helpful with language or reading difficulties.

Choosing the most desirable method for your own purposes is a central part of planning your communication.

Source: CITB-ConstructionSkills

Site and Workshop Communication

Within the construction industry there is a need to transmit information to an ever-changing base, for example, the building site itself and site workshops. The communication difficulty within workshops is usually solved by installing an intercom that allows messages to be transmitted through an amplified system, which is much more suitable for the workshop than the construction site.

The intercom is a one-way communication system, and the recipient of the message has to return to the source of the message or to an internal telephone, to report or exchange information.

Telephone

The telephone as a means of communication will provide immediate and constant contact with head office, the architect, builders' suppliers and all statutory authorities involved in the building process. An internal telephone system allows managers and supervisors on a large site to coordinate their resources without the delays caused by circulating written information. Figure 2.1 illustrates a telephone message form.

For	Time
From	Date
of	
Tel	Fax
Message	

No. 184691

O telephoned O will ring back O returned your call O called to see you O please call O urgent

Fig 2.1 **Telephone message form**

Points to remember when using a telephone:

- Speak clearly and give the receiver of your call time to take notes
- Listen carefully
- Do not shout
- Give the receiver of your call time to answer your questions
- Remember facial expressions cannot be seen

Before dialing:

Make short notes about the key points of the topic; this will help you not to forget important information. Whenever possible, find out who you need to speak to before dialling.

Types of call:

■ Own exchange calls
■ Local area calls
■ National and international calls.

All codes are available in the British Telecom phone book.

Fax

Fax machines transmit visual information from one location to another by turning it into digital impulses and passing them to the receiving machine at the other end of the telephone line. They can be used to transmit letters or other written information very quickly, to locations all over the world. All faxes are capable of both transmitting and receiving documents.

E-mail

This is a communication method that uses the Internet. It enables you and your company to communicate effectively and simply on a worldwide basis. Messages are stored on a network until the recipient accesses them.

Internet

This is a network of electronic communications that allows the communication of text files, artwork or multimedia clips on the World Wide Web.

The Internet is a vast source of information. It connects millions of computers around the world: computers belonging to governments, colleges, universities, schools, libraries, trade organizations, companies and many more. All these computers hold information, some of which is free for everyone to use, once you are connected.

The Internet can be used to find information:

For study – to help with coursework, essays and assignments.

For work – to help with professional updating and for keeping up with the latest trends, techniques, training and news.

For leisure – to encourage and stimulate learning.

Be warned – the Internet does not have all the information and not all of it is up to date or fit to use. Some information has to be paid for.

Two-Way Radio

On large sites, direct communications can be provided by the two-way radio-telephone which enables an operative to move freely around the site and yet remain in contact with the main site office, as well as with other operatives or vehicles similarly equipped. Complete site coverage can be obtained by distributing handsets to all key personnel, with the control point situated at the main site office.

Written Communication

The aim of written communication is to get a message across by:

■ Being clear
■ Being brief

- Keeping it simple and straightforward
- Setting the right tone
- Using the most suitable words for the purpose
- Keeping the reader's interest
- Having a clear and attractive layout.

Points to Note

If you require support with written communication talk to your tutor about your needs.

Ensure you obtain the help you need to develop your understanding and skills.

Memos and Letters

The two most common forms of communication within an organization are memos and letters.

Memos – Memos are used within a company, between individuals and departments.

Business Letters – These are used externally with anyone outside of the company.

Memos

The majority of firms have a standard printed memo form, similar to the example shown in Figure 2.2.

```
                                    Academy Construction Co.
                                              Training Road
                                                    Esford
                                                    PL4 7GH

                        MEMO

To:  Site Manager              From:

Date:                          Subject:  Material Change
```

Fig 2.2 **Standard memo form**
Source: LLIT and E

Memos are usually used for the following reasons:

- Giving or asking for information
- Directing someone to take certain actions
- Confirming an event that is to take place
- Confirming telephone conversations or verbal instructions.

Explaining things, for example a new programme of work, a change of manager, a new induction policy and so on.

Memos are usually short and to the point, but they still need to be effective. Remember the reader of the memo will usually be familiar with the topic area. Which means you are able to be direct and concise.

Business Letter

A business letter is a more effective form of communication than say talking to someone. A letter:

- Is a permanent record that you can store and refer to at a later stage
- Enables you to prepare ideas and organize them in a coherent way
- Effectively conveys detailed information and complex ideas.

A business letter should give a positive impression of you and your company. Any letter should be clear, concise, logically written to enable the reader to understand it and above all without mistakes.

The majority of business letters follow a standard format regarding layout and will be on a company's headed notepaper. You will probably write business letters for the following reasons:

- Obtaining information or quotations from other companies
- Placing orders for materials or services
- Making arrangements with other companies
- Seeking advice from consultants and the like.

Business letters need a structure, otherwise they will not make sense, they require a clear beginning and end, and a logical format for everything in between.

Points to Note

Be clear – give all the relevant points and details, so plan it out carefully beforehand.

Be concise – keep to the point, so do not include unnecessary information.

Be courteous – write in a polite way and the person you are writing to will look favourably on your request.

Follow the layout of a business letter shown in Figure 2.3.

Communicating Information

The following documents communicate information to enable construction activities to function effectively.

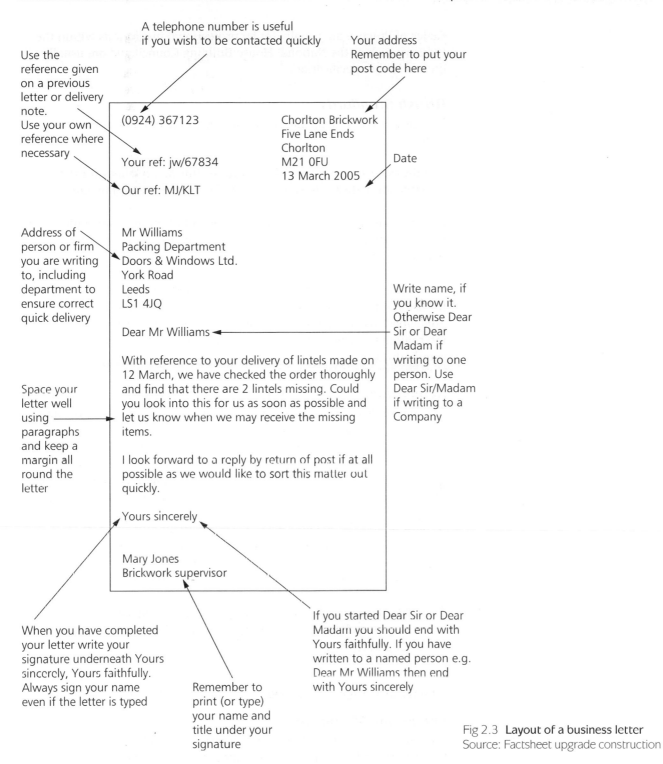

A telephone number is useful if you wish to be contacted quickly

Your address Remember to put your post code here

Use the reference given on a previous letter or delivery note.
Use your own reference where necessary

(0924) 367123

Your ref: jw/67834

Our ref: MJ/KLT

Chorlton Brickwork
Five Lane Ends
Chorlton
M21 0FU
13 March 2005

Date

Address of person or firm you are writing to, including department to ensure correct quick delivery

Mr Williams
Packing Department
Doors & Windows Ltd.
York Road
Leeds
LS1 4JQ

Dear Mr Williams

Write name, if you know it. Otherwise Dear Sir or Dear Madam if writing to one person. Use Dear Sir/Madam if writing to a Company

Space your letter well using paragraphs and keep a margin all round the letter

With reference to your delivery of lintels made on 12 March, we have checked the order thoroughly and find that there are 2 lintels missing. Could you look into this for us as soon as possible and let us know when we may receive the missing items.

I look forward to a reply by return of post if at all possible as we would like to sort this matter out quickly.

Yours sincerely

Mary Jones
Brickwork supervisor

When you have completed your letter write your signature underneath Yours sincerely, Yours faithfully. Always sign your name even if the letter is typed

Remember to print (or type) your name and title under your signature

If you started Dear Sir or Dear Madam you should end with Yours faithfully. If you have written to a named person e.g. Dear Mr Williams then end with Yours sincerely

Fig 2.3 **Layout of a business letter**
Source: Factsheet upgrade construction

Codes of Practice

The codes of practice are normally issued as part of the specification.
They give instructions to the contractor about:

- Protection of materials
- Procedure for fixing of materials
- Precautions that should be taken with materials.

Codes of Practice are usually set by professional institutions within the industry such as the National House Building Council and are usually quoted in the specification.

British Standards

Standards exist to make life safer and more efficient and to facilitate trade.

Standards cover every area of life from technical guidelines for the construction industry to specifications for new access equipment.

British Standards pioneered the development of these, along with BS 5750, which alongside BS 9000, are the world's most popular management system series.

British standards is the National Standards Body of the UK, responsible for facilitating, publishing and marketing British Standards and other guidelines. With collaborative ventures and a strong national and international profile, British Standards are at the heart of the world of standardization.

Regulations by Institutions

The majority of the specialist councils and professional bodies within the construction industry provide standards against which the work can be measured. An example quoted previously and one that you may be familiar with is the National House-Building Council (NHBC) which publishes rules and guidelines on the building of houses which outline methods of work, and the necessary standard expected from the builder.

If these standards are met, then after inspection of the completed property, the NHBC ten year guarantee is awarded. A measure of the importance of this guarantee is the fact that the majority of Building Societies will not grant a mortgage on the property without it.

The NHBC also provide guides and handbooks for informing the industry of the ways to achieve quality on site, with check lists for highlighting common problems and so on.

Contract Documents

Conditions of Contract

The majority of construction work is carried out under a Standard Form of Contract such as the Joint Contractors (JCT) or the Builders Employers Confederation (BEC) forms of contract. The actual contract will depend on the following:

- The type of client, for example, local authority, public limited company or private company
- Size and type of project, for example, small, major, subcontract or design and build
- The type of contract documents, that is, with or without a Bill of Quantities.

Schedules

Schedules are prepared by the building team on a small contract or by the design team, usually led by the quantity surveyor on a large contract. Schedules are normally prepared to record repetitive information for medium to large contracts, and their preparation is to simplify the presentation of information. They can be referred to in conjunction with the working drawings. The information that schedules contain is essential when preparing estimates and tenders. They also assist when measuring quantities, locating a particular item of work and checking off materials on site (see Figure 2.4).

A schedule should give information such as:

- Quantities of materials
- Types, sizes, thickness of materials
- Where material or item is to be placed.

DOOR SCHEDULE – INTERNAL							CONTRACT COMMON FARM ESTATE				
ORDER NO.	2431 2601					Supplier:	William Nolan Ltd.				

Item	Total Qty	Type	Size	Hand	Lock Latch	Hinge	Wall	Fanlight	Threshold	Head Height	Remarks
1	70	D7	2040 × 526	LH	1521 Roller catch	2 No. L/Pin	Frame 57	6 mm plywood	NIL	2374	Adjustable head 10 mm clearance between bottom of door and bottom of frame
2	72	D7	2040 × 526	RH	1521 Roller catch	2 No. L/Pin	"	"	NIL	2374	"
3	163	D9	2040 × 726	LH	915 Tubular latch	2 No. L/Pin	"	BDS	NIL	2374	"
4	162	D9	2040 × 726	RH		2 No. L/Pin	"	BDS	NIL	2374	"
5	72	D9	2040 × 726	LH	2294–3 Bath lock	2 No. L/Pin	"	BDS	NIL	2374	"
6	74	D9	2040 × 726	RH	"	2 No. L/Pin	"	BDS	NIL	2374	"
7	75	D9	2040 × 726	LH	1521 Roller catch	2 No. L/Pin	"	6 mm Plywood	NIL	2374	"
8	75	D9	2040 × 726	RH	"	2 No. L/Pin	"	"	NIL	2374	"
9	34	D10	2040 × 826	LH	915 Tubular latch	2 No. L/Pin	"	BDS	NIL	2374	"
10	40	D10	2040 × 826	RH	"	2 No. L/Pin	"	BDS	NIL	2374	"
11	16	D13	2040 × 726	LH	"	2 No. L/Pin	"	NIL	NIL	2082	10 mm clearance between bottom of door and bottom of jamb
12	17	D13	2040 × 726	RH	"	2 No. L/Pin	"	NIL	NIL	2082	"

A typical door schedule

Fig 2.4 **Schedules form**
Source: J.E. Johnston

Bill of Quantities

The Bill of Quantities is a contract document that includes all of the information contained in:

- The architect's working drawings
- The specification
- The schedule.

The Bill of Quantities is used by contractors quoting for work on larger projects. It is prepared by a quantity surveyor employed by the architect or by individual contractors (see Figure 2.5).

Specifications

Specifications are produced in conjunction with the working drawings and their purpose is to communicate to the contractor additional

Fig 2.5 Bill of quantities form

BILL OF QUANTITIES				
Contract			DWG No.	
DESCRIPTION	QUANTITY	UNIT	RATE	AMOUNT

information that has not been included on the working drawings. For example:

■ Special problems regarding the work

■ Restrictions, such as limited access and working hours

■ Standard of workmanship expected

QUALITY SPECIFICATION		
Operation	**Standards**	**Comments**

Fig 2.6 **Specification form**

- Standards of materials to be used
- Types and sizes of timbers
- Internal finishes required.

A specification used in conjunction with the working drawings should ensure the total quality assurance of any project (see Figure 2.6).

Working Drawings

Working drawings should contain the total information required for a building team to convert the architect's proposed building into a completed structure. These drawings are divided into a number of main types and scales. For more information on drawings see Chapter five.

Construction Regulations

The Construction Regulations cover in detail the standard practice expected from a contractor in order to ensure that work carried out on site is to a set national quality standard. The regulations are always reflected in the building contract and specification and are used as a quality measure of the work being carried out. The builder is contractually bound to adhere to these standards on behalf of the client.

Building Regulations

The Building Regulations cover the components used in the construction of buildings and the manner in which they all interlock to make a whole. So in effect the Building Regulations are not strictly concerned with the quality of finish, but more the performance of the building.

The main purpose of the regulations is to provide safe and healthy buildings and accommodation for the public and to conserve energy. This is achieved by stipulating minimum acceptable standards of building work and the materials used. The regulations also state the standards expected regarding structural stability of a building, safety in fire, thermal and sound insulation, stairways, refuse disposal, open spaces around a building and ventilation, chimneys and fireplaces, installation of heat producing appliances, drainage and sanitation.

The local Town Hall controls the manner in which the Building Regulations are adhered to on site, therefore, certain phases of the construction process need to be inspected by local authority building inspectors. For example, the inspector can demand to see the excavations for say strip foundations before any concrete is placed into them.

The reasons for inspection are closely bound up in the scope of the regulations. Namely that inspectors are not so much concerned with the standards of finish, as they are with the performance of the finished product. So, an inspector will want to make sure, that the building will remain stable once it has been completed. Therefore the excavations and whether they have been dug correctly will help them to decide if this is the case.

TRY THIS OUT

- What communication needs do you want to satisfy at work? Think of your relationships with other members of the site team, and try to relate to the ways in which you wish to be treated. Discuss your finding with your supervisor and tutor and see what ideas they have.

Work-based Evidence Required

- **Communication with colleagues and clients to ensure that the work is carried out efficiently.**

To meet this requirement, ask your supervisor to fill out a witness testimony sheet explaining how you communicate with colleagues and clients to ensure that work is carried out efficiently.

When you have received the signed and dated witness testimony sheet from your supervisor, place them in your work-based evidence portfolio when next in college and map and record it against the syllabus.

Quick quiz Quick quiz Quick quiz Quick quiz Quick quiz

❶ Give the name of the document that will give the quality standards to be achieved on the contract.

❷ Describe three methods of communication.

❸ List three types of electronic communication.

❹ What information would you obtain from a schedule?

❺ What information does a working drawing communicate?

Documentation 2.2

In this section you will learn about documentation that includes:

- Job cards, worksheets, material and resources lists and time sheets.

When you have completed this section you will be able to:

- Maintain records in accordance with the organizational procedures.

Know and understand:

- How to maintain documentation in accordance with organizational procedures.

This section will now cover documentation.

Documents

Research has established that completion and storage of documents and information can save considerable time, effort and paperwork. One way to achieve this is to have reference forms that are designed for simple completion and contain the maximum amount of data necessary to inform, store or update information connected to a particular project or specification detail.

Information frequently required during a contract includes tender documents, delivery of materials, project reviews and handing-over documentation.

A construction site can only work efficiently when all administration factors are in operation. If one of these factors is missing it may well alter the efficiency in such a way that not only is your area affected, but it may also cause an ongoing build up to develop with regard to materials and staffing requirements.

A clear understanding of the various documents in common use and their effective completion is vital for you to become an efficient team member.

Source: Further Education National Consortium

Job Cards

A job card or sheet is a simple form allocating a job or jobs to a person for a specific day or week (see Figure 2.7).

Fig 2.7 Job card or sheet

JOB SHEET				
NAME		WEEK COMMENCING		
SITE		FOREMAN		
DESCRIPTION	EXPECTED TIME	RESOURCES	DIFFICULTIES	REMEDIAL ACTION REQUIRED

Daywork sheets

Daywork sheets are sometimes confused with time sheets in that they are thought to carry out the same purpose. This is not the case. Daywork is work which is carried out without an estimate. This may range from emergency or repair work carried out on behalf of the client to work that was unforeseen at the start of a large and detailed contract. This work could entail for example, repairs, replacements, demolition, extra ground work, alterations and so on (see Figure 2.8).

Daywork sheets are completed by the contractor, authorized by the client or his representative and usually passed on to the quantity surveyor for inclusion in the next interim payment to the contractor. This extra payment comes from the provisional contingency sum included in the Bill of Quantities for any such unforeseen work.

Fig 2.8 **Worksheet**

DAYWORK SHEET

Registered office

Sheet no. ....

Job title ....

Week commencing ....

Description of work

Labour	Name	Craft	Hours	Gross rate	Total
			Total labour		

Materials		Quantity	Rate	% Addition	
			Total materials		

Plant		Hours	Rate	% Addition	
			Total plant		

Note Gross labour rates include a percentage for overheads and profit as set out in the contract conditions	Sub total	
	VAT (where applicable)..........%	
	Total claim	

Site manager/foreman ....

Architect ....

Details of the daywork procedures are usually included in the main contract conditions. A variation order which is simply an architect's written instructions is normally required before any work commences.

Time Sheets

A time sheet is a form completed by each member of staff on a weekly basis. Included on the time sheet would be details of hours worked and a description of work carried out (see Figure 2.9). The employer uses time sheets to determine wages and expenditure, as information for future planning, to judge the accuracy of target programmes and as the basis for the payment of daywork activities. Time sheets are usually completed by the supervisor in association with the member of staff.

Reports

A weekly or daily report is used to convey information to head office and to provide a source for future reference, especially where queries arise or problems develop regarding promises made to individuals or firms; verbal instructions; delays or stoppages caused by late deliveries; dates of telephone calls; visitors to site and so on. Like all reports the purpose is to disclose or record facts, therefore it should be brief and to the point (see Figure 2.10).

Resource Documentation

Many of the important decisions concerning the organizing of resources are made before the contract is awarded. So effectively when the tender is submitted, potential suppliers have already been selected or

| NAME | | NVQ No | |
| CONTRACT | | W/C | |

DAY	ACTIVITY	HOURS	DIFFICULTIES
MON			
TUE			
WED			
THU			
FRI			
SAT			
SUN			

Fig 2.9 Time sheet

Fig 2.10 Daily report and weekly status sheet

DAILY REPORT/SITE DIARY

No. .... Date ....

Job title ....

Registered office

Labour force on site		Labour force required	
Our employ	Subcontract	Our employ	Subcontract

Materials Received (state delivery no.) Required by (state requisition no.)	Information Received Required by
Plant Received (state delivery no.) Required by (state requisition no.)	Drawings Received Required by
Telephone calls To From	Site visitors
Accidents	Stoppages
Weather conditions	Temperature a.m. p.m.
Brief report of progress and other items of importance	
Site manager/foreman .... *Note* Send top copy daily to head office and retain carbon copy as an on-site record.	

WEEKLY STATUS SHEET

CONTRACT AS AT DATE End Week 2

Activity No.	ACTIVITY DESCRIPTION	Total Planned Quantity	Adjusted Quantity (variations)	PROGRESS Total work completed at date shown: STATUS LAST WEEK %	Planned units	Actual units	Planned %	Actual %	STATUS THIS WEEK %	COSTS Total expenditure at date shown: Total budget for % complete	Total actual cost for % work to date	COST STATUS TOTAL
1	EXCAVATE O'SITE	800m^2	–	60	800m^2	800m^2	100	100	0	£1976	£1824	+152
2	EXCAVATE TRENCHES	110m^3	–	0	79m^3	63m^3	72	57	–15	£575	£527	+48
3	CONCRETE FOUNDATIONS	50m^3	–	0	12½m^3	25m^3	25	50	+25	£1250	£1322	–72

nominated. It will probably be the case that the estimator or buyer within the organization will have already obtained quotations and costings from those suppliers (see Figure 2.11a).

Information about materials will come from the initial site investigation, the Bill of quantities, materials schedules, plant schedules and method statements. So that when the contract is awarded, the company's

MATERIALS ORDER FORM		
Order Number		**Date**
Site Address		
Name/Address of Supplier		

Please supply the following order to the above address:

Description	Quantity	Date Required

Special Delivery Instructions:

Signature of Site Manager

Fig 2.11(a) **Materials order form**

contract programme may be drawn up without delay. It is then that the following procedures can be operated:

- Confirm the materials supply selection, using the specification
- Up-date earlier quotations, taking into account any price rises
- From this information evaluate and place orders
- Progress orders
- Receive and check materials once on site.

Material and Resource Forms

Advice Note – This states the description, quantities and dates of the delivery of goods. This information can be used to arrange labour for unloading and or checking and for storage requirements.

Order Confirmation – To be checked against your order.

Delivery Note – This needs to be checked and signed by a supervisor.

Invoice – This shows the price of the items supplied. Always check this carefully against the delivery note before payment is made.

Requisition Form – A note generally used on site to obtain resources from the site stores as required.

Materials Record Book – A record that is made on the actual delivery day, of all the resources received. This record book should always be completed before sending delivery notes to head office.

Materials Record Board Usually situated in one or more of the site offices, it is used to show when deliveries, especially phased bulk supplies such as sand, cement and plaster are due to arrive.

Materials Transfer – This document covers the transfer of materials within the company, usually from one site to another.

Employment Documentation

On appointment to a company, a contract of employment should be signed by the employee and be regularly updated during employment, so that a complete record of work can be maintained (see Figure 2.11b).

All site personnel should be given a copy of the company's safety policy and statement of the firm's terms of employment. Most companies also issue employees with details of any general policy, procedures and disciplinary rules.

Working Hours

The requirements covering working hours, overtime and site conditions arise from three main sources:

- The Working Rule Agreement
- The Health and Safety at Work Act (1974)
- The organization and layout of the particular site.

> **Points to note**
>
> Always check drawings, specifications and schedules. Calculate material requirements exactly, using measurements from the site drawings.
>
> Insist that all suppliers give advance notice of all deliveries.
>
> Always keep informed those people who need to know about the arrival of supplies, for example, labour for unloading and handling, storekeepers and security. As well as staff responsible for checking, inspecting, testing or providing special storage or protection.
>
> Ensure that all of the companies material records are fully up to date and accurate.

Fig 2.11(b) **Contract of employment**

CONTRACT OF EMPLOYMENT

Registered office

STATEMENT OF MAIN TERMS OF EMPLOYMENT

Name of employer ....
Name of employee ....
Title of job ....
Statement issue date ....
Employment commencement date ....

Your hours of work, rates of pay, overtime, pay-day, holiday entitlement and payment, pension scheme, disciplinary procedures, notice and termination of employment and disputes procedure are in accordance with the following documents:

1 The National Working Rules for the Building Industry, approved by the National Joint Council for the Building Industry.

2 The Company wages register.

3 The Company handbook
   (i) general policy and procedures
   (ii) safety policy
   (iii) disciplinary rules

Copies of the above documents are available for your inspection on request at all site offices. Any further changes in the terms of employment will be made to these documents within one month of the change.

The Working Rule Agreement

The majority of construction personnel are employed under the wage rates, terms and employment conditions as laid down in the National Working Rules by the Construction Industry Joint Council.

The Working Rule Agreement (WRA) is a collective agreement agreed upon by the building trade employers and trade unions that make up the Construction Industry Joint Council (CIJC). It is a three-year agreement for pay and conditions, and covers all aspects of general working conditions and industrial relations for the building industry.

Basic rates of pay and conditions are set at national level but regional offices and committees can negotiate local variations and additions to suit a particular area of work or regional practice.

Requirements of the WRA

The WRA is divided into a number of sections, some of which are described below:

■ Provisions for abnormal working conditions, such as excessive dust, dirt, heat or noise.

■ Providing shelter from bad weather, storage and drying facilities for clothes, canteen, site huts and so on

■ Provision of sanitary conditions, including washing and drinking water.

Note: The provisions above have to be met by the employer and not the employee.

Trade Union Rights

At times we all need advice or support in connection with employment.

Everyone has the right to join a union – it costs less than you think and your employer does not need to know you are thinking of joining one. Some of the benefits are:

- They help negotiate better pay and conditions.
- Everyday, unions help thousands of people at work. In 2003 unions won a record 330 million pounds' compensation for their members through legal action.
- Union workplaces are safer, and more likely to help employees get on with better training and development programmes.
- In the best workplaces employers and unions have put behind them outdated ideas of confrontation and work together in partnership.
- Partnership employers recognize that staff morale and commitment are improved when they are treated well, have their views taken into account and enjoy job security. In return staff take more pride in their work and are more ready to embrace the changes modern firms often need to make in order to compete with their competitors.

Holidays

The Working Time Regulations 1998 give a right to four weeks' holiday, paid at a normal week's wage. There are no separate provisions for public holidays and it is lawful for the employer to count public holidays as part of the entitlement. However, if they do so the public holiday must also be paid at normal pay.

You are entitled to take your holidays by giving double the notice to your employer. For example, if you want to take a week's holiday you must give your employer at least two weeks' notice. This is now a statutory right for all workers.

Sickness

Employees should normally receive statutory sick pay for any period of absence due to sickness. You will be paid by your employer in the same way you normally receive your wages. This is a right payable to every employee, and you cannot sign away your rights to the statutory payment unless it is replaced by a company scheme that is at least comparable.

Minimum Wage

The minimum wage is paid to those who are 22 or over, 18–21-year-olds and the 16 to 17 age bracket. Each age bracket attracting a different hourly rate.

The Health and Safety at Work Act etc. 1974 (HASWA)

The most important health and safety law for site personnel is HASWA. It specifies the general duty placed on employers, occupiers of the buildings, manufacturers, employees and the self-employed. Employers have a duty to protect the general public as well as site personnel.

All site personnel should be familiar with two regulations, which have updated and modernized construction safety law. These regulations are the main set of regulations for the construction industry, and provide much of the detail regarding safety on site.

They are:
- the Construction (Design and Management) Regulations 1994 (CDM)
- the Construction (Health, Safety and Welfare) Regulations 1996 (CHSW).

The CDM Regulations are a comprehensive framework of regulations that place specific safety duties on clients, planning supervisors, designers and architects and contractors.

The regulations are intended to ensure that health and safety requirements are planned and co-ordinated throughout all stages of a construction project from first designs right through to the planning of maintenance work.

The CHSW Regulations covers most aspects of site safety and welfare including:
- Safe places of work
- Preventing falls
- Preventing falling objects
- Work on structures
- Excavations
- Traffic routes, vehicles gates and doors
- Welfare facilities.

Note: There are many more regulations imposed on employers than those listed above.

Site Safety

As you are aware, health and safety applies to everyone on a construction site, it is everyone's responsibility. Every employer and employee is required by law to comply. This could mean an employer or an employee being prosecuted for not doing so.

Therefore you must at all times ensure your own safety, and see that your actions do not endanger anyone else's.

TRY THIS OUT

- You are expecting a large delivery of materials to your site. Make out a checklist of all the factors you need to consider before the delivery arrives. Show the list to your supervisor and ask him or her if it is similar to his version.

Work-based Evidence Required

- **Documentation required by the organization is completed.**

To meet this requirement, ask your supervisor to fill out a witness testimony sheet stating that the documentation required by the company has been completed. This could for example, be as simple as filling out your time sheet each week.

When you have received the signed and dated witness testimony sheet from your supervisor, place them in your work-based evidence portfolio when next in college and map and record it against the syllabus.

Quick quiz Quick quiz Quick quiz Quick quiz Quick quiz

❶ What is the difference between a day worksheet and a time sheet?

❷ List three types of material and resource forms.

❸ What must be signed on appointment to a company?

❹ Name three requirements of the WRA.

❺ What information is required on a job card?

Procedures and Programmes 2.3

In this section you will learn about the use of resources for your own and other's work requirements.

- The allocation of appropriate work to employees
- The organization of work sequence
- Types of progress charts, timetables and estimated times.

When you have completed this section you will be able to:

- Follow organizational procedures to maintain good work relationships
- Complete the work within the allocated time, in accordance with the programme of work.

Know and understand:

- How organizational procedures are applied to maintain good work relationships

■ What the programme is for the work to be carried out in the estimated, allocated time and why deadlines should be kept.

This section will now cover procedures and programmes.

Administrative and Organizational Procedures

Administrative and organizational procedures are important parts of the building process. A construction company would not know where things are, or whether they are getting good value from resources unless they kept a check on them.

The responsibility for administration and organizational procedures is divided between the site and head office. In larger companies the selection, pricing, ordering, preparation of schedules and payment of invoices are dealt with at head office. This leaves the receipt, storage and protection of materials to local management on site.

Procedures vary, but the majority of work programming is usually carried out at head office, although their implementation still remains with site personnel, which in itself should be efficient if losses are to be avoided.

Site administration and control can only be successful when carried out correctly; this requires a mixture of experience, discipline and initiative. On larger contracts, there is usually a separate administrative staff acting in unison with other site management and personnel, who on smaller jobs will have total responsibility.

Organization of Work Sequence

Ever increasing demands are made on all members of the construction team to build more quickly and more cheaply, maximizing profits yet maintaining high standards.

The successful completion of any project depends on sound planning, and this is equally true in construction. Before work starts on a site it is essential to produce a detailed programme of work as illustrated in Figure 2.12 and an accurate schedule of deliveries, if labour and materials are to be co-ordinated successfully. The plan should take into account the level of skill of the people who will be implementing it, failure to do so only results in time being wasted later.

The location and duration of the contract will generally dictate the choice of programme. On a small contract experienced staff can work successfully using a few key dates relating to the main building operations, but on a larger contract activities must link into one continuous sequence of events.

All the information fed into the programme is only as good as the person wishes to make it, and full benefit will only be obtained when the programme is updated daily, and prompt corrective action taken when the work falls behind. The programme of work must take into account capital outlay and the builder's cash flow.

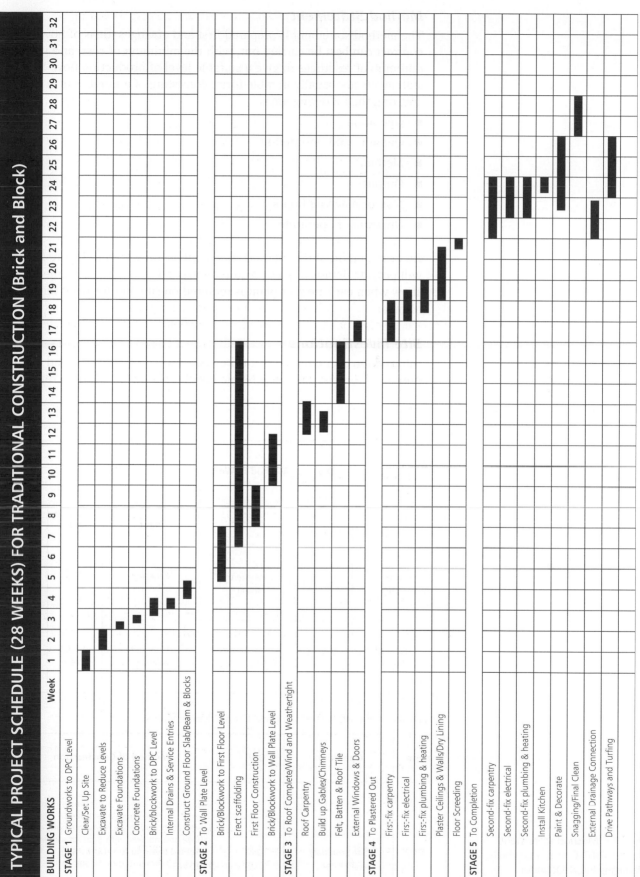

Fig 2.12 Programme of work

Method Statement

The method statement is prepared first and arranges ideas of how a contract can best be carried out, with the minimum of cost, and with the optimum of resources to give a suitable level of production flow. Method statements are usually in table form, consisting of a number of columns covering the following areas.

- Operation
- Quantity and description
- Method
- Output
- Man or machine hours
- Duration of operation.

An examination of the method statement as illustrated in Figure 2.13 will provide details of plant requirements and so on. The statement will show when each item of plant is required on site and for what length of time.

Site Investigations

Information accumulated from site visits should be recorded and presented for easy reference by means of tables listed within a report.

Description of Item	Qty.	Method of Work	Resources		
			Plant	Labour	Days
Excavate oversite	200m³	Excavate by dozer	1 tracked bulldozer	1 lab. 2 ops.	1
Excavate to reduced	1025m³	Excavate by dozer with ripper att.	1 tracked bulldozer	1 lab. 2 ops.	6

Compare that with a detailed MS for a single item of Preparatory Work:

Item	Operation	Qty	Method of Construction
3/1	Site boundary fencing	1040 lin. m	Excavate post holes at 2440 centres using post hole auger attachment. Erect 100 × 100 fence posts to height of 2250 above ground level with 3 no. triangular rails. Set old plywood formwork 2440 × 1220 sheets 150 mm into ground and secure to rails.

Fig 2.13 **Method statement**
Source: CITB-ConstructionSkills: Managing Information for Operations 1994

Programmes

Programmes of Work

The programme of work is the key document containing the duration and sequence of operations for the completion of the building. It covers three critical areas.

The master programme shows start and finish dates, duration, sequencing and relationships for the whole contract.

The stage programme covers a precise stage of the contract, or the overall programme for a one to two month period in much greater detail.

The weekly programme functions at the level where the work takes place; it requires frequent up-dating and reviews.

Monitoring and Control of Operations

It requires a great deal of information to be able to monitor and control work progress. Programmes of work do this for us. They let us know:

- What resources have been allocated
- The planned output to achieve the programme
- The productivity rates used in the tender or contract plan
- The key control operations.

When we have this information we can monitor and control work progress. Information for the work programme comes from various sources, for example the tender and contract programme will be based on calculations of the resources needed and the planned output to achieve the programme. There will usually be stage programmes that list the resources and output for different parts of the contract.

In order to measure progress we need to compare the actual output against the planned output. So, we measure against what was planned.

There are a number of factors, some outside the control of management, which can lead to a programme's modification. These include:

- Bad weather
- Labour shortages
- Industrial action
- Contract variations
- Bad planning.

Recording Progress

There are a number of methods of recording progress, for example:

- Bar charts
- Annotated plans
- Numerical schedules
- Histograms
- Graphs and other similar methods.

> **Points to note**
>
> It is far better to make regular comparisons of output because the sooner we are aware that things are not taking place, then the easier it is to find the cause and take the necessary action.
>
> Important tasks, those that could have an effect on other jobs if they were not to finish on time, should be checked more regularly
>
> Rather than using the usual calculated targets, such as square metres of brickwork per day, it might be better to convert these targets into units of activity. For example, the number of walls per day or foundations per day and so on. This method is usually easier to understand, and just as important, to check.

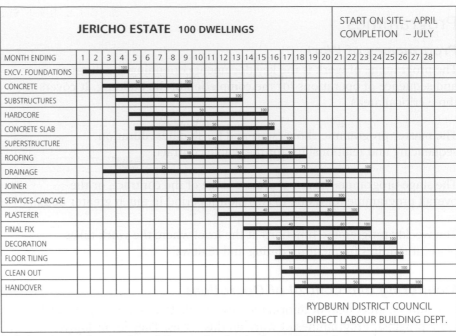

Typical programme for rate of completion on a housing development contract

Fig 2.14 **Gannt chart**
Source: J.E. Johnston

The type of programme adopted for small and medium sized contracts is usually based on the Gannt chart, which provides a graphic description of each operation as illustrated in Figure 2.14. Because Gannt charts are presented as a series of horizontal bars they are generally referred to as bar charts.

Operations are shown separately with the length of each bar depending on the duration of the activity. These bars have a limited dependency upon each other, and this is one of the shortcomings of the system because some operations can be in advance of others that may have fallen behind. The results can be interpreted in different ways, which means that agreement is not always unanimous when assessing progress at meetings.

Types of Bar Charts

Bar charts are the most common form of monitoring progress on a construction site. The main advantage of bar charts is that they relate to the programme of work. There are several ways of monitoring progress, using a bar chart.

Single Bar System

This chart involves a single bar indicating the activity and, as work progresses, the bar is filled to indicate the amount of work completed as shown in Figure 2.15.

The single bar system is very simple and probably the least informative of bar chart systems.

Two-bar Systems

Using the two-bar system you can tell how much work has been completed for each week of operation, as shown in Figure 2.16.

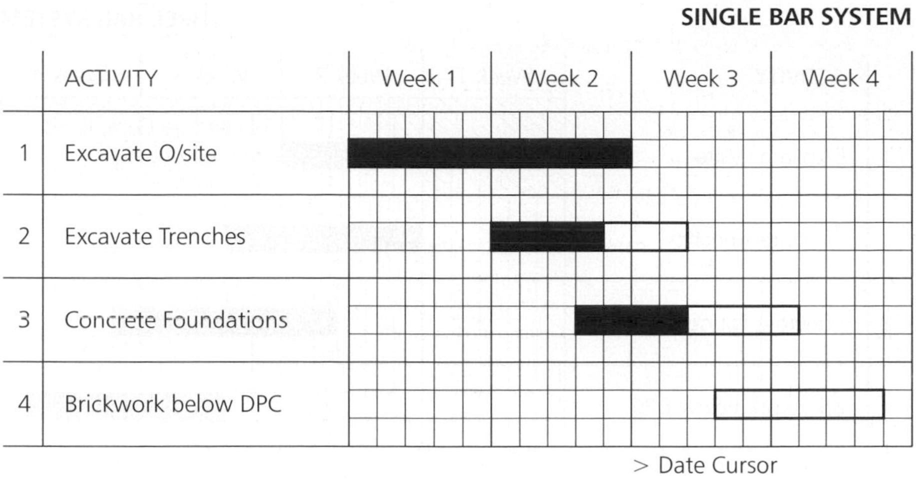

SINGLE BAR SYSTEM

	ACTIVITY	Week 1	Week 2	Week 3	Week 4
1	Excavate O/site				
2	Excavate Trenches				
3	Concrete Foundations				
4	Brickwork below DPC				

> Date Cursor

Fig 2.15 **Single bar chart**
Source: CITB-ConstructionSkills

TWO BAR SYSTEM

	ACTIVITY	Week 1	Week 2	Week 3	Week 4
1	Excavate O/site		Percentage Completed		
			Planned Activity		
2	Excavate Trenches				
3	Concrete Foundations				
4	Brickwork below DPC				

> Date Cursor

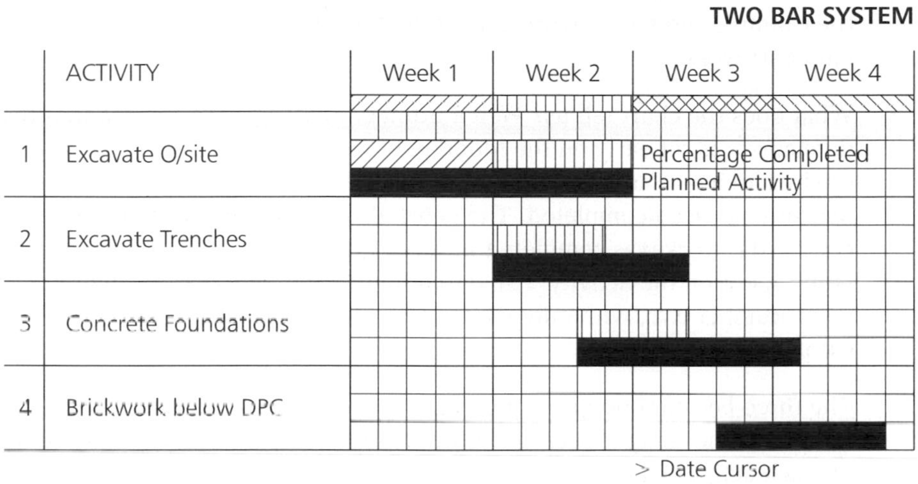

Fig 2.16 **Two-bar system**
Source: CITB ConstructionSkills

We can see from the chart that the following activities have been carried out:

Item 1

It is clear that 50 per cent of the work has been completed in week one, leaving 50 per cent to be completed in week two.

Item 2

This task is behind schedule, only just above half of the excavation has been carried out at the end of week two, whereas it had been planned for some 70 per cent to have been done.

Item 3

On the programme it was planned to have some 25 per cent of the work competed by the end of week two, whereas 50 per cent has been carried out. So the two bar system tells us that the contract is 100 per cent ahead of schedule.

Three-bar Systems

Three-bar systems are basically the same as two-bar systems but with the addition of a bar which indicates how many days have been worked on each activity. The system shows the percentage of tasks completed, the

ACTIVITY		Week 1	Week 2	Week 3	Week 4
1	Excavate O/site			Percentage Completed Planned Activity Days worked	
2	Excavate Trenches				
3	Concrete Foundations				
4	Brickwork below DPC				

> Date Cursor

Fig 2.17 **Three-bar system**
Source: CITB-ConstructionSkills

planned duration of the activity, and the number of days worked. Study the example shown in Figure 2.17 to better understand how the three-bar chart works.

What does the chart tell us? Well a number of things! We can see that the date cursor is set early on the Monday of week number three. You can see by looking at activity number one that all of the excavation of the oversite has been completed. The chart also tells us that some 60 per cent of the work was completed in week number one, only four days being spent on the activity. The remaining 40 per cent was finished in week number two, with only Wednesday and Thursday needed to complete the job.

The three-bar method gives more information than the earlier bar charts. However, one thing it does not inform us of, is what resources were used on each activity.

Source: CITB-ConstructionSkills

Annotated Plans

This system uses drawings to show what progress is being made. An easy way of explaining the system is to use a housing development as an example, as shown in Figure 2.18

Illustrated is a small estate of eight houses. From the shaded areas we can tell how much of the work has been carried out, for example.

■ All eight houses have had their substructures completed

■ Seven houses have had their services completed

■ Two-and-a-half of the roofs have been finished, out of the eight.

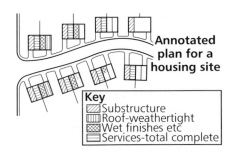

Fig 2.18 **Annotated plan**
Source: CITB-ConstructionSkills

Approximately four-and-a-half of the eight wet finishes have been completed, which is just over half of the total required. This is a simple method that relies on graphic imagery. It is easy to see how much progress has been made.

Roads, paths, fences and drains could also be included using different colours or different patterns or various hatchings.

Numerical Schedules

Schedules are useful for activities on a construction site that repeat themselves, such as on a block of flats or housing development

The method is very simple, you enter the start dates and finish dates for each activity. If you look at the example shown in Figure 2.19 this illustrates activities on a block of flats that are duplicated on every floor.

From the schedule it is easy to see that the electrical carcassing has been completed for the first three floors. The fourth floor carcassing is still being carried out.

PROGRESS AS AT	NOV. 25TH			FINISHES BLOCK 3				
	FLOOR NUMBER							
ACTIVITIES	1st	2nd	3rd	4th	5th	6th	7th	8th
ELECTRICAL CARCASSING	14/11 / 16/11	17/11 / 21/11	22/11 / 24/11	25/11 /				
HOT AND COLD WATER DISTRIBUTION	7/11 / 10/11	11/11 / 16/11	17/11 / 22/11	23/11 /				
JOINER FIRST FIX	14/11 / 18/11	21/11 /						
PLASTERING TO AREA 'A'	21/11 /							
DITTO TO AREA 'B'								

Fig 2.19 **Numerical schedule**
Source: CITB-ConstructionSkills, Monitoring and Controlling Work Progress, 1994

Graphs

Graphs are used to show cumulative progress, as they are highly visible and usually instantly understood.

There is no limitation on the variations that can be used for the representation of work activities carried out on a site and it is for this reason that graphs remain popular. The industry however, is increasingly using software programs for computer application, it is still useful though to understand the basic principles which underpin the techniques of plotting graphs.

TRY THIS OUT

- Try and think of the forms that are used for administration and organization on your site or at head office.

- Prepare a list of the ones that you use and know about.

- Find out who has the responsibility of completing records and forms and what happens to them after completion.

- Get your tutor to check if your work is accurate.

Work-based Evidence Required

■ **Procedures and use of resources, allocation of work and method of work.**

To meet this requirement obtain a witness testimony sheet from your supervisor stating that you have followed company procedures in the use of resources, allocation of work and method of work For example:

To whom it may concern.

I would like to confirm that between 1 November 2004 and 3 November 2004 Ravi Singh carried out company procedures for the following:

Ordered 140 aircrete blocks and 300 common bricks from D. Whatmough and Son Builders' Merchants.

Checked and signed off a delivery of ready mixed mortar.

Carried out all necessary safety checks on an angle grinder before use.

Allocation of work:
Ravi was instructed to build a one brick wall to the front of the client's house, he carried this out to the Industrial Standard using the standard specification and site drawings.

Method of Work:
Ravi follows a method of work that is organized and competent, from first instructions he shows initiative and an understanding of the work programme. He at all times follows the company's health and safety policies.

Yours faithfully
Darren Howells (site supervisor)

When you have received the signed and dated witness testimony sheets from your supervisor, place them in your work-based evidence portfolio when next in college and map and record it against the syllabus.

Quick quiz Quick quiz Quick quiz Quick quiz Quick quiz

❶ What type of information would be contained in a site schedule.

❷ Bar charts are used to plan and record progress of work operations. Name two other methods that could be used.

❸ List five factors that could delay the progress of work operations.

❹ State four benefits for evaluating the progress of work.

❺ State four advantages of planning work activities.

Relationships

In this section you will learn about relationships that include:

- Individuals, workplace groups, client and other operatives, line management, own occupation and allied occupations.

When you have completed this section you will be able to:

- Communicate with others to establish productive work relationships.

Know and understand:

- The methods of communication with other workplace personnel and, or the client.

This section will now cover relationships.

Relationships with the Client

As a member of the site personnel team you may at times be the first point of contact with the client. Some important points when dealing with clients are:

- The client in whatever form pays your salary, so always be helpful and polite
- Deal with their questions as quickly as possible, if you are not sure of an answer say so and find someone who does
- You are usually working on the client's property, so treat it with respect
- Keep your work area clean and tidy
- Clean up at regular intervals, this will project pride in your work and give confidence to the client that you are a competent person
- At times breakages may occur, always be honest, inform the client and your supervisor
- Your appearance is important, a clean and tidy person will project confidence and a professional image

Visitors should be greeted properly and politely, they could be any one of the following:

- The architect, local authority inspectors, prospective clients, any one of whom might wish to give your company work, and if treated badly might be put off doing so.

Workplace Groups

In order for a construction company to make a profit and thereby pay site personnel their wages, it is important that personnel are content and relaxed about their role within the company. This means that people need to communicate and that working conditions are as beneficial as possible, for example, salaries, holidays, job security, future opportunities and a safe working environment are all available.

TRY THIS OUT

- What do you think are the advantages of involving site personnel in decision making? Make a list of five and show them to your supervisor to see if he agrees with your findings.

When you join a construction company you are often the odd one out and therefore you should try harder than most to co-operate with your new colleagues. This will entail being polite, acting on a request as quickly as possible and forming a good working relationship with all site personnel. All of these factors will make your time at work better and more rewarding.

Source: CITB-ConstructionSkills. Team Building, 1994.

Work-based Evidence Required

■ Work carried out in conjunction with others

To meet this requirement obtain a witness testimony sheet from your supervisor stating that your work is carried out in conjunction with others. For example:

To whom it may concern.

I would like to confirm that between 3 November 2004 and 5 November 2004 Anel Amin was working on the contract at St Marys Gate college. Anel was involved in building a large boundary wall with two of our other bricklayers, Donna Howells and Frank Watson. Anel worked extremely well with Frank and Donna and helped them as a team to carry out the job on time and to budget.

Yours faithfully
Paul Keilty (site supervisor)

Place the evidence in your work-based evidence portfolio when next in college and map and record it against the syllabus.

Quick quiz Quick quiz Quick quiz Quick quiz Quick quiz

❶ List the key points of good relations with the client.
❷ How should visitors be greeted when arriving on site?

Information on Communication

For more information about the topics identified in this section why not visit the following websites.

British Standards Institution
www.bsi–global.com

Health and Safety Executive
www.hse.gov.uk

National House Building Council
www.nhbc.co.uk

Information on Documentation

For more information about the topics discussed in this section why not visit the following websites.

HSE
www.hse.gov.uk

Construction Confederation
http://www.theCC.org.uk

The Construction Confederation is a Trade Association that gives advice to members of the member federations, e.g. National Federation of Builders. The members pay a subscription to their member federation for certain services the Construction Confederations part being purely advisory.

To find out more about how to join a union and which union is the right one for you, phone the TUCs Know Your Rights Line on 0870 600 4882 or visit the following website.

Worksmart
www.worksmart.org.uk

CITB-ConstructionSkills
citb-ConstructionSkills.co.uk

The CITB have an excellent series of learning modules entitled Open Learning for Supervising Managers in the Construction Industry which cover in detail the monitoring and controlling of work progress. They are highly recommended as a learning resource.

City and Guilds
www.city–guilds.co.uk

Information about Relationships

For more information about relationships on site, why not visit the following websites.

CITB-ConstructionSkills
citb-ConstructionSkills.co.uk

Chapter Three

Move and Handle Resources

NVQ Level 2   Unit No. VR 03   Move and Handle Resources

This Unit, in the context of brickwork and the construction industry work environment, is about:

- ❡ **Following instructions**
- ❡ **Adopting safe and healthy working practices**
- ❡ **Selecting materials, components and equipment**
- ❡ **Handling, moving and storage of materials and components by manual procedures and lifting aids.**

There are four sections in this chapter, disposal of waste, information, methods of work and problems.

This chapter will now cover methods of moving and handling resources.

Disposal of Waste ▬▬▬▬▬▬ 3.1

In this section you will learn about environmental responsibilities, organizational procedures, manufacturers' information, statutory regulations and official guidance related to the disposal of waste.

When you have completed this section you will be able to :

■ Comply with the given information to prevent damage to the product and surrounding environment.

Know and understand:

■ Why disposal of waste should be carried out safely and how it is achieved.

This section will now cover the disposal of waste.

Introduction

Waste is all substances that the holder wishes or is required to dispose of in solid, liquid or gaseous form.

Over 70 million tonnes of waste is produced in the construction industry each year. This amounts to 24 kg per week for every person in the UK, about four times the rate of household waste production. Government strategy and guidance, suggests we should follow a hierarchical approach to reduce the amount of waste we produce, and to reuse and recycle what waste is produced.

Whilst the trend is questioning the traditional routes of waste disposal in favour of sustainable waste management strategies, the majority of the construction industry has placed waste reduction at the bottom of research agendas because of complexities over reuse and recycling.

Source: A. Keys, A. Baldwin and S. Austin, *Designing to Encourage Waste Minimisation in the Construction Industry,* Department of Civil and Building Engineering, Loughborough University, Leicestershire, LE11 3TU

Environmental Responsibilities

Every business produces waste of some kind or other, but what waste is and how much is produced will vary greatly across sectors. With changes in environmental legislation affecting how we handle and dispose of waste, attitudes will have to change or businesses will risk high costs and prosecution.

Behind all this legislation is a drive towards a more sustainable planet through reductions in natural resource use. Minimizing the waste we produce is one way of doing this, as waste is a symptom of inefficient consumption.

But having produced the waste, it all has to be disposed of in a way that inevitably causes some environmental impact and the challenge is to reduce the effect of waste both today and on future generations.

Traditionally, the UK has relied on landfill for the bulk of its waste disposal. Over 70 per cent of commercial waste is still landfilled whilst for household waste, that figure is over 80 per cent. There is plentiful availability and therefore cost has been has been the key factor in inhibiting the development of alternatives, but that now has to change as European pressure demands reductions in landfill through targets for reduction, recycling and, potentially, re-use.

By 2009 the current methods of waste collection will all but disappear. Segregation, treatment and landfill diversion will become the norm as costs rise and legislation bites. Acting now will reduce those costs and improve business.

Recycling

Recycling should not be expensive and should cost no more than general waste disposal. But cost is a function of material type, volume, location and quality together with the savings that can be made on disposal of residual waste. So for instance, a small office might well find that having an office paper recycling scheme adds to the cost of waste disposal if they simply add it to their existing waste arrangements. But by reducing their residual waste costs by reducing the number of times waste is removed or had a larger container, they might well be able to save overall costs.

Did you know

Aluminium cans could be recycled indefinitely saving 95 per cent of the energy needed to make new.

key terms

Controlled Waste means household, commercial and industrial waste. It includes office waste and waste from a house, shop factory or other business premises. A substance is controlled waste whether it is solid or liquid and even if it is not hazardous or toxic.

Special Waste is the most dangerous (including toxic and hazardous) and difficult commercial and industrial waste. The 1996 Special Waste Regulations define the term special waste. Examples of special waste include oils, lead–acid and nickel–cadmium batteries and asbestos. Asbestos from households is also treated as special waste. There are separate controls on radioactive waste.

Did you know Composting of plant-based, kitchen and garden waste is a growth process for the domestic market, and collected via various means including Civic Amenity sites and kerbside collection.

The problem is that the UK is starting from a much lower baseline than most of Europe, so we have much more to do. Approximately 60 million tonnes of industrial, commercial and household waste goes to landfill each year in the UK. To meet all the targets, 20 million of this has to be diverted down alternative uses or simply not produced. But not only will it make a difference to business. It should also cut costs.

Recycling – it's worth thinking about.

Source: Biffa. Recycling an Overview.

Methods

There are three important reasons for the disposal of waste:

- SAFETY
- HEALTH
- ECONOMY

Waste materials left lying around can cause accidents.

Scaffolds and other work areas, doorways and runways must be kept clear.

Waste left lying about makes a breeding ground for vermin.

Materials are expensive; therefore do not waste materials.

Broken bricks, tiles stone and so on; can be reused as hardcore beneath concrete slabs and so on.

Offcuts of timber can be used as pegs or for making profiles.

Sweeping up Debris

On site a brush can be used to sweep fine debris into heaps.

In confined spaces or in the workshop lay the dust by sprinkling water on the area to be swept.

If dust cannot be avoided always wear a dust mask.

Mortar Bay

The mortar used on site is a mixture of lime sand and cement and usually has a shelf life of some 48 hours. Once the mortar has been used, any surplus should be returned to the mortar bay to be remixed. When returning the mortar to the mortar bay, always ensure no particles of brick or block are mixed in with it as this will damage the mixer.

Waste Bins

All brick and block waste should be deposited in waste bins for reuse or recycling.

Materials are expensive do not throw away good bricks and blocks.

Good Practice

Good Working Practice

- When you have waste, you have a duty to stop it escaping, store it safely and securely.

- If the waste is loose, bag it or cover it.

- Keep it in the confines of the container.

- Do not pile waste higher than the sides of the container.

- Keep lids and doors locked and shut when not in use.

- Do not burn waste, it causes damage to the environment.

- Prevent unauthorized access to containers by children or vagrants.

- DO NOT – enter any container or skip.

- DO NOT – pile waste beyond the sides of any container (see Figure 3.1). Waste blowing about the site contravenes the Environmental Protection Act duty of care regulations.

- DO NOT – overload containers, it is unsafe to site personnel and dangerous for waste disposal staff to handle the containers.

Source: Biffa.
Adding Value —
How Do Biffa Measure Up?

Step 1 Apply the brake to all wheeled containers before using.

Step 2 Open lids fully to load

Step 3 Lock and close the lids when finished loading

Step 4 Use the correct handles to manoeuvre the containers around

Fig 3.1 (a) Container badly filled; (b) Wheeled container trade waste guidelines
Source: Biffa

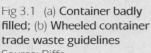

Statutory Regulations and Official Guidance

3.2

Landfill Tax

Landfill tax has been in operation since 1996 and has risen by a pound a year to a figure that is now £15 per tonne. But from early 2005, that figure will rise by at least £3 per tonne to a government stated target figure of £35 per tonne within a short space of time (see Figure 3.2). This could see landfill costs double in five years, placing a huge additional cost on business.

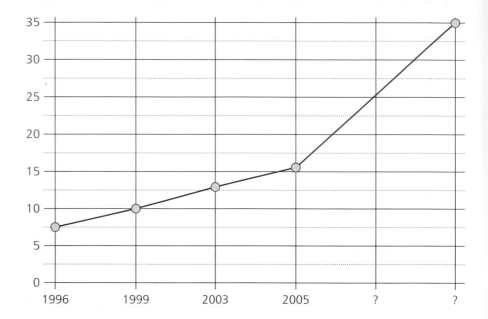

Fig 3.2 **Graph showing rise in landfill tax**
Source: Biffa. Recycling: An Overview

Other legislation is beginning to apply more and more producer responsibility pressures where the environmental impact of end of life disposal is charged to those who produced the product and placed it on the market.

Did you know

For recycling, waste office paper is the quality end of the paper market, and the average office worker will generate approximately 35 kg of paper per year.

The waste packaging regulations have been with us since 1997, requiring those in the packaging chain to pay towards increasing recycling of packaging. Other producer responsibility legislation is being developed for waste electrical and electronic equipment and scrap cars whilst batteries, newspapers, tyres, office paper and junk mail are all in the firing line (see Figure 3.3).

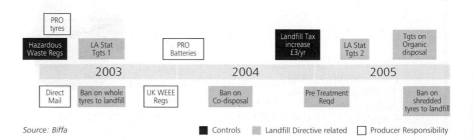

Fig 3.3 **Environmental timetable**
Source: Biffa. Recycling: An Overview

Work-based Evidence Required

- **Disposal of waste packaging in accordance with legislation to minimize damage and maintain a clean work space.**

To meet this requirement, obtain from your supervisor a witness testimony sheet stating that you have disposed of waste packaging in accordance with legislation to minimize damage and maintain a clean work space. It would also be useful if you could obtain some photographs of yourself carrying out these activities.

When you have received the signed and dated witness testimony sheets from your supervisor, place them in your work-based evidence portfolio when next in college and map and record it against the syllabus.

Information 3.3

In this section you will learn about technical, product and regulatory information in oral, written and graphical forms.

When you have completed this section you will be able to:

- comply with the given product information to carry out the work efficiently to the required guidance

Know and understand:

- the level of understanding operatives must have of information for relevant, current legislation and official guidance and how it is applied.

This section will now cover information.

Sources of Information

It is not possible to recall all the information required for a particular job or contract. To record this information a variety of systems are installed within the administration of companies. A vital feature of these systems is the need to regularly update information to account for such instances as technical developments, financial alterations and legislative change.

Site managers and supervisors would be well advised to collect suitable quick reference information as soon as possible on the award of a contract. This may then be used to instruct, notify or advise individuals, and determine solutions to problems that from time to time may well arise.

Throughout your career in construction you will be called upon to make decisions in order to solve a variety of problems, both material and personal, and contribute effectively towards the organization of the companies involved. To be an effective member of a team of building personnel you will need to be actively researching the sources of information and regulatory publications available to you and the information included in each.

Types and Sources of Information

People

One of the best sources of information is other people. As a member of the site team you are part of a large network of people, who for example include:

- Members of the site team
- Supervisors
- Managers
- Sub-contractors
- Company specialist, e.g. safety officer.

Any one of these people may be able to help you. All you have to do is ask.

Libraries

Libraries are able to provide a wealth of information material from books and leaflets on a wide range of subjects, to computers to access the Internet. Most libraries have a reference section that will include dictionaries and directories as well as a host of other information sources. All libraries are part of the inter-library loan scheme, through which it is possible to order books, provided you know the title, author and publisher, which are not held in the library. Libraries also hold indexes of periodicals giving details of articles, and most have copies of past newspapers and magazines on file.

College and University Libraries

College and university libraries exist to provide you with facilities and resources to extend your learning and support you in the successful completion of your course.

If you are a student on a NVQ course in brickwork at your local college then you will automatically be a member of the college library. Most college libraries will have the following resources in printed, audio-visual and electronic formats:

Printed
Books – there are books to support you in your coursework as well as fiction for leisure reading.

Journals – There are subject specific journals such as *Building* magazine and *Construction News* but there are also easy reading magazines

Audio-visual
Videos – these are usually available for a one week loan period.

Cassettes – cassettes include audio stories and language learning cassettes.

Electronic

Internet – usually available on all personal computers free of charge.

Intranet – each college usually has its own web site that can be accessed from the student Intranet.

Online Resources Booklet – an in-house guide to electronic sources which can be accessed from the library Intranet.

Facilities

Study Areas – both group and individual study areas are usually available.

Drop-in computers – with access to electronic sources and packages to produce your assignments such as, Word, Access, Excel, PowerPoint, Publisher, Photo draw, FrontPage.

Laser Printing – black and white printing is usually available.

Video viewing – videos can usually be watched on an individual basis.

Photocopying – in colour and black and white is usually available.

Services

All libraries offer a range of services to provide you with access to the resources you need. These will include:

Inter-library loans – they can borrow books from the British Library on your behalf.

Reservations – traps can be placed on items that are checked out so that they will be held for you on return.

Advanced computer booking – to ensure you have access to a personal computer when you need it.

Information

Libraries have a wide variety of information sources for you to use and you can find the items you require by the following:

Library staff – ask a member of staff to help you locate the items you want.

On-line catalogue – based on a computer, this is a database of all resources held in the library. You can search by author, title and subject.

Shelf guides – these labels give an indication of which subject books can be found on which shelves.

Subject guides – there will be a range of guides on different subjects which will outline where you can find book, internet, journal and CD-ROM sources for your subject area.

If you are not a student but have an interest in brickwork, do not despair. Most college and university libraries are open to outside users, with the payment of a small fee, or you may simply need to produce a letter from your employer explaining why you need to use the service and for how long.

The British Library now holds a wealth of information about construction and the built environment on public shelving.

Quick quiz Quick quiz Quick quiz Quick quiz Quick quiz

❶ State three information sources that would provide information on materials required to complete a contract.

❷ State five methods by which information can be communicated on site.

❸ Name three information sources that will provide information on the type and quantity materials required on a construction project.

❹ Which document will provide information on the correct use of material?

Note – the text does not necessarily include all the answers to these questions. In which case refer to other sources of information.

Methods of Work 3.4

In this section you will learn about the application of knowledge for safe work practices, procedures, skills and transference of competence for:

■ Manual handling and storage.

When you have completed this section you will be able to safely carry out manual activities which require:

■ Complying with the given information to move and store resources to maintain safe working practices
■ Handling and storing heavy bagged material
■ Handling and storing sheet materials
■ Handling concrete building components
■ Handling masonry building components
■ Handling and storing lengthy materials.

Know and understand:

■ the hazards associated with the resources and methods of work and how they are overcome.

This section will now cover methods of work.

Manual Handling and Storage

Introduction

More than a third of all over-three day injuries reported each year to the Health and Safety Executive (HSE) and local authorities are caused by manual handling, that is, the transporting or supporting of loads by hand or bodily force.

Most of the reported accidents cause back injury, although hands, arms and feet are also vulnerable. In 1995, an estimated average of 11 working days per sufferer was lost through musculoskeletal disorders affecting the back, caused by work. HSE estimated that such conditions cost employers up to £335 million (based on 1995/6 prices).

Many manual handling injuries build up over a period rather than being caused by a single handling incident. These injuries occur wherever people are at work – on building sites, in factories, offices, warehouses and while making deliveries.

Source: HSE

Legislation

In addition to the responsibilities of the employer and employee as set out in the Health and Safety at Work Act, there are regulations relating to manual handling. The manual handling Operations Regulations place a requirement on the employer to deal with risks to the safety and health of employees who have to carry out manual handling at work.

Duties of the Employer

- Avoid the need for hazardous manual handling, as far as reasonably practicable
- Assess the risk of injury from any hazardous manual handling that cannot be avoided
- Reduce the risk of injury from hazardous manual handling, as far as reasonably practicable.

Duties of the Employee

- Follow appropriate systems of work laid down for their safety
- Make proper use of equipment provided for their safety
- Co-operate with their employer on health and safety matters
- Inform the employer if they identify hazardous handling activities
- Take care to ensure that their activities do not put others at risk.

There is no such thing as a completely safe manual handling operation. But working within the guidelines will cut the risk and reduce the need for a more detailed assessment.

Typical Hazards

Care must be taken at all times when handling construction materials and components. Typical hazards are:

- Splinters – wood or metal
- Jagged edges – wood, metal or clay products

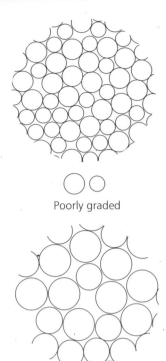

Poorly graded

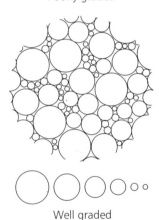

Poorly graded

Well graded

Fig 3.4 **Examples of sand**
Source: Hanson

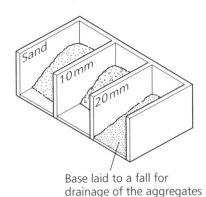

Base laid to a fall for
drainage of the aggregates

Fig 3.5 **Storage bays for aggregates**

- Sharp edges on materials – corners of bricks, metal cladding, cut wall ties
- Falling objects – collapsing stacks, items falling on to hands and feet
- Chemical burns or irritants – cement, lime
- Trapped fingers – lifting or lowering heavy objects
- Muscular strains – lifting or lowering heavy/awkward objects
- Damage to eyes or lungs – dust, powder, fumes
- Sharp objects – nails left sticking out of wood, sharp metal offcuts.

Methods of Handling and Storage

Aggregates

Aggregates are granules or particles that are mixed with cement, lime and water to make mortar and concrete. Aggregates should be hard, durable and should not contain any form of plant life, or anything that could be dissolved in water.

Aggregates are classified into two groups :

- Fine aggregates – composed of granules which pass through a 5 mm sieve
- Coarse aggregates – composed of particles which are retained by a 5 mm sieve.

The most commonly used fine aggregate is sand.

Mortar should be mixed using soft or building sand, it should be well graded having an equal quantity of fine medium and large grains.

Concreting should be carried out using a sharp sand which has more angular grains and a coarser feel than soft sand, which has more rounded grains as shown in Figure 3.4.

When concreting we also require coarse aggregate to be used. The most common coarse aggregate is usually limestone chippings, which are quarried and crushed to graded sizes, usually 10 mm, 20 mm or larger.

Storage of Aggregates

Aggregates are normally delivered from lorries either being tipped, or more usually in one tonne bags that are crane handled off the lorry. Aggregates should be stored on a concrete base, with a fall to allow for any water to drain away. The different sizes of aggregates should be stored separately to prevent them from getting mixed together as illustrated in Figure. 3.5.

Aggregate stores should be sited away from any trees to prevent leaf contamination. Tarpaulin or plastic sheets may be used to cover the aggregates to prevent rainwater and rubbish from affecting the materials.

Notes on Handling Aggregates

- They are usually delivered by high-sided lorry to prevent spillage
- Always check the quality, grade and quantity to ensure it matches the order form

- Tip into prepared bays or selected areas
- Transfer by grab, mechanical shovel or power-assisted equipment on weigh batcher
- Transport on site by bucket, hopper, dumper and barrow
- Loss or waste can occur through:
  - Indiscriminate handling
  - Contamination of any kind
  - Using the aggregate as site dressing or to fill site voids.

Cement and Plaster

Cement

Cement is a material which when water is added to it undergoes a chemical change, which causes the cement powder to turn very hard. Cement is made from chalk or limestone and clay, which is crushed into a powder and mixed together and heated in a rotary kiln before being ground into a fine powder. It is then bagged and distributed to builders' merchants. There are many different types of cement for various situations.

Plaster

Plaster is applied on internal walls and ceilings to provide a joint free, smooth, easily decorated surface. Plaster is a mixture that hardens after being applied, it is made from gypsum, cement or lime and water, with or without the addition of fine aggregates depending on the background finish.

Gypsum Plaster

This plaster is for internal use only, there are different types and grades available, depending on the background finish. On undercoats, Browning plaster is usually used.

Cement and Sand Plaster Rendering

This type of plaster or render is used for external finishes, internal undercoats and waterproof finishing coats.

Lime and Sand Rendering

This type of plaster or rendering is usually used as an undercoat, but may also be used as a finishing coat depending on the specification.

Storage of Cement and Plaster

Both cement and plaster are usually available in 25 kg bags. These bags are made from a multi-wall layer of paper with a polythene liner. Great care should be taken not to puncture the bags before use as this could result in moisture entering the material, which will adversely affect it. Each bag may be off-loaded manually or with a machine and then stored in a well ventilated, waterproof shed or room on a dry floor stacked on wooden pallets as shown in Figure 3.6.

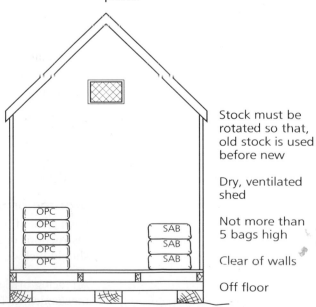

Fig 3.6 Storage shed for cement or plaster

Stock must be rotated so that, old stock is used before new

Dry, ventilated shed

Not more than 5 bags high

Clear of walls

Off floor

The bags of cement or plaster should be kept clear of all walls, and be stacked no higher than five bags high. It is important that the bags are used in the same order as they were delivered, this is to minimize the length of time that the bags are in storage. Lengthy storage times may result in the contents setting over the duration of the building project.

Notes on Handling Cement and Plaster

- Delivered in 25 kg paper sacks on timber pallets
- May also be delivered by tanker and pumped into a silo
- Offload by forklift or crane
- Use bagged cement and plaster in order of delivery.

Loss or waste can occur through:
- Humidity causing materials to lump
- Dampness initiating set
- Indiscriminate handling causing bags to burst
- Failure to use deliveries in rotation
- Pilfering
- Leaving stocks unused.

Self Levelling Compounds

In order to level uneven floors before laying the final covering, a self levelling compound is used which creates a smooth and level surface, which should be covered within 24 hours of application. Levelling compounds are available in bags of 10, 15 and 25 kg.

Storage is the same as for cement and plaster.

Notes on Handling

- Delivered by supplier in drums
- Keep different materials separate
- Loss or waste can occur through:
  - not using for the specified purpose
  - leaving drums open.

Containers

Many materials are supplied in metal or plastic containers with airtight lids. These include paints and adhesives. Frost or extreme heat can affect the contents and so they must be stored in dry, cool conditions.

Bricks

Bricks are components that are used for building walls, they are classified by the type of walls that they can be used for and its situation in the building.

Storage of Bricks

Each pack of bricks that arrives on site should contain a sheet of relevant instructions or information for the use of site personnel. This information should include storage, off-loading and site handling advice.

All facing bricks are supplied in strapped packs and normally off-loaded mechanically. This should be carried out as near to the place of work as possible. A standard pack of facing bricks can weigh anything up to 1600 kg and any lifting equipment used for off-loading or transportation on site must be capable of safely handling this weight.

Safe Offloading

Packs of bricks should never be lifted by their packing straps – the strapping is only designed for safe and convenient transport from the brick manufacturer to the building site. Repeated lifting will loosen the straps and could cause subsequent damage to the bricks. Caution should also be used when cutting straps. Only wire cutters should be used, with site personnel standing well away from the line of the strap to avoid any possible back-lash.

When moving and handling bricks on site, it is important that safety helmets and protective gloves be worn. When lifting pallets by crane and above head height, avoid the use of poles and chains. Always use an enclosed cage or net as a safeguard should a pack become unstable.

Work-based Evidence Required

- **Selection of resources to be moved and/or stored**
- **Own work and that of the team**
- **Materials, components and fixings**
- **Tools and equipment.**

To meet these requirements, obtain a witness testimony sheet from your supervisor stating that you selected resources to be moved and stored. For example:

To whom it may concern.

I would like to confirm that between 6 November 2004 and the 8 November 2004 Mirriam Smith was working on the contract at St Marys Gate College. Mirriam helped with others move a large number of scaffold boards and scaffold clips that were in the way of the building of a boundary wall. They stored the boards and clips in the site compound on the appropriate racks and under cover. Mirriam then helped load out bricks and mortar for the new walling.

At the end of each working day Mirriam is responsible for cleaning and storing the cement mixer and other equipment and tools in the site hut which is then locked and secured. Mirriam always carries out these tasks competently and treats the responsibility in a proper manner.

Yours faithfully
Paul Keilty (site supervisor)

Place the evidence in your work-based evidence portfolio when next in college and map and record it against the syllabus.

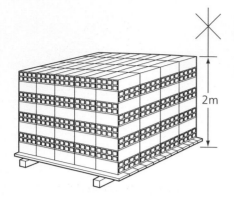

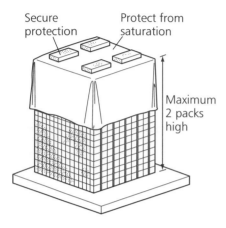

Secure protection

Protect from saturation

Maximum 2 packs high

Fig 3.7 **Storage of bricks**

Method of Storing Bricks

Designated storage areas for bricks should be reasonably accessible to delivery lorries and site handling plant. Bricks should be stored on dry, level ground, or on a well-drained level hardstanding, as shown in Figure 3.7, ensuring they are not in contact with soil, sulphate bearing ground or ash.

Bricks should be stored no more than two packs high and protected from the elements, as well as from splashing by passing vehicles, with tarpaulin or polythene sheets.

It is important to protect stored bricks from becoming wet as they may become difficult to lay, due to their lack of suction. Wet, dense bricks also tend to float on the mortar bed. Lack of protection during storage may ultimately lead to problems of efflorescence, lime leaching and an increased risk of frost attack in the finished brickwork.

Notes on Handling Bricks

- Delivered in packs or on pallets
- Offload by vehicle-crane, forklift or mobile crane
- Transfer on site by forklift, dumper, crane, hoist or elevator
- Sort all chipped or damaged bricks and set aside
- Do not tip facing bricks
- Cut bands holding packs with proper cutters.

Loss or waste can occur through:
- Using facings for common work or as supports and packings
- Faulty workmanship
- Double handling.

Blocks

Blocks tend to be of the concrete or aerated type. The former being heavy and dense and the latter being lightweight and less dense.

Storage of Blocks

The storage of blocks is the same as it is for bricks.

Notes on Handling Blocks

- Delivered on pallets or in polythene-covered packs
- Offload by vehicle crane, forklift or mobile crane
- Transfer on site by forklift, crane and so on
- Keep stacks secure: not too high.

Loss or waste can occur through:
- Using blocks as packings
- Excess breakages.

> *Points to note*

Do not stack materials more than two metres high.

Paving Slabs

Paving slabs are made from concrete, and are available in a variety of sizes, shapes and colours. They are used for pavements and patios, with some slabs being given a textured finish to improve their appearance.

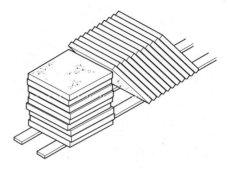

Fig 3.8 **Storage of paving slabs**

Storage of Paving Slabs

Paving slabs are stored outside and stacked on edge to prevent the lower slabs if stored flat, from being damaged by the weight of the stack. The stack is started by laying about eight to ten slabs flat with the other slabs leaning against them as illustrated in Figure 3.8.

It is good practice to put an intermediate flat stack of slabs in long rows of slabs to prevent them from toppling. Slabs should be stored on firm, level ground with timber bearers below to prevent the edges from being damaged. To provide protection from rain and frost, it is advisable to keep the slabs under cover, by placing tarpaulin or polythene sheet over them.

Kerbs

Kerbs are concrete components laid at the edge of a road. The size of a normal kerb is 150 mm wide, 300 mm high and 1 m long.

Pre-Cast Concrete Lintels

Lintels are components placed above openings in brick and block walls to bridge the opening and support the brick and blockwork above. Lintels made from concrete have a steel reinforcement placed on the bottom, which is why pre-cast concrete lintels will have a 'T' or 'top' etched into their top surface. Pre-cast concrete lintels come in a variety of sizes to suit the opening width.

Storage of Pre-cast Concrete Lintels and Kerbs

Kerbs and lintels should be stacked flat on timber bearers, this will assist in lifting and lowering these components by providing a space for hands or lifting slings if machine lifting is to be used.

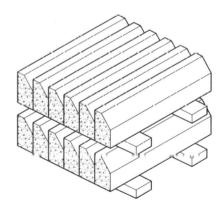

Fig 3.9 **Storage of kerbs**

When stacking kerbs on top of each other, the stack must not be more than three kerbs high. To protect the kerbs and lintels from rain and frost, it is advisable to cover them with a tarpaulin or polythene sheet as illustrated in Figure 3.9.

Notes on Handling

- Offload and transport with care using correct equipment and any lifting points provided in the casting
- Protect edges where slings or cables are used for lifting
- Lifting equipment to be fully capable of raising the load.

Loss or waste can occur through:

- Damaged or broken units will be expensive to replace: repeated orders cost money
- Duplication of items means waste
- Shortage of precast items can create delays.

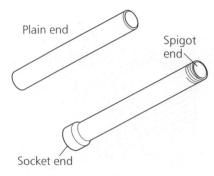

Plain end

Spigot end

Socket end

Fig 3.10 Drainage pipe

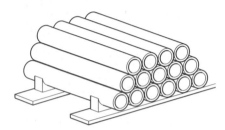

Fig 3.11 Correct method of stacking pipes

Shaped timber cross bearer

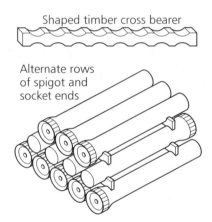

Alternate rows of spigot and socket ends

Fig 3.12 Storage of pipes with socket and spigot ends

Fig 3.13 Storage rack for bars and tubes

Drainage Pipes

Made from vitrified clay or plastic, drainage pipes may have a socket and spigot end or be plain as shown in Figure 3.10.

Clay pipes are easily broken if misused, so care must be taken when handling these items.

Storage of Drainage Pipes and Fittings

Pipes should be stored on a firm, level base and prevented from rolling by placing wedges or stakes on either side of the stack as shown in Figure. 3.11.

Clay pipes with socket and spigot ends, should be stored by alternating the ends on each row, they should also be stacked on shaped timber cross-bearers to prevent them from rolling as illustrated in Figure 3.12.

Do not stack pipes any higher than 1.5 m and taper the stack towards the top.

Fittings and special shaped pipes, like bends, should be stored separately, and if possible in a wooden crate until required.

Notes on Handling

- Fix as work proceeds to avoid damage to structure
- Check angles, offsets and bends for any damage.

Loss or waste can occur through:

- Pilfering
- Damage by site traffic
- Vandalism
- Failure to collect surplus lengths and fittings
- Plastic materials brittle in low temperatures.

Storing Bars, Tubes and Similar Materials

Often it is necessary to store metal bars, tubes and similar materials for short periods or for maintaining a stock.

The type of rack illustrated in Figure 3.13 is frequently used in workshops and allows for separation of materials which allows quick identification of sizes and types.

This type of rack can also be used for storing scaffolding tubes or pipes.

Storage of Pipes and Cylindrical Materials

Pipes and other types of cylindrical items are often brought to a site for immediate use. These materials can be stored on the floor. Use a wedge or some other blocking device to prevent the stacked pipes from moving or rolling during stacking or removal as shown in Figure 3.14.

Remove large diameter pipes from a stack by pulling them out from the ends as shown in Figure 3.15. Do not remove by lifting from the sides.

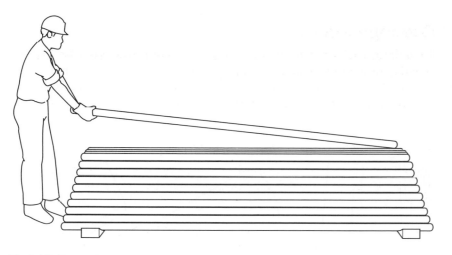

Fig 3.15 Removing pipes from a stack

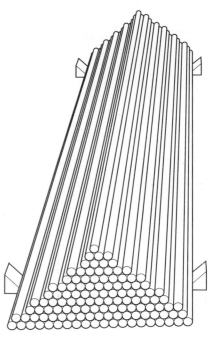

Fig 3.14 Storage of pipes

Reinforcing and Structural Steel

Reinforcing steel should be stored and grouped by diameter in order to facilitate identity and handling as shown in Figure 3.16.

Notes on Handling

- Offload as close to fixing point as possible
- Lay on timber skids to keep steel above ground
- Check type and quantity delivered
- Cut with proper tools
- Hoist bundles of bars or sheet reinforcement with care.

Loss or waste can occur through:
- Careless handling
- Leaving bars behind in fixing areas
- Failing to fix steel as specified
- Cutting bars incorrectly.

> Points to note
>
> To avoid accidents, do not stand or walk on stacked pipes when placing or removing pieces.

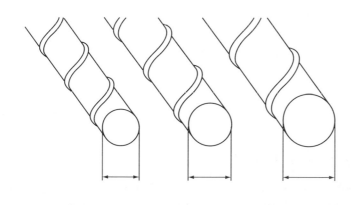

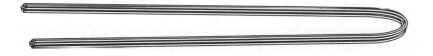

Fig 3.16 Grouping of steel items

Roofing Tiles

Roofing tiles are made from either clay or concrete. They may be machine or handmade and are available in a variety of shapes and colours. Many roofing tiles are able to interlock to prevent rain from entering the building as illustrated in Figure 3.17.

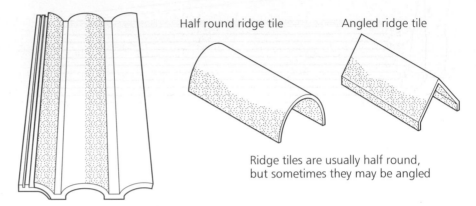

Half round ridge tile

Angled ridge tile

Ridge tiles are usually half round, but sometimes they may be angled

Fig 3.17 **Roof tile showing method of interlocking**

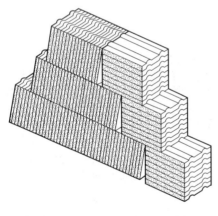

Fig 3.18 **Correct method of stacking tiles**

Storage of Roofing Tiles

Roofing tiles are stacked on edge usually in special crates to protect their nibs, and in rows on level, firm, well drained ground. If the tiles are not in crates or strapped on pallets they should not be stacked any higher than six rows high and tapered towards the top to prevent them from toppling over. If stacked in this way the tiles at the end of the rows should be placed flat to provide the support for the rows as illustrated in Figure 3.18.

Ridge tiles may be stacked on top of each other, but not any higher than ten tiles as shown in Figure 3.19

To protect roofing tiles from rain and frost before use, they should be covered with a tarpaulin or polythene sheet.

Notes on Handling

- Delivered by supplier
- Offloaded manually unless in packs
- Take care in handling to avoid breakages.

Loss or waste can occur through:

- Mishandling materials at all stages
- Damage from site traffic.

Flexible Damp Proof Course

Damp proof course (DPC) may be made from polythene, bitumen or lead and are supplied in rolls of various widths for different uses.

Storage of Rolled Materials

Rolled materials, whether damp proof course or roofing felt should be stored in a shed or room on a level, dry surface. Narrow rolls may be best

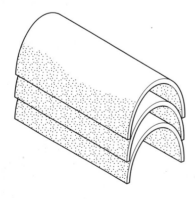

Fig 3.19 **Ridge tiles stacked correctly**

stored on shelves, but in all cases they should be stacked on end to prevent them from rolling, and to reduce the possibility of damage being caused by compression, as layers of bitumen melt together when under pressure (see Figure 3.20).

Notes on Handling

- Unroll quantity to be used only
- Replace surplus amounts in safe storage
- Use proper knife for cutting to length
- Use correct widths as specified.

Loss or waste can occur through:

- Leaving unused rolls lying around
- Using incorrect widths or cutting unnecessarily.

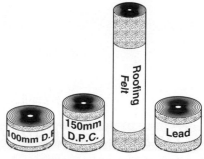

Rolled materials stored on end

Fig 3.20 **Rolled material stored correctly**

Sheet Materials

Flat sheets, such as plywood, plasterboard, hardboard and chipboard, are called sheet materials. They are obtained in packs or individually. Sizes vary but a common size is 2440 mm × 1220 mm. Thickness also varies.

Plywood and Plasterboard

Plywood consists of an odd number of thin layers of timber glued together with their grains alternating in direction, used for flooring, formwork and stud partition walling.

Plasterboard is made from gypsum plaster centre sandwiched between two sheets of heavy paper, used for ceilings and stud partition walling.

Storage of Sheet Materials

Plywood and plasterboard is best stored flat on racks in a warm dry place as illustrated in Figure 3.21. Plasterboard with a foil-backed surface should be stacked in pairs with their foil surface together.

Where space is limited sheet materials can be stored on edge in a specially made rack which allows the outer board to be supported on the previous board and keep its shape, as shown in Figure 3.22.

Once off-loaded, it is the building contractor's responsibility to move all materials to a safe and secure place until they are required for use.

Notes on Handling

- Delivered by supplier
- Offloaded by forklift; requires platform to support the boards
- Manual handling and stacking requires two men to each board
- Plastic or foil-backed boards should be handled with reverse face to face.

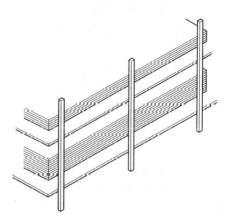

Fig 3.21 **Plasterboard stacked on racks**

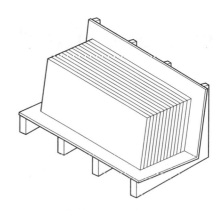

Fig 3.22 **Plasterboard stacked on specially made rack**

Loss or waste can occur through:

- Using wrong size boards causing excess cutting
- Poor stacking
- Indiscriminate handling
- Lack of protection from weather.

Work-based Evidence Required

■ Handling and storing occupational resources

Handle and store occupational resources to meet product information and/or organizational requirements relating to:

- Sheet material
- Loose material
- Bagged or wrapped material
- Components
- Liquid material.

To meet these requirements, ask your supervisor to fill out a witness testimony sheet stating that you have handled and stored occupational resources to meet product information and organizational requirements related to the above. It would be also useful if you could obtain photographs of yourself carrying out some of these activities.

When you have received the signed and dated witness testimony sheets from your supervisor, place them in your work based evidence portfolio when next in college and map and record them against the syllabus.

Manual Handling Techniques　　　3.5

Lifting heavy or awkward objects, such as bags of cement and plaster, can cause injury if not performed correctly. Incorrect lifting techniques can put stress on the lower back and after years of bad lifting, the discs between the various vertebrae become disjointed and are prone to slipping. By using the kinetic method of manual handling, injuries to the back can be avoided.

Kinetic Method

The kinetic method is based on two principles:

Fig 3.23 Correct lifting techniques

- Fully employing the strong leg muscles for lifting, rather than the weaker muscles of the back
- Using the momentum of the weight of the body to begin horizontal movement.

These two motions are combined in smooth continuous movements by correct positioning of the feet, maintaining a straight back and flexing and extending the knees.

In practice, this requires: correct positioning of the feet, a straight back, arms close to the body when lifting or carrying, the correct hold, keeping the chin tucked in and using the body weight (see Figure 3.23).

Safe Handling

The Health and Safety Executive outline important handling points, using a basic lifting operation as an example.

Stop and Think

Plan the lift. Where is the load to be placed? Use appropriate handling aids if possible. Do you need help with the load? Remove obstructions such as discarded wrapping materials. For a long lift, such as floor to shoulder height, consider resting the load mid-way on a table or bench to change grip (see Figure 3.24).

Position the Feet

Feet apart, giving a balanced and stable base for lifting. Leading leg as far forward as is comfortable and if possible, pointing in the direction you intend to go (see Figure 3.25).

Adopt a Good Posture

When lifting from a low level, bend the knees. But do not kneel or over flex the knees. Keep the back straight, maintaining its natural curve. Lean forwards a little over the load if necessary to get a good grip. Keep the shoulders level and facing in the same direction as the hips (see Figure 3.26).

Fig 3.24 **Stop and think**
Source: HSE

Fig 3.25 **Positioning the feet**
Source: HSE

Fig 3.26 **Good posture**
Source: HSE

Fig 3.27
Firm grip
Source: HSE

Points to note

Wear protective gloves to avoid cuts, abrasions and splinters.

Get a Firm Grip

Try to keep the arms within the boundary formed by the legs. The best position and type of grip depends on the circumstances and individual preference, but must be secure. A hook grip is less tiring than keeping the fingers straight. If you need to vary the grip as the lift proceeds, do it as smoothly as possible (see Figure 3.27).

Keep Close to the Load

Keep the load close to the trunk for as long as possible. Keep the heaviest side of the load next to the trunk. If a close approach to the load is not possible, slide it towards you before trying to lift.

Do Not Jerk

Lift smoothly, raising the chin as the lift begins, keeping control of the load.

Move the Feet

Do not twist the trunk when turning to the side.

Put Down, Then Adjust

If precise positioning of the load is necessary, put it down first, then slide it into the desired position (see Figure 3.28).

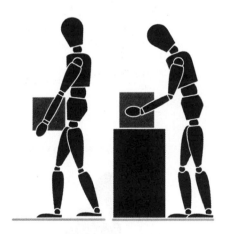

Fig 3.28 **Put down, then adjust**
Source: HSE

Lifting a Load From a Bench

Keep your back straight, extend your arms in front of you and bend your knees slightly, until you can grasp the load firmly (see Figure 3.29).

Pull the load towards you, straighten up and lean back slightly (see Figure 3.30).

Lifting and Carrying Long Loads

In general, a load longer than six metres requires more than one person to lift and carry it (see Figure 3.31).

When being lifted by one person, one end is raised above shoulder level (see Figure 3.32).

Fig 3.29 **Lifting a load from a bench 1**   Fig 3.30 **Lifting a load from a bench 2**

Fig 3.31 **Carrying long loads**

Fig 3.32 **One person carrying a long load**

Fig 3.33 **Handling sheet materials**

The operative then walks forward, moving his hands along the length until the point of balance is reached. The load is then balanced.

Handling Sheet Materials

Large sheets of material are awkward shapes to pick up. By using an easily made hook, with a long handle, a large sheet of material can be lifted and carried quite easily as shown in Figure 3.33.

Alternatively, sheet materials and other large items can be moved by a walking process. This is done by lifting one side and swivelling the item on the opposite corner, repeating the process on alternate corners. Care should be taken to avoid damaging corners when walking items.

> **Points to note**
>
> It is recommended that the feet are placed about 50 cm apart. This distance is suitable for a person having a height of about 175 cm.
>
> Do not attempt to lift or carry any load exceeding 25 kg alone.

Work-based Evidence Required

■ Safe lifting techniques

Work skills to:

■   Move, position, secure and use lifting aids and kinetic lifting techniques.

To meet these requirements, obtain a witness testimony sheet from your supervisor stating that you have moved, positioned and used lifting aids employing kinetic lifting techniques. Place the evidence in your work-based evidence portfolio when next in college and map and record it against the syllabus.

Team Lifting

If an object has been assessed as being too heavy or awkward for one person to lift, then a colleague should help you. When team lifting, those lifting should be approximately the same height and build as each other. The effort, should be the same for each person, and only one person should be responsible for giving instructions.

These instructions should be clearly given, using a recognized call such as, 'lift after three: one, two, three, lift'. Prior to lifting, any objects that

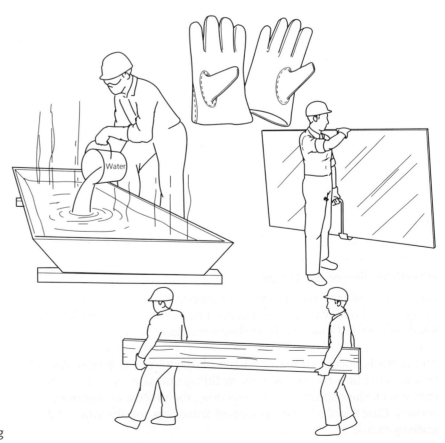

Fig 3.34 **Person wearing PPE when lifting**

are in the immediate area should be removed. It is important that you wear suitable protective clothing such as boots, gloves and overalls as illustrated in Figure 3.34.

Examining Loads

Always examine the load in order to ascertain whether you can lift it, if you feel that this is not possible, then obtain help. Always check the route in which you are to take the object for any obstructions and that the area you are to place the object is clear.

Bagged Materials

The carrying of bagged materials such as cement and plaster can be very tiring, as the bags are awkward to lift, the easiest way being to place the bag on the shoulder. This is made easier if you support the shoulder. It may make it easier still if you support your shoulder by putting your hand on your hip, and hold the bag with your other hand.

Loose Materials

Loose materials such as aggregates, bricks, blocks and bags of cement may be moved by using a wheelbarrow or trolley. Building sites can form rough terrain, and it may be hard work pushing loaded barrows over such rough ground. In these circumstances barrow runs may be used, these are boards laid down over the ground. If the board run is to be over trenches, always ensure that the boards are thick enough to carry the weight imposed on them. Always load the barrow evenly with most of the weight above the wheel as shown in Figure 3.35.

Fig 3.35 Correct method of using a wheelbarrow

Do not throw bricks into a wheelbarrow, place them in neatly. When unloading bricks from a barrow, it is important that they are taken out by hand and not tipped, this saves any damage to the bricks. When moving any material, care must be taken not to damage the material or the packaging.

Trolleys are best used for moving items on hard surfaces such as in warehouses or workshops, since the relatively small wheels will sink into soft surfaces. It is better to take several smaller loads than to risk injury by overloading wheelbarrows or trolleys.

Delivery of Materials

It is the manufacturer's responsibility to ensure that his products conform with the established standard and are brought to the customer safely and efficiently. Products should arrive at the point of delivery in a satisfactory condition for use.

Delivery Notes

When materials are delivered on to a construction site, someone must sign a delivery note, this note is evidence that a delivery has been made and that all the items on the note have been received in good condition. Before any delivery note is signed, the delivery must be checked ensuring that all items have been received in good condition and in the correct quantity.

If there is any discrepancy between the delivery note and the materials, the note must not be signed, and the supervisor or foreman informed. If the delivery note was signed in such circumstances and the delivery not checked, it could result in the company, or even the person who signed paying for materials that were not delivered. If a supervisor is not available and a shortage is noted in the delivery, the person signing should write on the note what is missing, and then sign the copy

Work-based Evidence Required

- **Safe use and storage of lifting aids and equipment**

To meet this requirement, obtain a witness testimony sheet from your supervisor stating that you have safely used and stored lifting aids and equipment. Place the evidence in your work-based evidence portfolio when next in college and map and record it against the syllabus.

Quick quiz Quick quiz Quick quiz Quick quiz Quick quiz

❶ Before a delivery of materials is received on site, state the actions that should be taken.

❷ State the regulations that control the handling and storing of materials on site.

❸ State the actions you would take if you identify unsafe storage conditions.

❹ Give four factors that need to be considered when requesting a delivery of materials.

❺ What is meant by the term 'just in time delivery'?

❻ What is the maximum height that cement bags should be stacked?

❼ Describe the storage requirements for cement and plaster.

❽ Give the storage conditions for materials that contain noxious fumes.

❾ What are the storage conditions for aggregates?

❿ Describe the procedure for stacking roof trusses.

Problems

In this section you will learn about problems arising from information, resources and methods of work that include:

■ Own authority to rectify

■ Organizational reporting procedures.

When you have completed this section you will be able to:

■ Comply with the given product information to carry out the work efficiently to the required guidance.

Know and understand:

■ How methods of work, to meet the specification, are carried out and problems are reported.

This section will now cover problems.

Defining Problems

We come up against problems every day and in many different ways. It is therefore important in this section to decide on a definition that relates closely to the information, resources and methods of work you employ.

Problems at work could include items such as:

■ Site personnel absent

■ Bad weather conditions preventing work from being carried out

■ Breakdowns with machinery and equipment

■ Injuries or accidents on site

■ Shortages of labour and or materials.

The examples above would be described by most people as problems. Problems can be defined as:

■ Difficult situations

■ Occurrences causing work to stop

■ Situations where decisions need to be made

■ A situation preventing site personnel from getting the job done.

However, for the purposes of this section the last idea is probably closest to the definition we require. Which is:

A problem is a situation that causes a deviation from a known plan.

This definition assumes that we have a plan; in other words, we know what is supposed to happen. No building project would get very far without a plan, even if it is in note form; a situation more common for a small company.

Of course, the planning of events makes us take decisions and decisions are closely allied to problems. This is because we solve them by deciding between different possible scenarios. Therefore, a suitable definition of a decision would be the following:

A decision is a choice between alternatives, where we choose the one that best meets our objectives.

Therefore, one of the benefits of having a plan is that we can sometimes predict a problem occurring. This is a potential problem.

The problem has not occurred yet, but our planning suggests it might. We therefore take action to prevent this happening, like wearing personal protective equipment on site. Or we have a contingency plan ready for it, like following the drill precautions in the event of a fire alarm sounding.

So we can say that this section is about three ideas:

- Problems and how we effectively deal with them
- Making effective decisions
- Dealing with potential problems.

Solving Problems

The ability to solve a problem involves planning because when you trying to solve a problem, planning helps you work through the problem. If you follow the plan you will know the logical actions to take to arrive at a suitable solution.

Following the plan should enable you to use your time more effectively. It should also reduce the risk of making a decision that may turn out to be the wrong one. Not that making decisions is wrong, it just sometimes happens that you will make the wrong one. If this happens, what reasons could you give for making a wrong decision? What about the following:

- The problem was not thought through adequately
- The situation demanded that I act to prevent further losses
- Because of pressure of work I did not have time to look at the alternatives
- I lost sight of what the company were trying to achieve
- More information was required, but I did not know how to go about finding it
- I should have asked more questions.

The list above gives some of the reasons for failing to solve problems during the decision making process. You may have noticed that reasons two and three often occur at work, and that is something you may have to take into account. A building contract never runs as smoothly as it might or as it was planned. Always remember you will never have enough time to think things through properly, that is the nature of the industry.

However, if you have a plan to follow, then your problem-solving will improve, as long as you use each stage of the plan as thoroughly as possible.

Planning

The activity of solving problems falls into three areas:

- Understanding the problem
- Thinking of solutions and using the best one
- Putting the solution into effect and then evaluating it.

In other words:

- This is what I think is wrong
- This decision should fix it
- Did the solution work?

Remember every activity has several important stages that make up the whole problem-solving plan.

The Plan is a device towards understanding the problem. So what might be the structure of a plan? The answers lie in the plan itself, the plan must be problem-solving and include the following ideas:

Understanding the problem:

- Recognize the problem
- Define the problem
- Identify its causes.

Creating and choosing solutions :

- Think of possible solutions
- Decide on the best solution.

Implement and evaluate

- Implement the chosen solution
- Monitor the outcome and evaluate the results.

Remember decision making is an important part of solving problems.

Source: CITB-ConstructionSkills. Problems and Decisions, 1994.

Information on Official Guidance

The following bodies provide official guidance and useful information on materials, general recycling and waste disposal issues.

Environment and Energy Helpline
0800 585 794

Free telephone advice on waste minimization and management.

Environmental Technology Best Practice Programme

http://www.etbpp.gov.uk

Provides impartial authoritative information on best practice and managing resource use. Their publications are disseminated through many channels including Trade associations, Business Links and the Environment Agency. These include:

Finding Hidden Profit – 200 Tips for reducing Waste

Green Efficiency: Running a Cost Effective, Environmentally Aware Office

Saving Money Through Waste Minimization: teams and champions

BSI

www.bsi.org.uk

SO 14001 is the international standard which specifies the requirements for an environmental management system. ISO 14001 is a management tool which organizations of any type can use to help them control the impact on the environment of their activities, products and services in a structured and systematic way.

Information about DETR

Department of the Environment, Transport and the Regions

Eland House, Bressenden Place, London SW1E 5DU Tel 0207 944 300, Fax: 0207 944 4242. www.environment.detr.gov.uk

Guidelines for company Reporting on Greenhouse Gas Emissions *and* Environmental Reporting – Getting Started www.environment.detr.gov.uk/envrp/index.htm

Packaging Regulations Registered Compliance Schemes
For information contact
Paul_McKinnney@detr.gsi.gov.uk

Quality of Life Counts

Indicators for a Strategy for sustainable development for the United Kingdom: A Baseline Assessment: *a publication of the Government Statistical Service, available from DETR Publication Sales Centre, Unit 21, Goldthorpe Industrial Estate, Goldthorpe, Rotheram S63 9BL.*

Waste Strategy 2000 for England and Wales, Available from DETR Publications Sales Centre.

DETR Greening Government

http://www.environment.detr.gov.uk/greening/gghome.htm

Information on Regulatory Information

The British Standards Institution (BSI)

www.bsi–global.com

British Standards is the National Standards body of the UK, responsible for facilitating, publishing and marketing British Standards and other guidelines.

BSI provides:

- *The development of private, national and international standards*
- *Information on standards and international trade*
- *Independent certification of management systems and products*
- *Product testing services*
- *Training and seminars*
- *Commodity inspection services.*

With collaborative ventures and a strong national and international profile, British Standards are at the heart of the world of standardization.

The Building Research Establishment (BRE)

www.bre.co.uk

The BRE is committed to providing impartial and authoritative information on all aspects of the built environment for clients, designers, contractors, occupants and so on. They make every effort to ensure the accuracy and quality of information and guidance when it is first published.

BRE is the UKs leading centre of expertise on building and construction, and the prevention and control of fire. Contact BRE for information about its services, or for technical advice, at BRE, Garston, Watford WD25 9XX. Tel: 01923 664000.

Details of BRE publications are available from the BRE bookshop, 151 Rosebery Avenue, London EC1R 4GB. Tel: 020 7505 6622 or the BRE website.

The Health and Safety Executive (HSE)

HSE Infoline

08701 545500

Infoline is the HSEs public enquiry contact centre. Its a one stop shop, providing rapid access to the HSEs wealth of health and safety information, and access to expert advice and guidance.

HSE and the Internet

www.hse.gov.uk

HSE has a website on the Internet, this contains information about the objectives of HSE, how to contact HSE, how to complain, recent press releases and research and current initiatives. Information about risks at work and information about different workplaces is also available.

HSELINE

01634 574592

HSELINE is a computer database of bibliographic references to published documents on health and safety at work. It contains over 230,000 references and over 9000 additions are made each year.

The Stationery Office Shops

www.tso.co.uk

The Stationery Office (TSO) Shops are the ideal place to purchase a large range of official, regulatory and specialist publications. In addition to stocking their own titles, TSO Shops offer a large range of publications from other authoritative organizations. For example:

Health and Safety Executive Publications

TSO shops are a main stockist for HSE books, and carry around 1000 HSE titles. If you require a HSE publication that they do not have in stock, they will order it for you.

British Standards

TSO Shops are official distributors for the British Standards Institution and offer a unique print on demand service that enables them to provide any British Standard immediately.

Ordnance Survey

In addition to stocking the full range of Ordnance Survey products, all TSO shops have become Options agents. This large scale mapping service from Ordnance Survey offers three main mapping products that meet the needs of domestic planning applicants through to professional users.

Information on Technical Information

Brick Development Association (BDA)

www.brick.org.uk

The BDA provides a comprehensive range of advice and information on every aspect of brick construction. Dedicated to promoting the use of brickwork in our environment in the most effective and attractive way. The BDA offers an inclusive service supported by a wide range of publications and online advice either through professional experts on the phone or via their website.

In addition the BDA supports ongoing international research into construction and the use of brickwork to develop confidence in the industry and encourages excellence in design, innovation and craftsmanship by hosting the annual Brick Awards.

The BDA publish a wide choice of specialist books, including recommended texts for industry standard training and expert guides on developing brickwork skills and fostering best practice in brickwork design and construction.

If you want to know literally anything about brickwork and its uses, contact the BDA. They have qualified in-house architects able to offer expert, impartial information and who have access to the full BDA library of technical data.

CITB – ConstructionSkills

www.citb.org.uk

CITB – Construction Skills have published over 400 aids to training. These include videos, tape slide programmes, open learning packages, books, manuals, training support packages, study notes, case studies and worksheets.

Through these, CITB makes directly available the results of on-going development of industry approved methods of working, safe practices, management techniques, craft and technical know-how, career guidance and training schemes.

There are publications to help you at every stage of your career in construction and allied industries. Each is dedicated to training site personnel in correct methods of working and safe practices.

Details of CITB publications are available from CITB – Construction Skills Publications, Bircham Newton, Kings Lynn, Norfolk PE31 6RH.

Concrete Block Association (CBA)

www.cba–blocks.org.uk

The CBA is the trade body representing an industry producing around 60 million square metres of dense and lightweight aggregate concrete building blocks per year.

The CBA consult closely with organizations including DETR, BRE and HSE and have pioneered product innovation, testing and research initiatives for a number of years, many of which have proved instrumental in the development of new design and construction solutions.

The Quarry Products Association (QPA)

www.qpa.org

The Quarry Products Association is the trade association for companies involved in supplying crushed rock and sand and gravel from land and marine sources, asphalt and flexible paving, ready-mixed concrete, silica sand, industrial lime, mortar, recycled materials and construction and quarrying plant. In representing the interests of over 90 per cent of the UK quarrying industry, they are the key national contact on every aspect of the UK quarrying industry.

Information on Manufacturers Technical Information

The majority of companies involved in construction produce information about their products or services, most of which is extremely well presented and very useful.

The information obtainable from companies is vast, most have websites from which you can download information, or if that is not available, by ordinary mail. Manufacturers' technical information is of relevance and of use to you in your studies, as in most cases it is up to date, informative, relevant and usually free.

Information on Manual Handling

For more information about manual handling and storage of materials, why not visit the following websites.

Health and Safety Executive

www.hse.gov.uk

The HSE website contains information about the objectives of HSE, how to contact HSE, how to complain, recent press releases and research and current initiatives. Information about risks at work and information about different workplaces is also available.

Information on Problem Solving

For more information about problem solving why not visit the following websites.

CITB – ConstructionSkills

www.citb-constructionskills.co.uk.co.org

The CITB have an excellent series of learning modules entitled 'Supervisor Development in the Construction Industry' that cover in detail problems and decisions. They are highly recommended as a learning resource.

Chapter Four

Erect Masonry Structures

NVQ Level 2   Unit No. VR 40   Erect Masonry Structures

This unit is about:
- **Interpreting information**
- **Adopting safe and healthy working practices**
- **Selecting materials, components and equipment**
- **Preparing and erecting brickwork and blockwork structures.**

There are three sections in this chapter, methods of work, protect work and resources.

METHODS OF WORK

In this section you will learn about bricklaying relating to the area of work and material used, to:

- Erect cavity and solid walling using brick and block
- Lay blocks (traditional and thin joint)
- Determine brick and block bonds
- Form joint finishes
- Form openings for doors and windows
- Position damp proof barriers
- Mix mortar
- Use hand tools, power tools and equipment.

When you have completed this section you will be able to:

- Select the required quantity and quality of resources for the methods of work
- Comply with the given contract information to carry out the work efficiently to the required specification.

Know and understand:

- How methods of work, to meet the specification, are carried out and problems reported
- How maintenance of tools and equipment is carried out
- What the programme is for the work to be carried out in the estimated, allocated time and why deadlines should be kept.

This section will now cover methods of work relating to the erection of masonry structures.

Tools
4.1

Hand Tools

Bricklaying Tools and Their Uses

The bricklayer requires few tools as compared with many other trades, but care should be taken in their selection. Try to obtain the best quality, this will avoid frequent renewals and the necessity of having to get to know the feel of new tools at frequent intervals.

It is useful to classify the tools required by a bricklayer, together with a description of their uses, under the following headings:

- Laying Tools – the brick trowel

- Levelling Tools – spirit levels, straight-edge, gauge staff, line and pins and tingle plate, steel tape measure, square and bevel

- Cutting and Marking Tools – club hammer, bolster chisel, brick and comb hammer, cold chisels, brick cutting gauge

- Finishing Tools – pointing trowel, hawk, jointer and chariot.

Laying Tools

The Brick Trowel

Definition: The brick trowel is a hand tool with a thin flat blade, usually diamond shaped, for applying mortar.

Like most other tools, the bricklayer's trowel is the end product of many years of evolution, in fact brick trowels can be traced back to the fifteenth century. The oldest surviving UK brand was started by William Hunt and Son in 1793.

Of all the tools used by a bricklayer, the brick trowel is by far the most important as it is in almost continuous use. Trowels come in various sizes and shapes ranging between 260 mm and 360 mm in length, from the back of the shank to the tip of the blade; the width varying from 80 mm to 130 mm. Figure 4.1 is an illustration of a brick trowel with the various parts named.

The right hand side of the trowel has a more rounded edge, this is for rough cutting, however, this practice is not recommended as it tends to damage the trowel. Whereas the left-hand edge is almost straight, the object of this being to provide a straight edge for removing surplus mortar. (For left-handed people, left-handed trowels are available with these features reversed.)

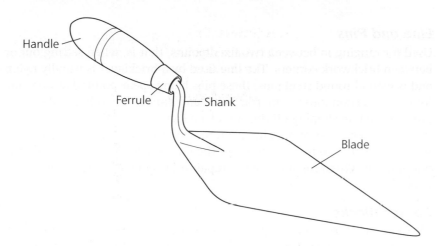

Fig 4.1 Brick trowel

Trowel Sizes and Lifts

Trowels are also made with various lifts, this referring to the angle that the handle makes with the blade, and for this reason several trowels should be considered before a final selection is made. The one chosen being obviously the most comfortable to use. A bricklayer usually has two trowels, one about 230 mm or 260 mm long which would be used on facework, while a larger trowel 280 mm to 300 mm long would be used on rough or heavy work. For the student or apprentice, however, it has been found that the most suitable size to use for all purposes is 230 mm to 260 mm long.

Levelling Tools

There are three main types of levelling tools:

- Spirit levels
- Line and pins
- Straight edge and gauge rod.

Spirit Levels

Used for the plumbing and levelling of bricks and blocks. They are essentially a metal straight edge fitted with glass tubes containing a spirit and a bubble of air. The glass tubes are set into the level with an adhesive or screws, so that when the level is placed across two points that are exactly level the air bubble will be exactly in the centre of the tube. This position being clearly marked on the glass tube with incised lines. In a similar manner, tubes are fitted to read correctly with the level held vertically. For the majority of bricklaying purposes the type of level shown in Figure 4.2 is used, the length usually being about 1 m.

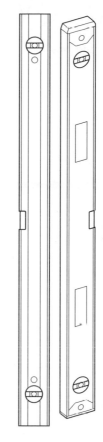

Fig 4.2 Spirit levels

Boat Level

A useful asset in any bricklayer's tool bag is the boat level as shown in Figure 4.3 which is similar in all respects to the longer level, except in length and shape. Boat levels are used for levelling single bricks on piers or plumbing in a single brick on a soldier course. They are usually 150 mm to 300 mm in length.

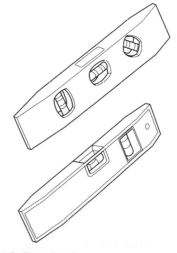

Fig 4.3 Boat levels

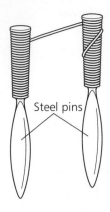

Fig 4.4 **Line and pins**

Line and Pins

Used for ranging in between two fixed points, that is, when setting out or between brickwork corners. The line used by a bricklayer is usually nylon and is wound round steel pins, these pins being spear pointed at one end for easy insertion into the mortar joints and flanged the other end to prevent the line slipping off the stem (see Figure 4.4). When winding lines on to pins, care should be taken to wind the line on the two pins in reverse direction so that when in use the line will come over the pin and not under it. When the line breaks, repair it by splicing, not by tying a knot.

Corner Blocks

These are used to secure ranging lines to brickwork corners or profiles. They are held in place by the tension of the line. Their advantage over line and pins being that the mortar joints are not touched in any way. They are inexpensive to buy or alternatively you could make your own (see Figure 4.5).

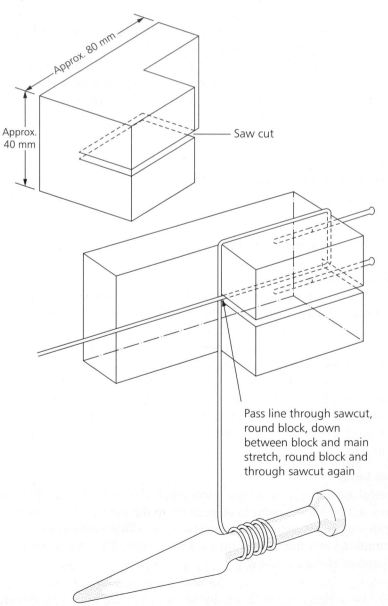

Fig 4.5 **Corner block**
Source: BDA

Tingle Plate

This is not an expensive tool but of great use (see Figure 4.6). A tingle plate is used to support the centre of ranging lines on brick or block walls, removing the sag and thus giving better alignment.

Straight Edge

Any length of timber that has parallel sides can be used for a straight edge (see Figure 4.7) but for a better degree of accuracy a purpose-made straight edge should be employed. A straight edge is used in conjunction with a spirit level as a method of transferring a spot level from one point to another. When using the straight edge for levelling it should be reversed end to end after each reading, this will do away with any inaccuracy in the straight edge or spirit level.

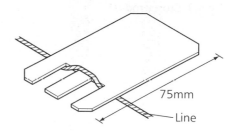

Fig 4.6 Tingle plate

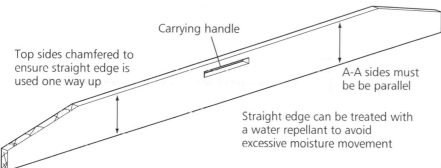

Fig 4.7 Straight edge

Gauge Rod

The gauge of brick and blockwork is maintained throughout the height of the wall by the use of a gauge rod.

The gauge rod itself is a length of timber usually 1 m long by 30 mm wide by 10 mm in thickness. For workshop use it is usually marked off with saw cuts to the required brick gauge, that is, one division on the gauge is equal to the height of a brick plus the bed joint, or four courses of brickwork to 300 mm as shown in Figure 4.8.

The gauge rod used on a construction site is usually sufficiently long to reach from one floor to another. In this case it is known as a storey rod or pole and, in addition to the brick courses, various other important levels such as cill level, window and door head levels and so on, are also marked on it (see Figure 4.9).

Cutting and Marking Tools

The bricklayer makes use of a number of tools of this kind whilst carrying out his craft.

Club or Lump hammer

The club Hammer consists of a steel head fixed to a handle approximately 200 mm long. The head varies in weight between 1 and 2 kg, the hammer normally use by the bricklayer being 1.5 kg in weight.

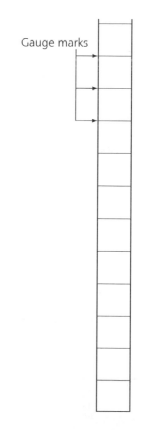

Fig 4.8 Gauge rod

Fig 4.9 **Storey rod**

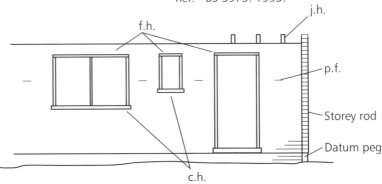

Storey rods

A storey rod is a guage rod that contains additional information.

Some typical information is:

jh = joist height
fh = top frame height (lintel/arch)
ps = putlog side
pf = putlog front
ch = cill height

Note: Cill heights will vary for different height windows.

Provision must be made for putlog scaffolding

Front and side heights differ by one course (ps) and (pf).

Putlog holes should be in the bed joint.
Ref. - BS 5973: 1993.

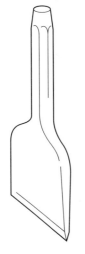

Fig 4.10 **Club hammer**

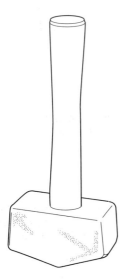

Fig 4.11 **Bolster chisel**

It is used with a bolster chisel or plugging chisel when cutting bricks or chasing out joints. Figure 4.10 illustrates the club hammer.

Bolster Chisel

Bolster chisels are used in conjunction with a lump hammer to cut bricks and blocks. They are forged from steel, with a very broad blade, the cutting edge of which has a very slight convex curve, as shown in Figure 4.11. The blade, which may vary in width from 50 mm to 100 mm, is hardened for cutting, but the striking end should be left comparatively soft to avoid pieces of metal breaking and flying off when it is struck with the hammer.

Brick Hammer

This type of hammer is used for the rough cutting of bricks. The chisel blade should always be kept sharp (see Figure 4.12).

Comb or Scutch Hammer

Similar to the brick hammer (see Figure 4.13) except that this hammer has detachable blades. When the teeth of the blades have worn down they can be renewed. The comb hammer can be used for a number of different jobs:

■ Tidying the edges of cuts to leave a clean edge
■ Rough cutting of bricks to form halves or quarters
■ Shaping of bricks.

Fig 4.12 **Brick hammer**

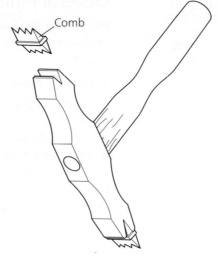

Comb

Fig 4.13 **Comb hammer**

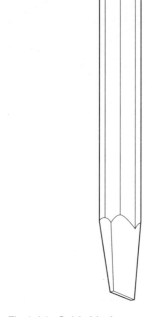

Fig 4.14 **Cold chisel**

Cold Chisels

These are made in varying lengths and thicknesses and should include sizes between 10 mm by 100 mm to 25 mm by 150 mm as illustrated in Figure 4.14. They are forged from steel with the cutting edge and the striking end treated in a similar manner to those on a bolster chisel.

Bricks reduced to various sizes and shapes are usually cut with the aid of a club hammer and bolster and trimmed to a fine finish, if required with a comb hammer. For very fine work, the face of the cut surface is finished by rubbing down with a carborundum stone.

Brick Marking Gauge

This is another inexpensive tool that is of great use to the bricklayer. It is easy to use where a lot of cutting is required and where maintaining a regular size to brickbats is important. Usually made for the three most basic brick cuts; half bat, three quarter bat and closer (see Figure 4.15).

Try Square

Before cutting a brick, the position of the cut must be measured off and a square mark pencilled on with the aid of a try square (see Figure 4.16).

Bevel

A bevel is used for marking off an angle in the manner previously described for a square. The blade is pivoted at the top of the stock and fixed to enclose the required angle by fastening with a set screw (see Figure 4.17). The bevel is excellent for raking cuts on gable end walling.

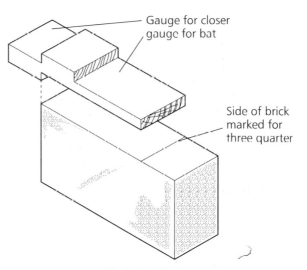

Gauge for closer
gauge for bat

Side of brick marked for three quarter

Fig 4.15 **Marking gauge**

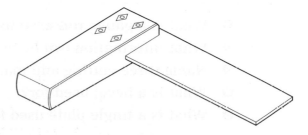

Fig 4.16 **Try square**

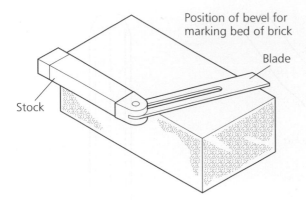

Position of bevel for marking bed of brick

Blade

Stock

Fig 4.17 **Bevel**

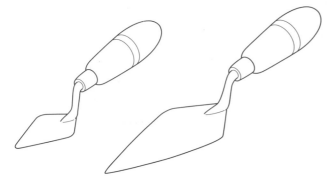

Fig 4.18 **Pointing trowels**

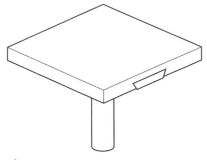

Fig 4.19 **Hawk**

General Finishing Tools

For putting the final touches to his or her work the bricklayer needs a number of special tools.

Pointing Trowels

These are similar in appearance to the ordinary brick trowel but the blades are proportionally smaller and usually made of a lighter gauge steel, the length of blade varying between 50 mm and 150 mm. It is the usual practice for the bricklayer to carry two pointing trowels, one about 50 mm long known as a dotter or cross joint trowel the other about 150 mm long and known as a bedder or bed joint trowel (see Figure 4.18)

Jointing Tools

Used for putting a finish to the joints in brick and blockwork, as work progresses, the resulting finish is called a half-round joint which is also known as a bucket handle joint.

Hawk

The bricklayer's hawk is usually made in two parts for convenience in carrying, the top part which is about 150 mm square and a handle about 175 mm long. The handle is attached to the top by means of a dovetailed slip, which slides easily into a prepared groove, thus forming a rigid connection as shown in Figure 4.19.

Quick quiz **Quick quiz** Quick quiz Quick quiz Quick quiz

❶ What is a gauge rod used for?
❷ What information can be marked on a storey rod?
❸ Name three cutting and marking tools.
❹ What is a bevel used for?
❺ What is a tingle plate used for?

Power Tools

Safe Methods of Using Portable Power Tools

If used correctly, powered hand tools can save time, money and effort. Skill in using them comes only through training and experience – it cannot be picked up on site. The following precautions must always be taken, when using power tools:

- Only use powered hand tools if you have been authorized to do so and have been taught how to use them correctly.

- Always choose the right tool for the job; check that it is in good condition and that any blade or cutter has been fitted correctly.

- If you are unfamiliar with the equipment read the instruction booklet and practise using the tool. Proceed with the job only when you are sure you can do so safely and be certain of producing good results.

- If the tool does not work, get it replaced – do not tamper with it. Repairs should only be carried out by a competent person.

- Before making any adjustments disconnect the tool or switch off at the source – just switching off at the tool is not good enough.

- Guards are fitted on machines for your protection. Do not remove them. Never put a tool down with rotating parts until they have stopped revolving.

- Wear goggles when there is any danger of flying particles. Sometimes a dust mask, ear protectors and safety helmet may also be necessary.

- Report any accident to your supervisor, whether or not it results in injury to yourself or others.

- If you are injured, even if it is only a minor wound or scratch, obtain immediate first aid treatment.

- Tools cannot be careless but you can.

- Do the job safely: it is quicker in the long run.

Source: P. Smith.

Power Supply

The power supply for power tools can be the normal 240 volts mains supply or 110 volts reduced voltage from a transformer. This is often centre tapped to earth so the maximum potential is 55 volts to earth. The use of lower voltages reduces the effects of electric shock, should this occur.

Tools should only be used on the appropriate power supply. All electric hand tools must comply with British Standard 2769 and, except for double insulated tools, must be effectively earthed.

Maintenance of Power Tools

Powered hand tools should be cleaned regularly. This is especially important with cutting and abrasive tools because the dust produced can easily pass into and damage the motor. Clean every tool regularly before dust accumulates to a harmful extent. This may mean a daily clean for tools in constant use.

Information for cleaning and maintaining power tools can be found in the instruction manual for each machine.

Mixing Machines

Equipment

There are two common types of mortar mixing machines:

1. The revolving drum
2. The mortar pan.

Revolving Drum Mixer

This machine consists of a drum with an open end and is obtainable in various sizes according to the number of bricklayers to be supplied with mortar. Fitted to the inside of the drum are blades that mix the materials as the drum revolves. The matrix and the aggregate are placed in the drum with sufficient water to make a pliable mortar when the drum is set in motion. The drum is revolved for a period of one or two minutes, after which the mortar is ready for use.

Common Types of Petrol and Diesel Powered Mixers

Mixers are commonly equipped with either petrol, diesel or electric engines or motors. All of these machines have certain features in common (see Figure 4.20).

When using any piece of machinery or equipment, always refer to the manufacturer's operating procedures.

Wheel Base – This supports the mixer and allows it to be moved safely and quickly (see Figure 4.21).

Mixing Drum – This holds the materials to be mixed.

Mixing Blades – The mixing blades inside the drum turn and blend the materials (see Figure 4.22).

The Motor and Cover – The motor provides the power required for loading, mixing and emptying the machine. The cover protects the motor from damage and also protects the operative from the motor's moving parts.

Shovel and Hopper Assembly – The shovel assembly provides the means of filling the hopper which holds the material for weighing (see Figure 4.23).

Water Storage Tank Assembly – The tank holds the water for mixing.

Weighing Dial – The weighing dial registers the weight of the materials in the hopper.

Drum and Hopper Controls – The drum is controlled by the wheel. The hopper is operated by a knob located near the wheel (see Figure 4.24).

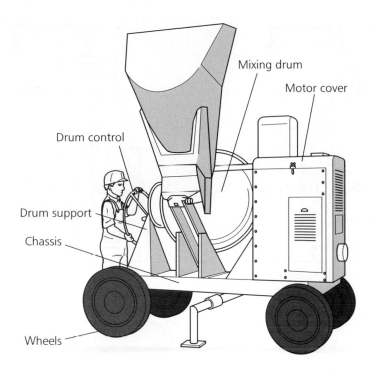

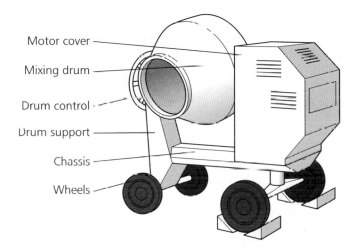

Fig 4.20 **Features of a mixer**
Source: ILO

Levelling and Stabilizing Devices – These devices prevent the machine from moving excessively when operating. Always position and stabilize the mixer on a level piece of ground.

One person cannot position large mixers. They are towed into position. Site conditions sometimes require even small machines to be towed to the mixing area.

When you have levelled and stabilized the mixer carry out the pre-start checks suggested in the manufacturer's operating manual. For example: fuel, safety, oil and switches.

Fig 4.21 **Wheel base of a mixer**
Source: ILO

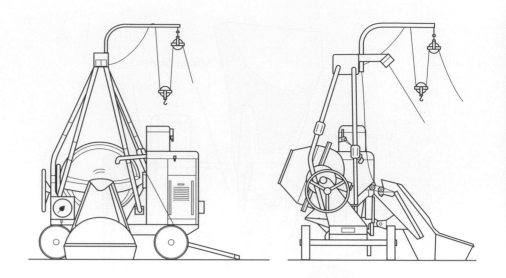

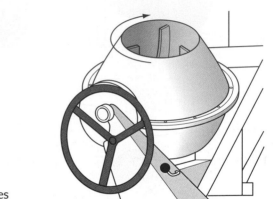

Fig 4.22 **Mixer blades**

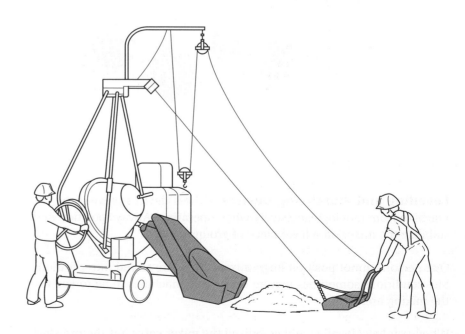

Fig 4.23 **Shovel and hopper**
Source: ILO

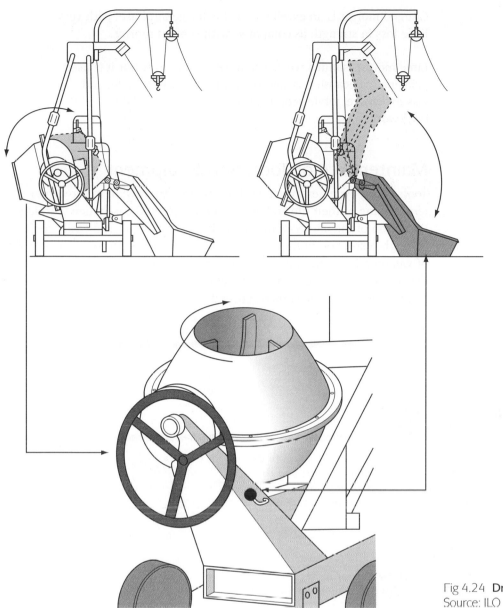

Fig 4.24 **Drum and hopper controls**
Source: ILO

Mortar Pan Mixer

This is a large pan pivoted on a central axle, with heavy rollers mounted inside the pan. With the pan revolving in an opposite direction to the rollers the matrix and the aggregate are added, together with the necessary amount of water. The action of the rollers serves to knead and mix the matrix and the aggregate, and to break down any large particles in the latter. Mainly used in training colleges, not on site.

Mortar for Mixers

Cement mortar is generally used where maximum strength and durability is required and where settlement is to be avoided. As it is quick setting it allows rapid progress in the building of brick and blockwork.

Gauged mortar is an excellent mortar for general use, with very little loss in strength as compared with cement mortar.

Lime mortar is much weaker than cement mortar but it is used principally because it is smoother and easier to handle, and less expensive, while producing sound and dependable brickwork.

Maintenance of Tools and Equipment

Tools of any type deserve careful treatment; the reward to the owner is a lengthening of their life and greater efficiency and ease when working. By reason of the nature of the work, bricklayers' tools can easily spoil through rusting or, in the case of timber tools, through constant changes of weather. It should, therefore, become a habit to thoroughly clean and dry all tools after each days work, with the spirit level greatly benefiting from a periodic application of linseed oil.

Good Practice

Whilst some brick trowels are strong enough to chop bricks, this is not advised due to the danger of flying chips and the damage which could be caused to the brick trowel edge – a specialist tool such as a brick hammer or brick bolster should always be used.

If attempting to chop bricks with the appropriate tools, goggles should always be worn to protect the eyes.

Always clean tools after use and do not allow mortar to set on to the tool. Ideally the tools should be cleaned with oil which helps prevent rusting.

Tools with wooden handles should not be left exposed to the sun, frost or rain, as the natural elements can cause cracking that could ultimately shatter the handle.

Take care when using the tools as many have sharp edges.

The tool bag should have a waterproof bottom to protect the tools from damp conditions as in the winter bricklayers are more exposed to the elements.

Always put your tools away – they provide you with a livelihood.

Work-based Evidence Required

■ Safe use and storage of tools and equipment

To meet this requirement, obtain photographs of yourself leaving tools and equipment safe and secure, this could be locking them up in a tool vault, placing them in a site security hut or locking them in the company's van.

When the photographs have been developed, place them on a photographic evidence sheet, then get your supervisor to authenticate the photographs by signing and dating them. Place the sheet in your work-based evidence portfolio, when next in college and map and record it against the syllabus.

Fig 4.25 **Always lock tools safely, for example, in the company's van**

Bricks and Blocks

Bricks

Types and Sizes of Standard Bricks

For the purpose of brick classification it is useful to note the difference between types of bricks according to:

■ Their method of manufacture; and

■ The general use for which they are suitable.

Classification by Method of Manufacture

Bricks may be broadly sub-divided under the following headings based upon the process of making and burning:

■ Hand Made or Soft Mud Moulded Bricks

■ Wire Cut or Extruded Bricks

■ Machine Moulded or Pressed Bricks

■ Sand Lime and Flint Lime Bricks.

Each of these processes produces in the finished brick certain characteristics which largely govern the use to which the brick is put, that is, general construction, decorative work, engineering work and so on.

Hand-made or Soft Mud Moulded Bricks

As the name suggests, these bricks are entirely hand-made. The mould in which the bricks are made consists of a bottomless box that fits over a stock board having the frog of the brick formed in reverse upon it. Clay is thrown into the mould that has been previously wetted or sanded to prevent the clay adhering to the sides. The surplus clay is cut off with a piece of wood known as a striker, or with a length of wire stretched over a wooden frame. The box is then removed leaving the brick ready for drying. When a mould is sanded it produces a sand-faced brick, and also tends to produce a variety of colours.

Wire Cut or Extruded Bricks

These bricks are partially machine made, the clay in a suitably plastic state being forced by revolving blades through a rectangular opening, which is the length by the width of a brick plus a shrinkage allowance, in one continuous length on to a steel table. A frame containing several wires spaced the thickness of a brick apart is brought down across the clay cutting it into a number of pieces, each piece being the size of a brick before baking. The brick has no frog and the wire marks can be seen on both beds of the brick.

Machine Moulded or Pressed Bricks

If it is desired to give bricks that have been wire cut a sharp arris and a frog the process of cutting off by wire is followed by machine pressing. The bricks are conveyed to a metal mould the sides and top of which are simultaneously compressed by mechanical means. This produces a good sound brick very regular in shape and size.

Sand lime and Flint lime Bricks

Sand lime and Flint lime bricks or calcium silicate bricks, as they are more properly called, are made from a mixture of sand, crushed flint, pebbles or rock, or a combination of such materials, with hydrated lime. They are moulded under pressure and hardened by exposure to steam at very high pressure. On cooling they are ready for immediate use.

Concrete Bricks

These types of bricks are made in a similar way to sand lime and flint lime bricks, except that sand and cement is used instead of sand and lime.

Classification by Use

Bricks may be classified according to their use as follows, bearing in mind that it is sometimes possible for a brick to come under more than one heading:

- Facing bricks
- Common bricks
- Engineering bricks
- Special bricks.

Facing Bricks

Definition: Facing bricks are intended to provide an attractive appearance. They are available in a wide range of facing brick types, colours and textures. Some may not be suitable in positions of extreme exposure. Some facing bricks have engineering properties.

The term facing covers a very wide range of bricks since it includes all those used for exterior and interior walls that are to be left as finished work. While it would not be possible to name all the bricks manufactured as facings, brief descriptions of the more general types are given below.

Reds – This type of brick is obtainable in various colours, and differ in character from a soft sand-faced brick to a hard brick with a smooth surface.

Flettons – These are smooth faced regular-shaped bricks and are a mottled pink in colour. While used chiefly as a common brick, they may also be used as a facing brick particularly for interior work. To make them suitable for use as a facing brick, they are produced with various surface treatments. They are entirely machine made, being handled only when placing them in and out of the kiln.

Stocks – This description originally referred to hand-made bricks in which it was the practice to mix ashes with the clay before moulding to assist in the burning. Similar quality bricks are now often machine-made and burnt in continuous kilns. There are other types of stocks similar in texture and quality, but usually with a variety of reds in the colouring.

Common Bricks

Definition – Common bricks are suitable for general building work not chosen for its appearance.

These are bricks for ordinary work that is not exposed to view for example, walls that are to be plastered or are built underground. Nearly all brick makers produce common bricks, which are often manufactured from the same clay as that used for better class products, but which lack the finer preparation and finish. Bricks to be included under this heading would be wire cuts of all descriptions, second and third class stocks, sand lime and flint lime bricks.

Engineering Bricks

Definition – Engineering bricks are hard burnt bricks that are very dense. They have a guaranteed minimum compressive strength and minimum water absorption. They are not chosen for appearance. There is no requirement for colour.

These are bricks suitable for ground works, manholes and sewers, retaining walls, or as a ground level damp proof course to free standing walls and situations where high strength and low water absorption are the most important factors.

Special Bricks

Definition – A wide variety of bricks are available in special shapes or sizes, to blend or contrast with most facing bricks.

Squints

These bricks are manufactured to special shapes that enable the bricklayer to build angled corners at 45 degrees or 60 degrees (see Figure 4.26). They are used to reduce the thickness of a wall and still maintain the face texture of the wall or remove the sharp corners from a brick wall or pier.

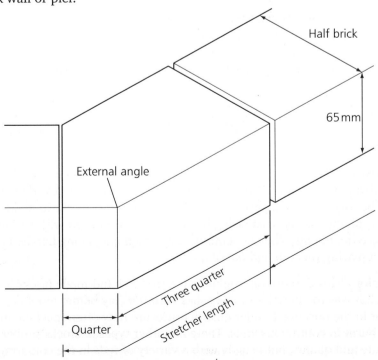

Fig 4.26 **Proportion of a squint brick**

Brick Dimensions

The dimensions and shapes of bricks vary according to the purpose that the bricks are intended to serve. Where bricks varying in size are used together, the task of the bricklayer is made difficult on account of the additional care required to produce work of good appearance. To overcome this difficulty, bricks should have standard dimensions, but even the most up-to-date methods of manufacture inevitably produce slight variations in size.

Sizes and Quantities of Bricks

The current British Standard brick size is 215 mm long, 102.5 mm wide and 65 mm thick.

Approximately 60 bricks are required per metre squared of half brick walling and 120 for full brick, including 10 mm mortar joints. Table 4.1 may be useful to calculate the numbers required and the mortar needed – but always remember to subtract an allowance for window and door openings.

Definition of Sizes

Co-ordinating Size – the size of a co-ordinating space allocated to a brick, including allowances for joints and tolerances (see Figure 4. 27).

Work Size – the size of a brick specified for its manufacture, to which its actual size should conform within specified permissible deviations (see Figure 4.27).

Dimensional Variation

During the brick manufacturing process there is sometimes considerable change in the size of the newly formed brick, as it dries out. For this reason the exact sizes of bricks are difficult to control.

Table 4.1 Quantities of bricks and mortar

Wall thickness mm	No. of bricks required per square metre of wall	Volume of mortar per square metre of all (m³)		Volume of mortar per 1000 bricks used (m³)	
		frog up	frog down	frog up	frog down
102.5	60	0.031	0.021	0.52	0.35
215	119	0.072	0.052	0.61	0.44

Notes to table

Note 1 The mix proportions given contain the minimum recommended cement content for durability. If, for any reasons, mortars with greater cement contents are required, then stronger mortars may be satisfactorily used with the London range of bricks

Note 2 The BS5628: Part 3 Table 15 mortar designation is given for each recommended mortar mix to assist these involved in structural design calculations to BS 5628: Parts 1 and 2.

Note 3 For work below finished ground level the mortar may have to be varied depending on the level of the sulphates in the soil or ground water. For details see Table 3. The same mortar should be used for all work up to ground level dpc, or at least two courses above finished ground level.

Note 4 Free-standing walls, parapet walls and chimneys must be finished with an overhanging coping.

Note 5 Retaining walls must have a water-proof backing and an overhanging coping.

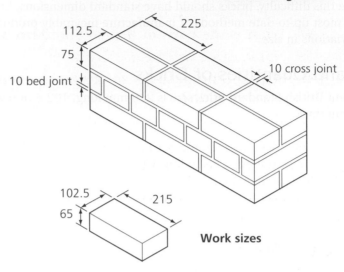

Sizes	Length mm	Width mm	Height mm
Co-ordinating size	225	112.5	75
Work size	215	102.5	65

Co-ordinating sizes

112.5 · 75 · 225 · 10 cross joint · 10 bed joint

102.5 · 65 · 215

Work sizes

Fig 4.27 **Bricks showing co-ordinating and work sizes**

British Standard 3921 specifies brick size and tolerances, based on the measurement of 24 bricks (see Figure 4.28).

Durability

Bricks are classified according to frost resistance and soluble salt content to distinguish different designations of durability (see Figure 4.29).

The chart shows us that frost resistant bricks are suitable for use in all normal situations, whilst, moderately frost resistant may also be used in most situations but should not be used in situations where they remain saturated and are subject to freezing and thawing. The not frost resistant bricks are only suitable for internal use.

Work Size mm	Maximum mm	Mean mm	Minimum mm
215	5235	5160	5085
102.5	2505	2460	2415
65	1605	1560	1515

Fig 4.28 **Chart showing size tolerances**
Source: Ibstock

Designation	Frost Resistance	Soluble Salts Content
FL	Frost Resistant (F)	Low (L)
FN	Frost Resistant (F)	Normal (N)
ML	Moderately Frost Resistant (M)	Low (L)
MN	Moderately Frost Resistant (M)	Normal (N)
OL	Not Frost Resistant (O)	Low (L)
ON	Not Frost Resistant (O)	Normal (N)

Fig 4.29 **Chart showing brick durability**
Source: Ibstock

Quick quiz Quick quiz Quick quiz Quick quiz Quick quiz

❶ What is the British Standard number for clay bricks?

❷ Approximately how many bricks are required in one square metre of half brick walling?

❸ What is the current British Standard brick size?

❹ Name three brick classifications.

❺ Why should packs of bricks be covered and what should they be covered with?

Types and Sizes of Blocks

There is a wide variety in the size and type of block used within the construction industry. Some of these are described below.

Lightweight Aircrete Blocks

- Manufactured in various widths of between 75, 100, 150 and 200 mm
- Designed for use in lightweight internal partitions and the inner leaves of cavity walls.

Cellular Blocks

- Manufactured in widths of 75, 100, and 150 mm
- Used for lightweight partitions.

Foundation Blocks

- Manufactured in widths from 100 mm and above
- Used below ground to carry cavity walls. They may be lightweight or dense.

Note: Dense foundation blocks should be lifted by two people.

Dense Concrete Blocks

- Manufactured in widths of 100, 150 and 225 mm
- Used for loadbearing and exposed work on industrial and agricultural buildings.

Hollow Blocks

- Manufactured in one size only – 440 mm long × 215 mm wide × 215 mm deep
- Used for loadbearing and hard-wearing walls in industrial and agricultural buildings.

Reveal Blocks

- Used to close the cavity at door and window openings.

Lightweight Aircrete Blocks

The block manufacturer Thermalite, introduced the autoclaved concrete block, now known as Aircrete over 50 years ago, and is now one of the largest producers along with Celcon of building blocks in the United Kingdom.

Aircrete is a lightweight, loadbearing and thermally insulating building material most commonly available in block format, but also as reinforced units. The blocks are light in weight, easy to work, and have excellent loadbearing capabilities (see Figure 4.30).

A combination of strength, moisture resistance and high thermal efficiency makes Aircrete blocks an ideal choice for cavity, solid, internal and party walls. Aircrete blocks are lightweight and easy to work, saving time and money. They are manufactured in widths of 75, 100, 150 and 200 mm.

Fig 4.30 **Aircrete blocks**
Source: Celcon

Over 50 per cent of the raw material used in the manufacture of Aircrete blocks is pulverized fuel ash, a stable by-product of coal burning power stations. This recycled material is mixed with sand, cement, lime and aluminum powder together with processed waste and water, to produce a range of blocks noted for their high thermal insulation properties.

High Strength Aircrete Blocks

High strength Aerated blocks combine strength with thermal performance and are lightweight and easy to use.

Larger Sized Aircrete Blocks

The block manufacturers Celcon and Thermalite have a range of larger block sizes available, named Plus and Jumbo in the Celcon range and similar from Thermalite, as illustrated in the work face dimensions chart, Figure 4.31. They are made to a size of 610 mm × 215 mm and 610 mm × 270 mm respectively, normal block size being 440 mm × 215 mm.

Work face dimensions	
Wall blocks	440 × 215 mm
Floor blocks	440 × 560 mm
Foundation blocks	440 × 215 mm
Coursing bricks	215 × 65 mm
Plus blocks	610 × 215 mm
Jumbo Plus blocks	610 × 270 mm

Fig 4.31 **Work face dimensions chart**
Source: Celcon

Foundation Blocks

Foundation blocks are mainly used below ground to carry cavity walls. They may be the lightweight Aircrete type or the dense concrete type depending on circumstances. They are manufactured in a range of thicknesses; 100 mm and above for cavity wall construction and 190 mm and above for solid wall construction (see Figure 4.32). The Aircrete blocks have an excellent thermal performance, and are equally suitable for the support of either cavity, solid walls or frame construction above ground level.

THERMALITE Product summary

Product		Available block thicknesses (mm)	Available[7] face dimensions (mm)
	Turbo	100 115 125 130 140 150 190 200 215 265 300[3]	440 × 215 440 × 430
	Shield	75 90 100 125 140 150 190 200	440 × 215 440 × 140 440 × 430 540 × 440[4]
	Hi-Strength 7	100 140 150 190 200 215	440 × 215 440 × 430
	Hi-Strength 10[3]	100 140 150 190 200 215	440 × 215
	Smooth Face	100 140 150 190 200 215	440 × 215 440 × 430
	Hi-Strength Smooth Face	100 140 150 190 200 215	440 × 215 440 × 430
	Party Wall	100 215	440 × 215 440 × 430
	Floorblock	100	440 × 350 440 × 215 440 × 540
	Floor Endblock	150 175	440 × 140
	Coursing Slip	40 65	215 × 100 (Plan dimensions)
	Trenchblock/ Tongue & Groove	255 275 300 355[3]	440 × 215 440 × 140[5]
	Hi-Strength Trenchblock/ Tongue & Groove	255 275 300 355[3]	440 × 215 440 × 140[5]
	Coursing Brick	100 115 125 130 140 150	215 × 65

Notes

(1) BRE Special Digest 1: Concrete in aggressive ground

(2) May be used in situations described in A1, A2, but not in situations described in A3 of Table 13 of BS 5628: Part 3

(3) Manufactured to special order only

(4) Compressive Strength 3 N/mm²

(5) Not available with Tongue and Groove jointing

(6) See notes on page 18

(7) Some thicknesses to special order only

Key

✔ = recommended use

4 Thermalite

Fig 4.32 **Range of block thicknesses**
Source: Thermalite

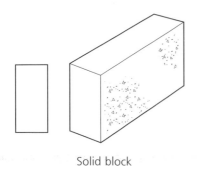

Solid block

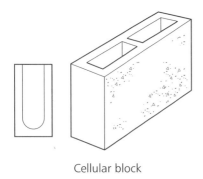

Cellular block

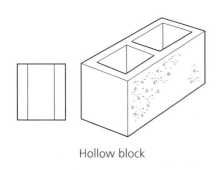

Hollow block

Fig 4.33 **Solid, cellular and hollow blocks**

Concrete Blocks

The aggregate concrete block is by far the most commonly used building block type in the construction industry, representing almost 70 per cent of new construction.

Aggregate concrete blocks are probably the most economical solution for house builders and have the best acoustic properties, provide an excellent fixing background and give unparalleled resistance to fires.

Aggregate concrete blocks are strong, durable, ideal for all wet finishes and for dry lining, and are easy to lay and position on mortar.

A single block type can be used in every situation on site, helping to control costs, improve delivery scheduling and reducing the risk of products being used in error. Aggregate concrete blocks are ideally suited to the building of inner and outer leaves of walling, cavity separating walls, beam and block flooring, partitions and work below the damp proof course.

Concrete blocks are manufactured under three headings:

Solid Blocks

These blocks are widely used in industrial and agricultural buildings, providing a hard-wearing load bearing structure (see Figure 4.33). Solid blocks contain no formed cavities.

Cellular Blocks

Used mainly for lightweight partitions. They are manufactured in widths of 75, 100 and 150 mm (see Figure 4.33). Cellular blocks contain one or more formed cavities that do not penetrate the block.

Hollow Blocks

These mainly concrete blocks are used for load bearing and hard wearing walls in industrial and agricultural buildings (see Figure 4.33). Hollow blocks contain one or more formed cavities that fully penetrate the block.

Reveal Blocks

These blocks, the majority of which are of the aerated type, are used to close cavities at door and window openings (see Figure 4.34). Closing cavities with aerated blocks provides a number of benefits, both at the design stage and during construction.

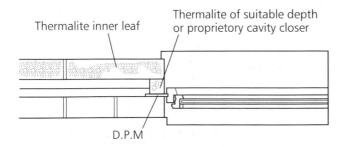

Window frame overlapping cavity closer – flush reveal

Window frame overlapping cavity closer – rebated reveal for very severe exposure zones

Fig 4.34 **Aerated blocks closing a reveal**

Aggregate concrete blocks are available in various strengths, weights, sizes, and surface textures. They can be used in the following situations:

- Inner and outer leaves of walling
- Separating walls
- Beam and block flooring
- Below the damp proof course.

Good Practice

The Concrete Block Association recommend the following good working practices when block laying.

High standards of workmanship should be encouraged at all times

All bed and perpend joints should be fully filled with mortar.

Cavities should be kept clear from mortar droppings and other debris.

Partially completed and new work should be protected at all times from bad weather.

Movement should be controlled by the inclusion of movement joints and or bed joint reinforcement appropriately positioned.

To maintain a satisfactory appearance in facing work, wall dimensions should be based on coordinating block sizes.

For facing work a sample panel should be built to enable specifications and standards of workmanship to be agreed before construction commences.

Special blocks should be used for lintels, sills and closing cavities.

Energy Conservation

Changes to the energy conservation requirements for buildings, mean that areas where thermal bridging may occur should be considered carefully and taken into account in the overall design of the building.

Please note, that the use of bricks and other dense materials for the closing of cavities is now not permitted by the Robust Details Document. The reason being that the use of aerated blocks enables the U-value of the wall construction to be maintained up to the door and window reveals and at roof level.

key terms

Thermal Bridge – A region within a building element, such as a mortar joint or a lintel, where the conduction of heat is higher compared with other parts of the building element.

Reference Panel – A panel of brick or blockwork built at the commencement of a contract to set standards of appearance and workmanship.

Sample Panel – A panel of brick or blockwork which may be built to compare material and workmanship with those of a reference panel.

Good Practice

Daily Lift Heights

Lift heights will be affected by block thickness, weight, type of block, wall type and mortar mix used. Weather conditions will also affect lift heights and they may need to be restricted in bad weather. Generally lift heights should be restricted to seven full block courses approximately 1575 mm in a working day.

In cavity walls, the two leaves should be brought up together and the difference in leaf height at any stage during construction should generally not exceed seven full block courses approximately 1575 mm in a working day.

Manual Handling

Careful consideration of the bricklayer's working area can contribute greatly to safe working. Points to take into consideration should include:

- Move blocks in packs by mechanical means whenever possible
- Load blocks out to just above two block courses in height
- Ensure that normal protective equipment that is appropriate to a building site is both provided and used.

Ensure that appropriate eye protection equipment and dust suppression or extraction measures are provided when mechanically cutting or chasing out blockwork.

Protection of Finished Work

Blockwork should be protected from bad weather and when required from other building operations with weatherproof sheeting which must be properly tied down. Care must be taken to cover all new work particularly if there is a likelihood of frost or extreme hot or cold weather.

Laying Blocks

Cold Weather Conditions

Blocks should not be laid when the temperature is at or below 3° Centigrade and falling, or unless it is at least 1° Centigrade and rising.

Laying

Solid and cellular blocks should be laid on a full bed of mortar and vertical joints substantially filled. Hollow blocks should be shell bedded with the vertical joints filled.

Do not wet the blocks before laying. Where necessary adjust the consistency of the mortar to suit the suction of the blocks.

When laying facing blocks select the blocks from more than one pack as work proceeds to reduce the risk of banding or patchiness of colour in the finished walling.

Quick quiz Quick quiz Quick quiz Quick quiz Quick quiz

❶ Draw and name a type of building block and say what it would be used for.

❷ What should newly built blockwork be protected from?

❸ Name three different types of concrete blocks.

❹ How high should packs of blocks be stacked?

❺ What is the minimum lap for blockwork?

Thin Joint Blockwork Systems

Thin Joint masonry is a fast, clean and accurate system of construction using aircrete blocks of close dimensional accuracy with the benefit of 2 to 3 mm mortar joints.

The block manufacturer Thermalite first began trials on thin joint construction in the 1980s, but there is a far longer history of this method of construction in Continental Europe. The increasing demands of the British construction industry for a higher build quality, greater productivity, improved thermal performance, air tightness and waste reduction, mean that the benefits offered by thin joint mortar systems are increasingly relevant.

Thin joint mortar systems have been developed to complement the overall performance of the standard aircrete block. Manufacturers claim that the thin joint system significantly improves productivity to the extent that it is now possible to build the supporting structure of a house in just a few days.

Thin joint mortar is a pre-mixed cement based product that only requires adding to water to make an easily applied mortar. It differs from the general use mortar in that it sets far more rapidly, therefore giving early stability to the construction. It provides an alternative to the traditional sand and cement mortar and allows the depth of the mortar to be reduced from at least 10 mm to 3 mm or less (see Figure 4.35).

Fig 4.35 **Materials and equipment for mixing thin joint mortar**
Source: Celcon

Benefits of the Thin Joint System

- Building time can be reduced
- Increased productivity
- Follow on trades can start sooner
- Much improved thermal performance
- Reduction of site waste, mortar and aircrete blocks
- Stability achieved earlier during construction
- Accuracy of walls allows thin-coat plaster finishes
- Speed and ease of fixing secondary insulation.

Installation

In common with all types of blockwork walling, the thin joint system should be built to the recommendations of the various British Standard Codes of Practice for the use of masonry – materials, components, design and workmanship.

Method of Construction

The building techniques employed for thin joint walling are similar to those used when working with general use mortar. It will, for example, remain necessary to maintain regular checks on level and line.

For the inner leaves of cavity walling a mix of standard, large format and cut blocks can be used to meet design datum levels for floor and wall plate levels. Thicker beds of mortar can of course be used if required to make up a level of a few millimetres or so (see Figure 4.36).

Setting Out the Base Course

The success of the thin joint system depends on the correct setting out of the base or first course. Base course blocks must be bedded in general use mortar and laid level, aligned, plumbed and allowed to fully set before commencement of the thin joint construction. Any inaccuracy in the base course cannot easily be corrected in the subsequent thin joint mortar beds.

Planning needs to be made so that any damp proof course can be incorporated into the base course bed joint.

Block and Brickwork Alignment

It is important to understand that thin joint walling combines 2 to 3 mm thick bed mortar with aircrete blocks of close dimensional accuracy. Therefore, bed joints will not align with standard brickwork coursing of the outer leaf as in normal practice, making necessary the use of special wall ties – see Figure 4.37.

Fig 4.36 Bricklayer working on a thin joint wall
Source: Celcon

Laying Blocks

With thin joint mortar, the construction process can be speeded up greatly. For example, mortar can be applied to the exposed block ends while still in the pack. Alternatively, blocks can be placed on a flat surface and several joint faces can be mortared, to an acceptable standard in one simple operation.

It should be noted that the bricklayer does not use his normal tools for the construction of thin joint walling, special tools designed specifically for thin joint walling must be used. The use of the recommended application tools will deliver the appropriate depth and spread of mortar to the surface bed of the block as well as the cross joint. When building long runs of walling, the thin joint mortar may be applied using a proprietary pumping system.

Subject to reasonable weather conditions, the exposed mortar bed will remain workable for up to 30 minutes. However, once blocks have been laid, initial setting takes place within 10 minutes, and any adjustment to the blockwork should be made during this period (see Figure 4.38).

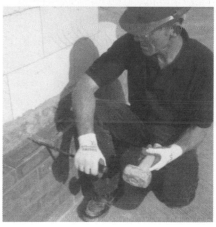

Applications for Cavity Walls

When building with thin joint walling, the inner leaf of blockwork may be built first, taking the outer leaf of brickwork off the planning pathway of the building programme. This enables internal work, such as first fix carpentry and services to proceed whilst the outer leaf is being built. This also enables easier installation of any added insulation. There is a wide variety of wall ties that may be used to connect the two leaves of thin joint construction, which will be covered later.

Fig 4.37 **Bricklayer fixing wall ties to a thin joint wall**
Source: Thermalite

Fig 4.38 **Bricklayer using the special tools designed for thin block walling**
Source: Thermalite

Application to External Solid Walls

Aircrete blocks are ideal for the building of solid external walls. The wide range of blocks available provides the designer with a choice of solutions, which offer both strength and thermal insulation. This results in a cost effective building in domestic, commercial and industrial construction. The use of thin joint techniques compared to conventional joints also gives greatly improved *U*-values for solid external walls.

Wall Ties

In standard cavity walling the two leaves of brick and blockwork are so designed, to ensure that courses meet every block course or every three brick courses. This enables tie wires of whatever type to be placed level and at right angles across the width of the cavity. We are not able to do this in thin joint walling, so when connecting two leaves of an external cavity wall together, there are a number of special wall ties available.

Generally, the most effective ties are the helical type that can be driven into the face of the blockwork at a level which will course with the outer leaf mortar joint. Insulation can be placed against the inner leaf before wall ties are inserted. These helical type ties can also incorporate clips for partial fill insulation and are positioned as the outer leaf is being built, thus reducing the risk of injury from projecting metal and reducing the build up of waste mortar on tie wires.

Ties are also available which allow the laying of ties in the thin joint beds as block laying proceeds. This is particularly useful when both inner and outer leaves are built together. All ties should conform to the relevant British Standard.

Helical Ties for Thin Joint Blockwork

Application

This is a hammer driven cavity wall tie, ideal for thin joint blockwork and other applications where the joints of the inner and outer leaves of masonry do not work to course.

Method of Installation

Keep the brickwork one course lower than the blockwork during installation of the ties. Position the tie against the inner leaf so that the outer end will be located in the bed joint of the external wall as shown in Figure 4.39.

Hammer the tie, through the insulation, and into the blockwork to the correct embedment as shown in Figure 4.39.

Install an insulation retaining clip to restrain the insulation as shown in Figure 4.40.

Build into the bed joint of the outer leaf of brickwork ensuring the tie is surrounded by mortar as shown in Figure 4.40.

Fig 4.39 **Placing a tie in blockwork with brickwork one course lower**
Source: Celcon

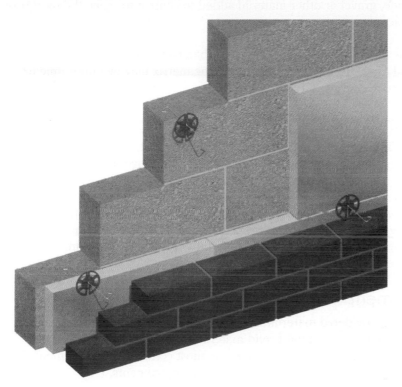

Fig 4.40 **Fixing retaining clip to insulation and tie built into brickwork**
Source: Celcon

Quick quiz Quick quiz Quick quiz Quick quiz Quick quiz

❶ Draw and name a type of building block used in thin joint walling.

❷ What size joints would you have in thin joint walling?

❸ What are the setting times of thin joint mortar once it is mixed with water?

❹ Where did thin joint blockwork originate?

❺ What quality improvement is there in the system over other blockwork systems?

Mortar

Mortars

Definition – The material in which bricks are usually bedded to form a wall is known as mortar. Mortar is a mixture of sand and cement or lime, or all three, which hardens as it dries.

Mortar is composed of a matrix and an aggregate which, when it is mixed with a certain quantity of water, becomes sufficiently plastic to be spread on the wall in thin layers. In a short while, varying with the matrix used, the mortar sets, becomes firm and eventually hardens.

The aggregate is the inert material forming the body of the mortar, sand being normally used for this purpose. It is composed of crushed stone, gravel or other material added to cement to make the mortar or concrete.

The matrix is the material which, when combined with water, hardens and binds the aggregate together. The matrix may be either lime or cement, or a mixture of the two.

Lime

Definition – Lime is a fine powdered material, with no appreciable setting and hardening properties, used to improve the workability and water retention of cement based mortars.

Lime improves the working properties of mortar. Non-hydraulic hydrated lime, as a finely ground powder, is available in the UK either in bulk or bagged. It has no setting (i.e. hydraulic) properties when mixed with water.

Cement

A fine powdered material which, when mixed with water, sets and binds together to form a hard solid material. It is used as a component of mortar and concrete. In the UK, the most commonly used cements in mortars are Portland cements and Masonry cements.

Purpose of Cements and Limes

Mortar is used to provide a means of placing together brick and block components into walling. In addition, loads are distributed more uniformly than they would otherwise be, if for example, we were to just place the bricks with their somewhat irregular bed surfaces together without mortar. Further, mortar joints contribute to stability and act as a resistance to weather.

Types of Commonly Used Cements

Ordinary Portland Cement (OPC)

Ordinary Portland cement is the most widely used cement for application where chemical or thermal attack is not to be encountered. These applications include ready-mixed and site-mixed concrete, pre-cast and pre-stressed concrete, grouts, screeds and mortars for brick and blocklaying.

Masonry Cement

Masonry cement has air entraining and plasticizing properties and produces a mortar having a high workability. Care must be taken to avoid adding too much water as the mix then becomes more fluid as air is entrained. Suitable for brickwork, blockwork and rendering.

Sulphate Resisting Cement

Portland cement is liable to sulphate attack in damp conditions, therefore the composition of sulphate resisting cement is adjusted so that it withstands sulphate action. Suitable for use in below ground concrete. Prevents the deterioration of concrete or mortar where sulphates are present.

Super Sulphate Cement

Super sulphate cement will resist attack by the strongest concentrations of sulphates normally found in soils. However, it must not be mixed with other cements. If soluble sulphates are present in materials or in the ground, then in damp conditions they combine with the alumina constituent of Portland cement, the resulting expansion causing splitting and cracking of mortar and concrete. In such conditions a sulphate resisting cement should be used.

Rapid Hardening Portland Cement

Where greater speed is required in the final setting time of concrete, rapid hardening cement may be used. The main difference between it and ordinary Portland cement is that it is burnt at a higher temperature, ground to a finer powder, and has a higher lime content, but the hardening process is much quicker, being completed in about four days to OPC's seven or longer.

High-Alumina Cement

This type of cement hardens much more quickly than those previously mentioned. The initial set is completed in two or three hours and the first hardening in one day; also the ultimate strength is greater. While the use of this cement for general purposes is unlikely by reason of the high cost of manufacture, there are many occasions where quick hardening justifies the cost. For example, formwork may be removed and re-used in a much shorter period than with ordinary cements. However, high alumina cement must not be used for structural concrete or masonry.

White Portland Cement

A white cement for architectural uses which provides an attractive and durable visual concrete, rendering and mortar. Its uses include: cast stone, architectural pre-cast concrete, paving slabs, street furniture and terrazzo. A wide variety of finishes can be achieved with the addition of coloured aggregates or pigments.

Types of Common Mortar Mix Proportions

Proportions of materials vary according to their nature. For example, a certain type of sand may require a greater proportion of cement or lime than a certain other type of sand, in order to produce mortar having the required strength and workability. Consequently, a fixed proportion cannot be wisely stated unless the nature of the materials to be used is known. However, it is accepted that proportions can be safely stated between certain limits in accordance with the various Codes of Practice as shown in Figure 4.41.

Lime Mortar

This usually consists of one part lime to three parts of sand by volume, but may vary in its proportions according to the type for which it is intended. If slaked quicklime is used, the method of preparation will differ from that required for powdered hydrated lime. When hydrated lime is used, being in powdered form it is more convenient to mix the lime with the sand before any water is added.

Application for Bricks	Exposure Category for site – Reference BS 5628: Part 3: Table 10	Recommended Mortart Mix (Note 1) Proportions of Cement: Lime: Sand Mortars based on Ordinary Portland Cement except where otherwise stated	BS 5628: Part 3 Table 15 Designation (Note 2)
Walls of buildings between ground level dpc and eaves – eaves and sills overhanging walls	Sheltered/Moderate or less Moderate/Sever or Severe/Very Severe	$1 : 1 : 5\frac{1}{2}$ + air-entraining agent or $1 : 4\frac{1}{2}$ masonary cement $1 : \frac{1}{2} : 4\frac{1}{2}$ + air-entraining agent or $1 : 3$ masonary cement $1 : \frac{1}{2} : 4\frac{1}{2}$ + air-entraining agent or using sulphate resisting cement	(iii) (iii) (ii) (ii) (ii)
Brickwork below ground level dpc, including brickwork below ground	All exposure categories	$1 : \frac{1}{2} : 4\frac{1}{2}$ + air-entraining agent (Note 3)	(ii)
Free-standing walls, parapet walls and chimneys (Note 4)	Sheltered/Moderate or less Moderate/Severe or greater	$1 : \frac{1}{2} : 4\frac{1}{2}$ + air-entraining agent or $1 : 4$ + air-entraining agent $1 : \frac{1}{2}: 4\frac{1}{2}$ + air-entraining agent using sulphate resisting cement or $1 : 4$ + air-entraining agent using sulphate resisting cement	(ii) (ii) (ii) (ii)
Retaining walls (Note 5)	All exposure categories	$1 : \frac{1}{2} : 4\frac{1}{2}$ + air-entraining agent using sulphate resisting cement or $1:4$ + air-entraining agent using sulphate resisting cement	(ii) (ii)
Rendered external walls of building between dpc and eaves	All exposure categories	$1 : \frac{1}{2} : 4\frac{1}{2}$ + air-entraining agent using sulphate resisting cement or $1 : 4$ + air-entraining agent using sulphate resisting cement	(ii) (ii)
Internal walls		$1 : 1 : 5\frac{1}{2}$ + air-entraining agent or $1 : 4\frac{1}{2}$ masonary cement	(iii) (iii)

Fig 4.41 **Code of practice**
Source: Hanson

144

Method of Mixing

The sand is placed in a heap to one side of the lime and the lime is spread over the sand, the two materials being then repeatedly turned with a shovel until a thorough mix is ensured. With the two materials thus mixed, a ring is formed, water is added and the procedure followed as for slaked quicklime.

Cement Mortar

This is a mixture of Portland cement and sand in proportions that will vary with the nature of the walling to be built. For all general purposes this is usually one part cement to four parts sand by volume.

Method of Mixing

The mixing of cement mortar follows the method outlined for hydrated lime mortar. With cement as a matrix the mortar begins to set about 30 minutes after the water has been added, and because of this it should be prepared in fairly small quantities and disturbed as little as possible after setting has commenced.

Gauging Mortar

Definition – The term used to describe measuring out quantities of material for a mortar mix.

The gauging of mortar carried out on a construction site is one of the most abused. It is generally the norm for the mixer to be filled by use of the shovel. This ensures that the mix proportions cannot be accurately gauged.

The only way that proportions can be controlled with a degree of accuracy is by using one of the two following methods:

■ Weight batching
■ Volume batching.

In the majority of cases the method employed will depend on the size of the building project being carried out.

Weight Batching

Of the two methods, weight batching is the more accurate. Weight batching is more likely to be found on larger construction sites as it involves large mixers fitted with automatic loading hoppers or separate weigh batch hoppers that discharge directly into the machine.

Volume Batching

This method is more likely to be used on smaller jobs where mixing is to be carried out by hand or by using a manually loaded mixer.

A simple form of mixing by volume is to use a bucket to gauge the quantity of each material. A more reliable method is to use a gauge box designed to the necessary size as shown in Figure 4.42. The gauge is a box with no bottom in which the dry materials are placed in order to gain the exact proportions required.

key terms

Slaked Quicklime – This is produced by the burning of calcium carbonate in the form of chalk, limestone, marble, the resultant being calcium oxide or quicklime. For building purposes quicklime requires slaking. Slaking is brought about by adding water to the quicklime, which becomes hot, swells and breaks down into small particles; as more water is added a putty-like substance is eventually produced. This is slaked quicklime in a saturated condition. In this state it is added to the sand to form a lime mortar.

Hydrated Lime – A fine powdered material, with no appreciable setting and hardening properties, used to improve the workability and water retention of cement-based mortars.

Compressive Strength – The average value of the crushing strengths of samples of bricks tested to assess load bearing capacity.

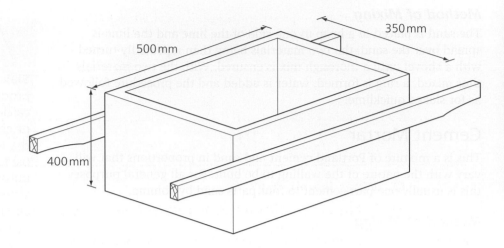

500mm
350mm
400mm

Fig 4.42 **Gauge box**

Method of Mixing

The dimensions of the box would usually equal four 25-kg bags of cement.

The gauge box is placed on a clean, firm base and filled in proportion to the design of the mix. For example:

- Five boxes of sand
- One box of cement
- One box of lime.

On filling, the box is removed and the dry materials placed into a mixer.

Gauged Mortar

It is now quite common to use a combination of lime and cement as a matrix with the usual aggregate of sand, this is known as gauged mortar. There are two methods of introducing the cement to the mixture, these are:

1. Lime mortar is prepared in bulk, as described earlier, and from this, sufficient is set aside for immediate use. To this lime mortar, cement is added as required, the usual proportion for general work being 10 per cent of the whole.

2. In this method all the dry materials are mixed as required in the proportion of one part cement, two parts hydrated lime, eight to ten parts of sand. The operation of mixing is similar to that described for hydrated lime or cement mortar. It must be remembered that since cement has been added it should only be prepared in small quantities.

Apart from the fact that lime and cement mortar is much easier to use than a cement mortar, it also has the advantage of rendering the brick and blockwork more damp proof. Recent studies have shown that cement mortar joints tend to shrink away from the surface of the brick, leaving capillary channels through which water may find access, while a gauged mortar will form a much better seal. The advantage is more apparent if the bricks have been laid in a dry state.

It appears that unless great compressive strength is required, gauged mortar is to be preferred for all general building purposes. For small quantities of mortar, mixing by hand as required is the more suitable method of preparation, but for large quantities machine mixing is usually adopted.

Quick quiz Quick quiz Quick quiz Quick quiz Quick quiz

❶ What is gauging?

❷ What is the difference between factory produced mortars and site mixed mortars?

❸ What is mortar?

❹ What is cement?

❺ Name the materials in a 1 : 1 : 6 mortar mix.

Suitable Sands for Mortars

Definition – Sand is a fine aggregate which forms the bulk of mortar.

Properties of Sand

The properties of sand influence, to a great extent, the quality of mortar. In selecting a sand suitable for general brick and blockwork the following points should be observed.

The sand should be:

■ Clean, that is, free from any impurities such as iron pyrites, salts, coal or other organic matter

■ Sharp, that is, having angular shaped grains

■ Well graded, that is, having proportionate amounts of varying sized grains combined to give the required texture, neither too fine nor too coarse, as shown in Figure 4.43.

Sharp sand, obtainable from pits or quarries, produces mortars of greater adhesive strength. Sand found in sea and river beds has rounded grains due to the continuous action of moving water; these grains are not only round but smooth and consequently cause a reduction in the adhesion between the cement or lime and sand. The use of sea sand should be avoided since it contains salt. With practice, sharpness of sand can be tested by rubbing the grains between the fingers.

Sand which is not clean may reduce the adhesive property of the mortar; dirty sand can usually be made suitable for use by washing, a process in which water is used to separate and convey the impurities from the sand.

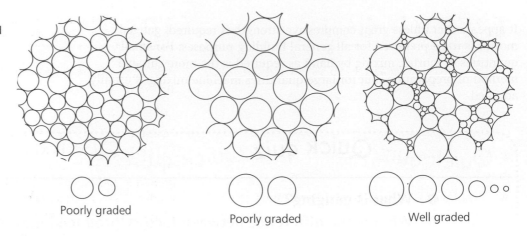

Fig 4.43 **Well graded sand and poorly graded sand**
Source: Hanson

Poorly graded   Poorly graded   Well graded

TRY THIS OUT

A Simple Experiment to Test for the Cleanliness of Sand.

The Silt Test

Sand can be tested for cleanliness by carrying out a silt test on a small quantity of sand taken from a load.

Material and Equipment required

● Glass measuring cylinder or jar

● Sample of sand

● Ruler or tape measure

● Water.

Method

Half fill the jar with water and add one teaspoon of salt.

Add 100 mm of sand.

The cylinder is then shaken vigorously, and the contents allowed to settle for three hours. Sand containing more than 8 per cent of silt should not be used for mortar as it will greatly reduce the bond between the brick and the mortar. Figure 4.44 shows an example of a completed silt test.

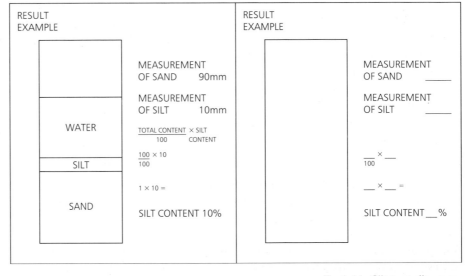

Fig 4.44 **Silt test diagram**

Results of Experiment

The sample of sand should not contain more than 8 per cent silt.

The sample of sand tested was suitable/ was not suitable for use in a concrete mix.

Delete as applicable.

TRY THIS OUT

A Simple Experiment to Test for the Good Grading of Sand.

Grading of Sand Test

To carry out the test you will require:

● Two containers
● Water
● Samples of sand from two different sources

Method

Take two containers of equal size and fill each one with sand obtained from two different sources. Pour water into the containers in turn, taking care to prevent overflowing.

The sand and water should be stirred to get rid of any air and sufficient water then added until it rises to the tops of each container.

The amounts of water used for filling each container should be noted down and compared. The better-graded sand will be the one that requires the smallest quantity of water.

Principle of the Experiment

The principle upon which the experiment is based is as follows:

Water that is absorbed into the sand fills voids that previously existed between the grains of sand. Therefore, the amount of water required in each case indicates the volume of the voids. From these amounts the comparative quantities of the voids can be obtained, the smaller amount being that of the well graded sand.

The Colour of Sand

Sand obtained from different sources may vary in colour from a reddish-brown to a pale yellow while in some cases there is almost an absence of colour, the term silver sand being given to the latter. Normally, the colour of the sand influences the colour of mortar but where, in the latter, a special mortar colour is required then the appropriate coloured cement or dye may be used.

TRY THIS OUT

A Simple Experiment to Test for the Bulking of Sand.

Bulking of Sand

Dry sand and saturated sand have approximately the same volume but a sample of damp sand will show a marked increase in volume. This effect is known as bulking. This increase when using fine grades of sand can amount to 30 per cent of the volume. Which may have an adverse affect on the mortar mix if it is being gauged by volume. Therefore, any bulking taking place due to bad weather should be calculated and additional sand added to make up the difference.

Materials and equipment required to carry out the test

● Glass measuring cylinder or jar
● Sample of wet sand
● Water
● Ruler or tape-measure.

Method

Place 100 mm of wet sand in the measuring cylinder or jar. Cover the sand with water and shake the cylinder. Allow the sand to settle and measure the reduction (see Figure 4.45).

Conclusion of Experiment.

The sample of sand has bulked by . . . . . per cent.

Result

The sand has bulked by ? per cent, requiring the sand stockpile to be replenished by the same amount.

Results Example

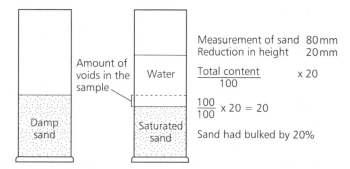

Measurement of sand 80 mm
Reduction in height   20 mm

$$\frac{\text{Total content}}{100} \times 20$$

$$\frac{100}{100} \times 20 = 20$$

Sand had bulked by 20%

Fig 4.45 Bulking of sand experiment

Mortar Additives, Plasticizers and Accelerators

Mortar additives usually come in two types: plasticizers and accelerators.

Plasticizers

Definition – A plasticizer is a substance that when added to a material, (in the case of brickwork sand and cement), produces a product which is flexible, resilient and easier to handle.

Accelerators

Definition – An accelerator is an admixture which increases the initial rate of chemical reaction between the cement and the water, so that the mortar or, more usually, concrete stiffens, hardens and develops strength more quickly. Accelerators have little or no affect on the workability of the mortar or concrete

Plasticizers and Accelerators

There are many types of plasticizers and accelerators on the market, some of those more commonly used are described below.

Plasticizers

Mortar Plasticizer

Description of Product

This is a liquid air entraining mortar plasticizer that replaces lime or other supplements in the mix and reduces the amount of water required to achieve the desired workability.

Fields of Application

This is an admixture for mortars that improves the workability of bricklaying mortars and significantly increases their resistance to freezing and thawing cycles.

Chloride Free Frostproofer and Mortar Plasticizer

Description of Product

Chloride free frost proofer, liquid admixture combines acceleration with the proven frost protection benefits of air entrapment in mortar, thus allowing work to continue even at sub-zero temperatures.

Fields of Application

The product is designed to be used as a mortar admixture throughout the winter period. The air entraining qualities of the product improve the workability of bricklaying mortars. This ensures that building operations can continue to be carried out at optimum rates.

It also includes frost-proofing chemicals which accelerate the setting time of the mortar during cold periods. The user will therefore find it unnecessary to change to a conventional frostproofer.

Powder Mortar Plasticizer

Description of Product

Mortar plasticizer in powder form is used as an alternative to lime or as a supplement to lime to aid mortar durability.

Fields of Application

For use as an admixture for mortars to improve workability in bricklaying. The product aids resistance of mortars to frost attack in both the wet and cured state. It also increases long term durability of cement, sand and cement, lime and sand mortars.

Accelerators

Chloride Free Powdered Accelerator and Frost-proofer

Description of Product

Chloride free accelerator admixture promotes accelerated strength gain in concrete and mortar and allows work to continue in lower temperature conditions.

Fields of Application

As a frostproofer:

In concrete or cement mortar when ambient temperatures fall, or are likely to fall, below freezing.

As a floor hardener:

For concrete floors, screeds and cement pavings, particularly where it is desirable to open the floor to traffic as early as possible.

As a chloride free accelerator:

In reinforced concrete in order to obtain higher earlier strengths.

The Use of Pre-mixed and Retarded Mortars

Pre-Mixed or Factory Produced Mortars

These are mortars which are produced in a quality controlled environment to ensure accurate mix proportions. There are two main types available:

Ready-to-use-Mortars

These mortars are produced in a factory and delivered to site ready-to-use. They may be:

- Wet ready-to-use, which requires no further mixing and is stored in tubs on site
- Dry ready-to-use delivered in silos or bags, which requires only the addition of mixing water.

Lime : Sand Mortars

These are prebatched materials which are delivered to site, with cement and water being added prior to use.

All production methods of factory produced mortars can offer both coloured and natural shades.

The Benefits of Factory Produced Mortars

- Accurate cement content
- Consistent strength
- Consistent colour
- Reduced mixing and labour costs
- Reduced wastage
- Compliance with the specification.

Factory Produced Mortars

Factory produced ready-to-use mortars fulfil the requirements of specifiers and users seeking the quality control of factory made materials. The mortar is delivered to site ready-to-use in every respect and requires no further mixing; no further materials should be added. The mortar has guaranteed mix proportions and should overcome any potential problems relating to site mixing.

Manufacturers' Recommendations

Workability

Premixed mortars are designed to have good workability and plasticity over their stated working period. However, in hot weather some stiffening of the mortar may occur which can be corrected by the addition of a small amount of water followed by trowel mixing on the spot board in the usual way.

Protection

Mortar should be protected against excessive rain or drying conditions. All newly built brick and blockwork should be covered at the end of the working day or when rained off.

Retarding Admixtures or Retarders

An admixture or retarder is composed of chemicals that slow down the initial reaction between cement and water by reducing the rate of water penetration to the cement and slowing down the growth of the hydration products. The mortar therefore stays workable longer than it would otherwise.

The inclusion of a cement set retarder into factory produced mortars makes it possible to produce mortars with an extended working life that will set normally when used for brick and blockwork. These types of mortar should now be included in the range of mortars available from your local supplier.

Factory Produced Silo Mortar for Brick and Blockwork

Factory produced silo mortars offer a range of mix proportions and should overcome any potential problems related to on site mixing.

Method

A silo as illustrated in Figure 4.46 is delivered to the site complete with internal mixer. Once power and water supplies are connected, mortar can be produced as required. Water being added as needed to produce the necessary consistency.

Fig 4.46 **Mortar silo**
Source: Tarmac

Two-Compartment Silo

This is a movable silo with two sealed compartments that are filled by the mortar manufacturer with the required amounts of sand and cement. The mixing ratio is decided on before delivery to ensure that the mix proportions are to the customer's requirements.

Single Compartment Silo

These are single compartment movable silos that are filled by the mortar manufacturer with dried sand, cement, or lime if required and other admixtures, pigments or additives that are premixed to the customer's requirements.

Water and pigment is added to both types of silo by means of a metered pump.

Manufacturer's Recommendations

The setting of cement is affected by the weather and will set more slowly when it is colder. This factor is taken into account when the mortar is manufactured. However, subsequent significant reductions in temperature may increase the setting period and extend the working life of the mortar. This will have no adverse affect on the brick or blockwork, but it is inadvisable to proceed with the building of brick or blockwork if the temperature falls below 3°C. If the mortar does freeze any frozen material or crust should not be used. Any unfrozen mortar may be used when the air temperature is suitable and the bricks or blocks are not frozen.

Factory Produced Lime : Sand Mortar for Brick and Blockwork

Factory produced lime : sand mortar is a blend of sand and lime to which cement is added whilst on site, to produce mortar for brick and block laying. Brickwork and blockwork built with a sand lime mortar should have adequate strength with a substantial built in safety margin. Yet the mortar should retain a degree of elasticity so that any movement in the building either during or after construction can be accommodated without cracking, which is unsightly and leads to expensive remedial costs. Sand : lime mortars are suitable for all types of brick and blockwork, particularly housing and other medium and low rise buildings.

Manufacturer's Recommendations

Deliveries of premixed lime and sand for mortar should be tipped, unless delivered in skips, on to a clean area with a sealed base, slab or similar area and covered with sheeting when not in use. Sheeting is very important when coloured mortar is required, as rain and weathering may otherwise cause separation of some of the materials.

To obtain the required mortar mix, considerable care should be taken on site to add the correct amount and type of cement. Gauge boxes as illustrated in Figure 4.42 or other accurate measuring aids should be used when mixing is carried out by volume. When using coloured mortars, it is advisable that the same brand, type and source of cement is used throughout the length of the contract. If possible, gauge mix proportions by weight.

Note: Only clean water should be used for obtaining the correct mortar consistency.

Although it is recommended that you use cement : lime : sand mortars within two to three hours, most mortars of this type will remain fairly soft for a working day, making cleaning up at the end of each day reasonably easy. If you have a reason to change the colour of the mortar, ensure all mixer spot boards and trowels are thoroughly cleaned so as to avoid contaminating any new colour of mortar.

Differences Between Factory Produced Mortars and Site Mixed Mortars

Factory produced mortars are mixed under controlled conditions in purpose-built production units. All materials are weigh batched to ensure the accuracy of mix proportions. All mix ingredients comply with the relevant British and European standards and are subject to testing to ensure quality control.

Site mixed mortars are generally produced by a site operative shovel loading bagged cement and sand from a heap into a small mixer. Water and plasticizers are added by hand to suit. Site mixed mortars cannot match the high degree of consistency that factory produced mortars achieve and they are unlikely to comply with on site specifications.

Quick quiz Quick quiz Quick quiz Quick quiz Quick quiz

❶ Describe two types of mortar silo.
❷ Name two ways of batching materials.
❸ What is a retarder used for?
❹ When mixing by machine, what should be added to the mixer first?
❺ What does a silt test measure?

Determine Brick and Block Bonds 4.4

Purpose of Bonding

Definition – The overlapping arrangement of bricks or blocks in order to unite or tie them together in a mass of brickwork or masonry, is known as bonding

When you have worked through this section you will be able to:

- Bond corners for half and one brick walls using half and quarter lap
- Understand the change direction, change bond rule
- Recognize the positioning of bricks
- Calculate short lengths of brickwork.
- Bond one and half brick walls and junctions in English and Flemish bonds.

At the end of this section you should be fully conversant with, the principles of quarter and half lap bonding. You should also be familiar with English and Flemish bonds used in one brick walling.

Vertical Joints

Good bonding should have a minimum of vertical joints in any part of the wall, since they are a source of weakness and should therefore be avoided where possible. Bricklayers sometimes concentrate solely upon the face bond and to some extent overlook the internal bond; it is essential to have good bonding throughout the wall.

Bonding, in addition to uniting a wall, also distributes a load from, say, a beam placed upon any individual brick to an increasing number of bricks forming the wall below, as illustrated in Figure 4.47, thereby reducing the tendency to settlement.

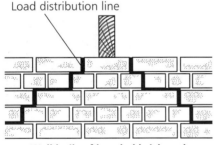

Load distribution line

Wall built of bonded brickwork

Fig 4.47 Load being distributed due to bonding

Purposes of Bonding Brickwork

- To strengthen the wall and ensure that any load carried is distributed over the whole wall.
- To ensure lateral stability and resistance to side thrust.
- To give a pleasing appearance to the face of the wall.

Before proceeding to describe the methods of bonding used, it is necessary briefly to define a few of the technical terms commonly used in this area.

Brick Terminology

Work Size and Co-ordinating Size

A standard building component with dimensions of approximately $215 \times 102.5 \times 65$ mm, is known as the work size (see Figure 4.48).

If a 10 mm mortar joint is added to each dimension, then the brick plus joint measures $225 \times 112.5 \times 75$ mm as illustrated in Figure 4.48, this is

Sizes

	Length mm	Width mm	Height mm
Co-ordinating size	225	112.5	75
Work size	215	102.5	65

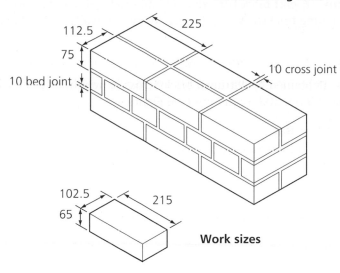

Fig 4.48 **Work and co-ordinating sizes**
Source: Ibstock

known as the co-ordinating size, and is usually used for design and setting out purposes. Always set out brickwork by using the co-ordinating size.

Face brickwork should be set out before brickwork commences using as a unit dimension the co-ordinating size of the brick. Wasteful cutting can be avoided and the appearance of the brickwork enhanced if the overall lengths and heights of walls and door openings are all multiples of the co-ordinating size.

Note: To avoid confusion, I will use the work size dimensions throughout this section and show an illustration again of work and co-ordinating size to reinforce its importance.

Standard Brick Sizes

When placed in a wall with the 102.5 × 65 mm face exposed, a brick is known as a header, while if the 215 × 65 mm face is exposed, it is known as a stretcher (see Figure 4.49).

The under surface of the brick measuring 215 × 102.5 mm is termed the bed, and the depression sometimes formed in the top of the brick is termed the frog. The sharp edge of the brick is referred to as the arris. An illustration of a brick with the various terms is given in Figure 4.50.

Brick Closer

Closers are formed from cut bricks, the brick surface exposed on the face of the wall measuring 46.25 × 65 mm. There are several types of closer but the two in general use are the ordinary closer and the queen closer as illustrated in Figure 4.50. The ordinary closer measures 46.25 × 102.5 × 65 mm and the queen closer measures 46.25 × 65 × 215 mm.

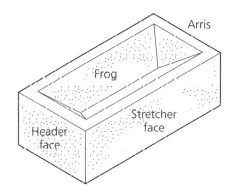

Fig 4.49 **Brick with terminology**

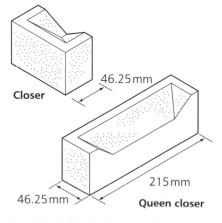

Fig 4.50 **Ordinary closer and queen closer**

157

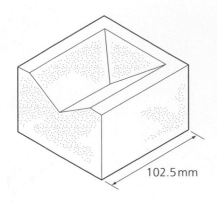

Fig 4.51 **Half bat**

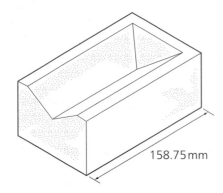

Fig 4.52 **Three-quarter bat**

It is general practice to use two ordinary closers to form a queen closer since, with certain bricks, it is difficult to satisfactorily cut queen closers.

Bats
Definition – A part brick For example half-bricks, three-quarters brick, used in bonding brickwork at corners and ends of walls and to break bond.

Half Bat
A half bat is obtained by cutting a brick across its width, its dimensions thus being 102.5 × 102.5 × 65mm (see Figure 4.51).

Three-Quarter Bat
This is also a cut brick measuring 158.75 × 102.5 × 65 mm (see Figure 4.52).

Bed Joint
The horizontal mortar joint between two courses of bricks.

Course
A row of bricks or other masonry units bedded in mortar, generally horizontal.

Cross Joints
The short, vertical joints between two bricks also referred to as perpends.

Transverse Joints
All joints formed at right angles to the face of the wall are transverse joints although they are sometimes referred to as sectional joints (see Figure 4.53).

Wall Joints
Continuous joints running parallel to the face of the wall and contained in the wall's thickness (see Figure 4.53).

Wall joint   Transverse joint

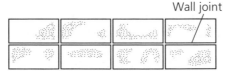 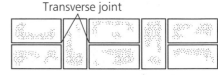

Fig 4.53 **Transverse joint**

Wall Junction
There are two main types, namely, Tee-junctions and Cross-junctions. A Tee-junction is an intersection of two walls which, on plan, has a T formation, while a cross-junction has a + formation (see Figure 4.55 and 4.56).

Stopped End
The termination of a wall usually finished with a flat surface similar to that of the wall face.

Quoins

A quoin is an external angle on the face side of a wall, the bricks forming the angle being referred to as quoin headers or quoin stretchers according to the face side of the angle viewed.

Quoins, junctions and stopped ends are classified as either square or squint according to their plan formation. Those in the square class form angles of 90° while the squint class form angles other than 90°.

Return Angle

A junction between two walls to enclose an angle, usually a right angle (see Figure 4.54).

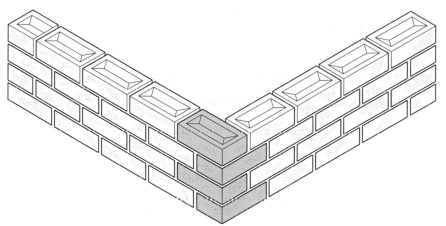

Fig 4.54 **Return angle**

Fig 4.55 **Cross junctions**

Toothed End

The form at the vertical end of a wall produced by recessing every alternate course in order that the wall may be extended and the bond maintained (see Figure 4.57).

Note: It is very important that toothing is staggered so as to avoid weak areas of walling and that all bed joints are full.

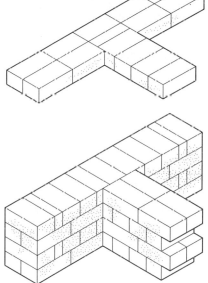

Fig 4.56 **Tee junctions**

Racking Back

As an alternative to toothing, the end of a wall may be set back on each course in relation to the course below. This is carried out so that later, the wall may be conveniently extended.

Note: Racking back and toothing can be combined.

The Bonding of Walls

Figure 4.58 shows a beam resting on a wall built without any form of bond, that is, a wall in which the connection between the various brick components is dependent upon the adhesive properties of the mortar only. With a load from a beam such as this imposed on any part of the

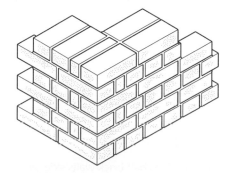

Fig 4.57 **Toothed end**

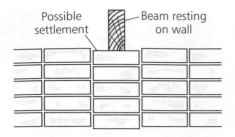

Fig 4.58 **Beam on an unbonded wall**

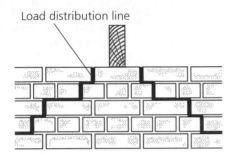

Fig 4.59 **Beam on a bonded wall**

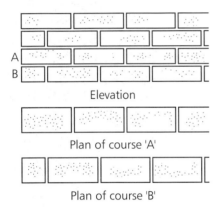

Elevation

Plan of course 'A'

Plan of course 'B'

Fig 4.60 **Half brick wall in plan and elevation**

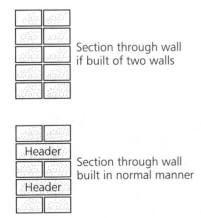

Section through wall if built of two walls

Section through wall built in normal manner

Fig 4.61 **Two half brick walls side by side and a bonded wall**

wall the tendency is for that part to subside, fracturing the mortar joints and leaving the remainder of the wall undisturbed.

To avoid the strain and possible fracture being set up in vertical cross joints it is necessary to bridge them with bricks, thereby causing the bricks in the respective courses to overlap and achieving the arrangement of bricks referred to as the bond.

Figure 4.59 shows the same beam bearing on a wall that is properly bonded and consequently has no continuous vertical cross joints. The result being that instead of the load pressing directly down on to one column of bricks it is spread out along the lines of the joints, thereby sharing it over many more bricks and in consequence a much greater area.

Brick Bonds

A Simple Bonded Wall

The simplest form of bonding is that for a half brick wall which is 102.5 mm wide, where all the bricks are laid down as stretchers, each lapping over the one below by half of its length as shown in Figure 4.60. This illustration shows an elevation and plan of the two alternate courses of the wall.

Note: The perpend is always central to the brick above and below.

This form of bonding, however, would only be suitable for half brick walling, since, if it were required to increase the thickness of the wall to 215 mm (a one brick wall), there would be no connection between the two half brick walls built face to face, as can be seen from the illustration in Figure 4.61.

It is therefore necessary to introduce ties across the two walls in the form of headers, and in this way a bonded wall 215 mm thick is formed, built of alternate courses of headers and stretchers as illustrated in Figure 4.61.

It is clear therefore that it is necessary to bond a wall along its length, so it is also necessary to bond it across the thickness in order that the entire wall may be tied together. In this way the distribution of the load takes place in both directions – that is, along its length and across the thickness.

Broken Bond

Definition – A broken bond is the arrangement of bats in a wall which become necessary where the lengths of brickwork courses are not multiples of the brick length.

Setting Out the Bond

In the foundations or certainly below ground level the bond is run out from each end of the wall, the position of window and door openings, at this stage, being ignored. At ground level however, the positions of all openings are carefully marked in position as illustrated in Figure 4.62 and the correct bond set out. Any broken bond that occurs should be

A With broken bond

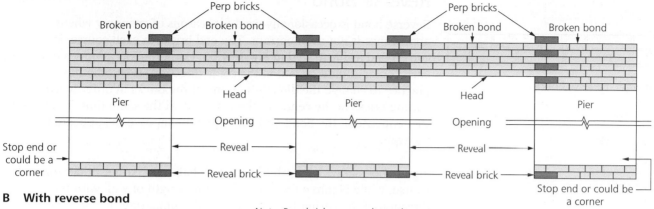

B With reverse bond

Note: Perp bricks are an alternative courses

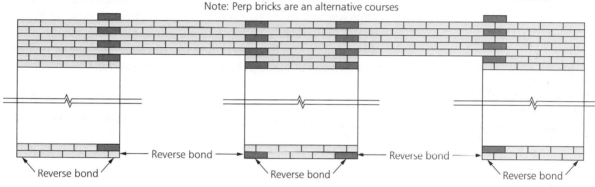

Fig 4.62 **Marking out the bond**
Source: STA

kept to the centre of piers and openings. The vertical joints are then kept plumb so that the reveal bricks are in the correct position when the openings are reached.

Good Practice

In long lengths of walling, broken bond may be avoided by increasing or decreasing the size of the cross joints. This is only permitted if it does not detract from the overall appearance of the wall and the perpends remain plumb.

The smallest piece that is allowed in the wall is a half bat.

Once the position of the cuts is worked out, the bond must then be maintained throughout the full height of the wall.

The size of cuts must be a constant size and perpends plumbed to ensure broken bond remains truly vertical. Once cuts have been established it is a good idea to cut all the bricks required before work commences.

When openings occur in a length of walling the broken bond must be positioned below them. They will then cease for the height of the opening and then re-occur above them.

Reverse Bond

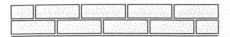

Fig 4.63 Reverse bond

Reverse bond is occasionally used for reasons of economy where appearance is not as important. The end bricks in each course do not correspond as illustrated in Figure 4.63. Corner bricks at opposite ends of each course should be laid in the same direction. It is sometimes the practice to change the direction of one of the bricks in order to avoid cutting bricks in the centre of the wall and, at the same time, to maintain the sequence of the bond and consequently improve the appearance of the wall.

Figure 4.64 shows a length of wall with balanced corner bricks for each course, while Figure 4.65 shows the same length of wall with the direction of the corner bricks reversed. By comparing the two, the improvement made by such a change is obvious. Reverse bond then may be used wherever its adoption will eliminate unnecessary cutting without the unbalanced effect becoming too obvious. The use of reverse bond is less obvious in Flemish bond than in English bond.

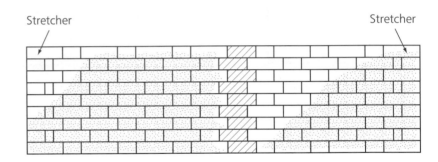

Fig 4.64 **Reverse bond method 1**

Fig 4.65 **Reverse bond method 2**

Bonding, therefore, is the systematic arrangement of bricks in a wall whereby each brick overlaps other bricks in the courses below in both directions, so distributing, over a wider area, a load imposed on any part of the wall. While the rules of bonding remain constant, the arrangement of bricks in a wall may be varied considerably; hence we have different names prefixing the term bond, each name denoting a recognized form of face bonding.

The Purpose and Method of Dry Bonding

Definition – Dry bonding is the term given to laying bricks without applying a bed or cross joint in order to establish the bond and size of cross joints required for a given dimension.

Purpose

Dry bonding enables the correct bond to be achieved and maintained in a wall.

Method

The bond is set out dry along the face of the wall working from each end to the centre, ensuring that the end bricks on each course are the same. If the length is such that a piece or cut is required then we have what is known as broken bond. It follows therefore that any broken bond will be in the centre of the wall.

Prevention of Banding of Brickwork

On projects involving the supply of large quantities of bricks over a significant time span, steps should be taken to ensure that possible between-batch variations in brick size, texture or colour are properly controlled. These include maintaining adequate stocks of bricks and inter-mixing deliveries as shown in Figure 4.66 to facilitate problem-free transitions over time.

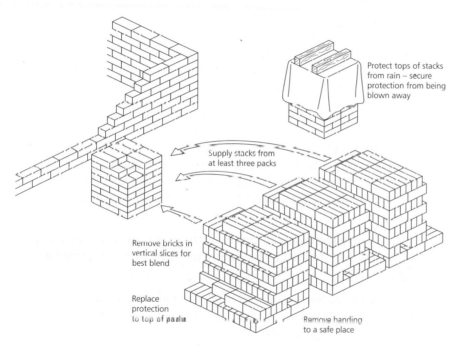

Protect tops of stacks from rain – secure protection from being blown away

Supply stacks from at least three packs

Remove bricks in vertical slices for best blend

Replace protection to top of pack

Remove banding to a safe place

Fig 4.66 **Mixing bricks from different packs**
Source: Butterly

In order to achieve a uniform appearance throughout the building and to avoid the possibility of patches or bands of differing shades, bricks should be used from a minimum of three packs at the same time. The placing of bricks from just one pack in one part of the wall only should be avoided.

The Rules of Bonding

When working out the bond a bricklayer applies a number of basic rules. These rules which are given below, are taken as a guide when solving a problem, but other relevant factors such as economical use of bricks, avoidance of wasteful cutting, strength requirements and so on are also considered.

1. The bond should be set out along the face of the wall, working from each end to the centre, as illustrated in Figure 4.67 with the end bricks in each course corresponding.

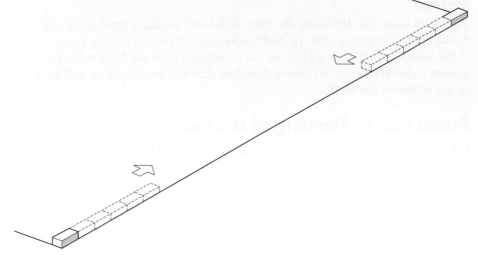

Fig 4.67 **Wall showing examples of working end to middle**

If the wall is of a length such that the bonding pattern does not work out, or a cut is required, then we have what is known as broken bond. If rule one is implemented, it follows that any broken bond will be as near to the centre of the wall as possible.

Note: No cut brick should be less than header width other than the closers at the end of the wall.

2. When half bond is used a half bat is used at a stopped end as illustrated in Figure 4.68. When quarter bond is used a closer is placed next to the header at the quoin or stopped end. Alternatively in some bonds a three-quarter brick may be used to achieve quarter bond.

3. All transverse joints should continue unbroken across the width of the wall unless stopped by the centre of a stretcher as illustrated in Figure 4.69.

4. In English bond where the wall is of odd half-brick thickness, stretchers are shown on the face, headers are shown on the back and vice versa (see Figure 4.70).

5. The bricks in the interior of thick walls are laid header wise as illustrated in Figure 4.71.

6. The tie-in brick at a corner is opposite the closer as illustrated in Figure 4.72.

Learn these rules well and it will save a good deal of time and money later.

Bond number 1

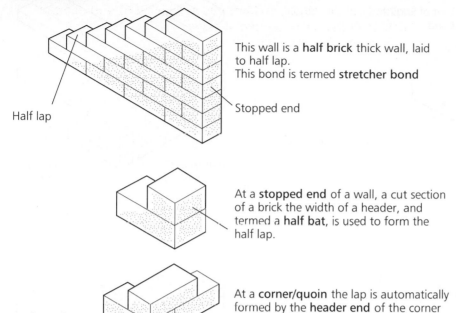

This wall is a **half brick** thick wall, laid to half lap.
This bond is termed **stretcher bond**

At a **stopped end** of a wall, a cut section of a brick the width of a header, and termed a **half bat**, is used to form the half lap.

At a **corner/quoin** the lap is automatically formed by the **header end** of the corner stretcher.

Bond number 2

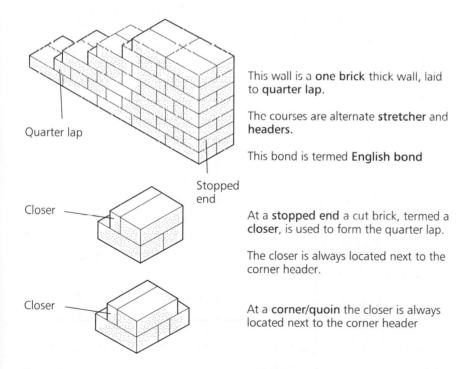

This wall is a **one brick** thick wall, laid to **quarter lap**.

The courses are alternate **stretcher** and **headers**.

This bond is termed **English bond**

At a **stopped end** a cut brick, termed a **closer**, is used to form the quarter lap.

The closer is always located next to the corner header.

At a **corner/quoin** the closer is always located next to the corner header

Fig 4.68 **Use of closers and halves to make the bond**

a. English bond

Transverse joint

Unit of English bond

Unit of English bond

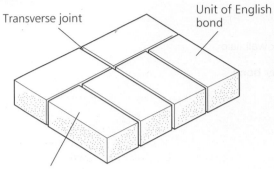

b. Flemish bond

Unit of Flemish bond

Transverse joint

Unit of Flemish bond

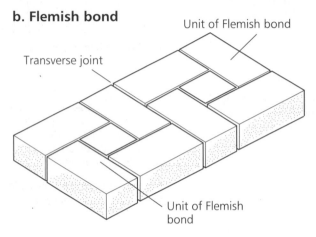

Fig 4.69 **Transverse joints**

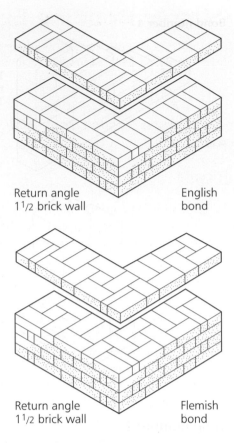

Return angle
1½ brick wall

English bond

Return angle
1½ brick wall

Flemish bond

Fig 4.70 **English and Flemish bond showing facers on face and headers behind**

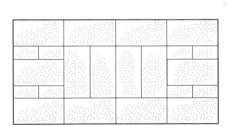

Heavy black line encloses unit of bond for *stretching* course

Fig 4.71 **Bricks laid header-wise in a thick wall**

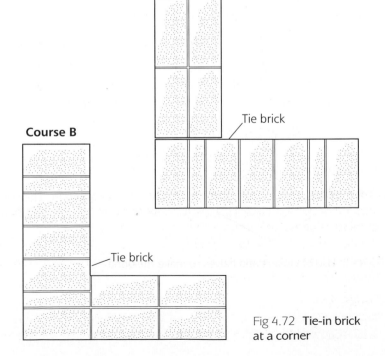

Course A

Tie brick

Course B

Tie brick

Fig 4.72 **Tie-in brick at a corner**

Simple Bonding Examples

This section sets out progressive stages in the development of bonding, and supplies simple examples for workshop practice.

Straight Walls

Bonding an English Bond Wall

Task – To set out in English bond a 215 mm wall, usually referred to as a one brick thick wall, 890 mm long, the stages are illustrated in Figure 4.73.

Note: It should be appreciated by the learner that the stages presented in the following text only apply to the bonding of the bricks as set out in the illustrations, and not the order in which the bricks are laid.

Stage One

The first step is to bond the face of the wall starting from each end and working towards the middle. Note that, irrespective of the length of the wall to be bonded, the bricks on the corners must be placed in the same direction. So that if a stretcher is placed at one end, then a stretcher must be placed at the opposite end. The same rule applies to the header course. Working towards the centre and numbering the bricks in the order in which they are placed in position, it is found that the face of one course consists of four stretchers, as illustrated in Figure 4.73.

Stage Two

The next course is a header course, in which a closer is introduced next to the quoin header to obtain the necessary 46.25 mm lap, the space between the closers being then filled with headers – as illustrated in Figure 4.73. The face bond is now clear for the stretcher and header courses. It should be noted that the bond on the face of the wall is the same for any wall of any thickness provided the length remains constant.

Stage Three

Proceed with the bonding to the back of the wall. The wall being two half bricks thick will obviously have stretchers on both sides in the same course. Therefore, the back of the stretcher course will be filled in with stretchers in the order and way illustrated in Figure 4.73. By reason of the fact that the width of a 215 mm wall is governed by the length of a header, the bonding to the header course is finished.

Bonding a Flemish Bond Wall

Now apply this method to a Flemish bond wall – that is, to a 215 mm wall, 890 mm long. The steps are illustrated in Figure 4.74.

Stage One

Outline the two rectangles in which the bricks are to be bonded. Follow the first example and set out the bond along the face of the wall. Place the two quoin stretchers in position, and continue with headers and stretchers alternately from each end towards the centre, so arriving at the bond illustrated in Figure 4.74.

Stage Two

To bond the next course, commence with headers at either end of the wall, followed by closers, and fill in towards the centre with alternate

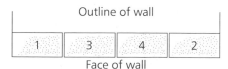
Outline of wall
1 | 3 | 4 | 2
Face of wall
Stage 1 Set out stretchers on face in order shown

1 | 3 | 5 | 7 | 9 | 8 | 6 | 4 | 2
Stage 2 Set out heading course in order shown

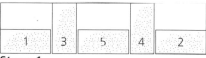
5 | 7 | 8 | 6
1 | 3 | 4 | 2
Stage 3 Complete bricks to back of stretching course

Fig 4.73 Stages in setting out bricks for short length of wall in English bond

1 | 3 | 5 | 4 | 2
Stage 1

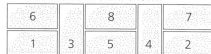
1 | 3 | 5 | 7 | 6 | 4 | 2
Stage 2
Stages 1 & 2 Set out bricks to face of each course in order shown

6 | 8 | 7
1 | 3 | 5 | 4 | 2
Stage 3

8 | 10 | 11 | 9
1 | 3 | 5 | 7 | 6 | 4 | 2
Stage 4
Stages 3 & 4 Complete bricks to back of wall as shown

Fig 4.74 Setting out of a wall

stretchers and headers in the order and manner illustrated in Figure 4.74.

Stage Three

The face bond is now completed for the first two courses of Flemish bond which, like English bond, will remain the same for walls any thickness, providing the length is constant.

Bond the bricks to the back of the stretcher course and think of the corner bricks first. These must be stretchers, the remaining space being filled in with a stretcher, as illustrated in Figure 4.74.

Stage Four

With the rule regarding transverse joints as a guide, the correct arrangement for the remainder of the bricks in the header course is carried out as illustrated in Figure 4.74.

Return Angles

All changes in the direction of walls are termed return angles, these may enclose an obtuse or acute angle or, more commonly a right angle. The stages are illustrated below.

Stage One: English Bond

When thinking about the bonding to a right angle return, it is simpler to consider two separate straight walls lapping one over the other on alternate courses and forming a right angle as illustrated in Figure 4.75. It follows that the rules of bonding that apply to straight lengths of walling will also apply to return angles, with only minor adjustments to be made.

Stage Two

Developing the outline as illustrated in Figure 4.75 and bonding the bricks in stages as for straight lengths of walling, first set out those bricks that are numbered one as shown in Figure 4.76. Note, that where the wall changes direction, the bond in the same course also changes.

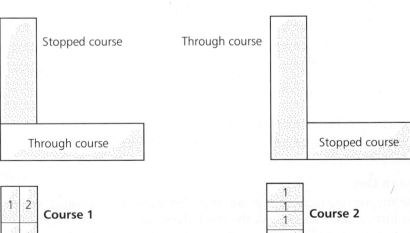

Fig 4.75 Lapping of walls for a return corner

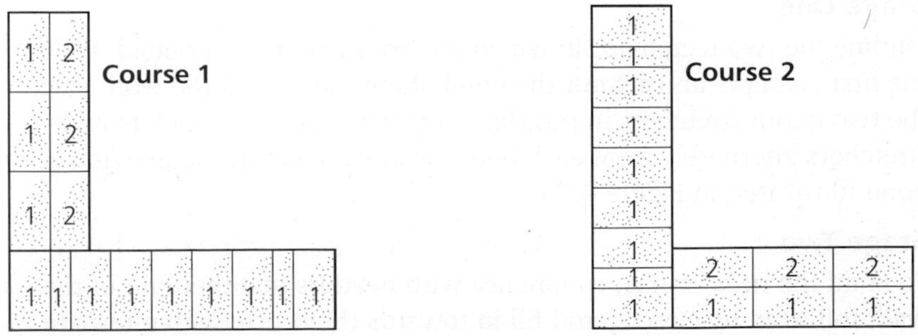

Fig 4.76 Stage 2, arrangement of bricks for completed courses in English bond

Moving on to the next part and filling in those bricks numbered two, we arrive at the bonding shown in Figure 4.76 thus completing the arrangement for this example.

Stage Three: Flemish Bond

Figure 4.77 illustrates an example of a return corner in Flemish bond that has been treated in a similar way.

The bonding to return angles presents very little more difficulty than that of straight lengths of walls, but the other illustrations in Figures 4.78 and 4.79 of a return angle in one-and-a-half brick walling should be studied and compared with the rules of bonding to fully appreciate the examples shown.

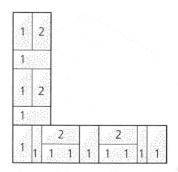

Fig 4.77 Flemish bond wall

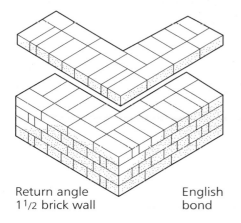

Return angle
1 1/2 brick wall

English bond

Fig 4.78 **One-and-a-half brick wall return in English bond**

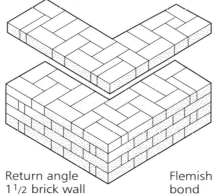

Return angle
1 1/2 brick wall

Flemish bond

Fig 4.79 **One-and-a-half brick wall return in Flemish bond**

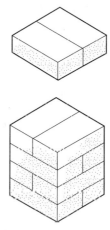

Fig 4.80 One brick pier

Piers

Pier and pillar in construction are considered to be synonymous terms for a large mass of masonry intended to provide additional strength and stability to a structure.

Piers are separate short lengths of wall which, though usually thought of as being square on plan, may, in fact, be of any shape or size within the considerations of the work being carried out. For the purpose of bonding, each side of the pier is treated as facework and must be treated differently to that given to a short length of wall.

The smallest bonded brick pier will be 215 × 215 mm on plan and should be built of two bricks laid side by side, their direction being changed for alternate courses, as illustrated in Figure 4.80.

Piers 327.5 × 327.5 mm and larger may be bonded in English and Flemish bond. Figures 4.81 and 4.82 illustrate two alternative methods of bonding a 327.5 mm square pier in English bond but, since the second method involves the cutting of every brick, it is usually avoided even though, in the first method, the transverse joints are not carried through the full thickness of the pier.

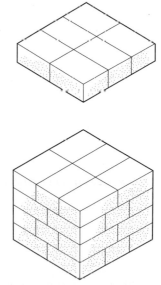

Fig 4.81 One-and-a-half pier in English bond

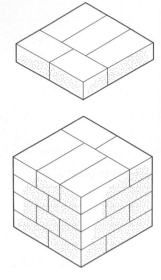

The other examples illustrated in Figures 4.83 to 4.86 show the bonding for various sized piers producing, on all faces, a representation of the bond used and, at the same time, carrying out the main principles of bonding.

The bonding of bricks, together with the correct mortar mix will give pillars and piers their strength. Brick bonding is an essential part of wall strength.

Fig 4.82 **Alternative arrangement**

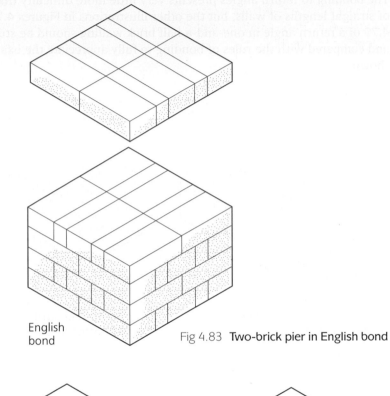

English bond

Fig 4.83 **Two-brick pier in English bond**

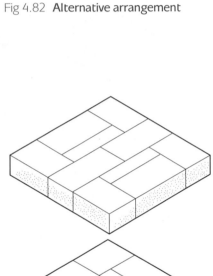

Flemish bond

Fig 4.84 **Two-brick pier in Flemish bond**

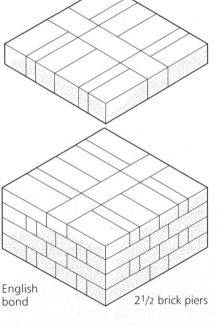

English bond

2¹/₂ brick piers

Fig 4.85 **Two-and-a-half brick pier in English bond**

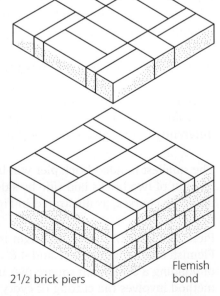

2¹/₂ brick piers

Flemish bond

Fig 4.86 **Two-and-a-half pier in Flemish bond**

Attached Piers

This is the term given to connections between walls that form the shape of a letter T, or a cross on plan, although it is not essential that the angles enclosed are right angles. Figures 4.87 to 4.88 illustrate various examples in English and Flemish bond for walls of different thickness. Similar principles are used to the bonding of walls that cross, some examples are also shown in Figure 4.89

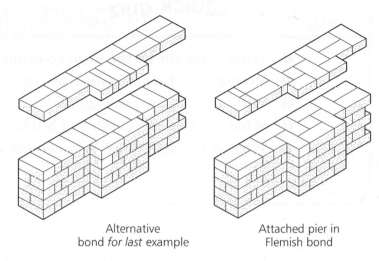

Alternative bond *for last* example

Attached pier in Flemish bond

Fig 4.87 **Attached piers in English and Flemish bonds**

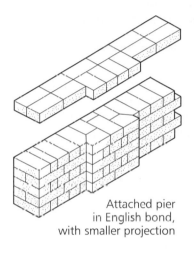

Attached pier in English bond, with smaller projection

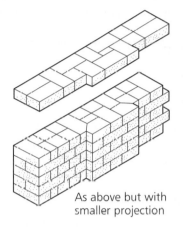

As above but with smaller projection

Fig 4.88 **Alternative attached piers in English and Flemish bonds**

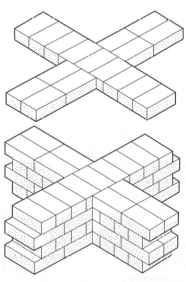

Fig 4.89 **Cross junction between walls in English bond**

Common Types of Bond

There are several types of bond; some are employed to obtain maximum strength while others are used for their appearance or economy.

English Bond

Header courses alternate with courses appearing as stretchers on the outer face or elevation as illustrated in Figure 4.90. The header course is commenced with a quoin header followed by a queen closer and continued with successive headers. The stretcher course is formed, on its outer face, of stretchers having a minimum of one-quarter their length over the headers.

Stretcher Bond

In this kind of bond each successive course is formed with bricks so laid, that their stretcher face appears in elevation as shown in Figure 4.91. The amount of overlap is half the length of the bricks and is obtained by commencing each alternate course with a half brick. Stretcher bond is suitable for half-brick thick walls and cavity walls. Stretcher bond is by far the most common bond used.

Flemish Bond

Successive courses are formed with alternating stretchers and headers as illustrated in Figure 4.92. In order to obtain the lap, which is one-quarter the length of the bricks, a queen closer is introduced next to the quoin header in alternate courses followed by a stretcher. The succeeding course commences with a stretcher followed by a header, which is placed centrally on the stretcher below.

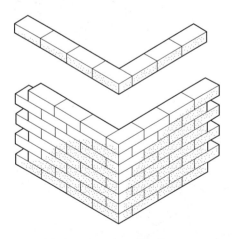
Return angle 1½ brick wall — English bond

Fig 4.90 **English bond wall**

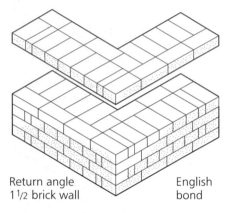

Fig 4.91 **Stretcher bond wall**

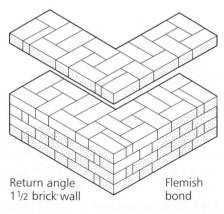
Return angle 1½ brick wall — Flemish bond

Fig 4.92 **Flemish bond**

172

Heading Bond

Each successive course is formed with headers, that is, bricks so laid that their header faces are parallel to or, appear in the elevation of the work as shown in Figure 4.93. The overlap, which is half the width of the brick, is obtained by introducing a three-quarter bat in each alternate course at the quoins. Header bond is seldom used for straight walling, but is suitable for walls that are curved on plan and in foundations.

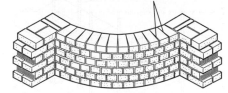
Note wedged shaped joints

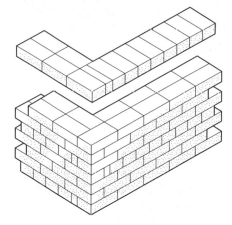
Fig 4.93 Heading bond

Garden Wall Bonds

These bonds are named according to the kind of bond to which they are related.

English Garden Wall Bond

English garden wall bond consists of a course of headers, with the necessary queen closer next to the quoin header as illustrated in Figure 4.94. There are then three, or sometimes five, courses of stretchers in series running the full height of the wall.

Flemish Garden Wall Bond

Flemish garden wall bond consists of alternate courses composed of one header to three, sometimes five, stretchers in series throughout the length of the courses as illustrated in Figure 4.95. The lap is obtained by either introducing the necessary queen closer next to the quoin header or by use of a three-quarter bat. Headers, other than quoin headers are placed centrally on the centre stretcher of the series.

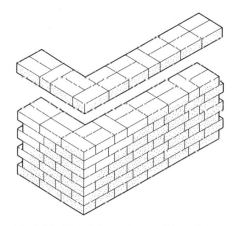
Fig 4.94 English garden wall bond

Flemish garden wall bond is also known as Sussex bond and Scotch bond. Fair faces to both sides of one-brick walls is more easily attained with garden wall bonds than it would be by using the true English or Flemish bonds.

Quantities

One square metre of brickwork, a half brick thick, requires the following number of bricks:

- English Bond. 86.
- Flemish Bond. 77.
- English Garden Wall Bond. 72.
- Flemish Garden Wall Bond. 67.
- Stretcher Bond. 60.

Figures are assuming one header per brick.

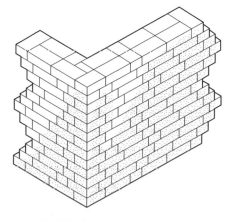
Fig 4.95 Flemish garden wall bond

Monk Bond

Monk bond is composed of two stretchers and one header, alternately, in each course, various arrangements of this bond have been used by different specifiers. Figure 4.96 illustrates a typical example of several courses, but it is not claimed to be the only bonding possible under this title. Monk bond has been used extensively as a facing bond and, owing to the reduction in the number of headers, is also an economical bond.

Fig 4.96 Monk bond

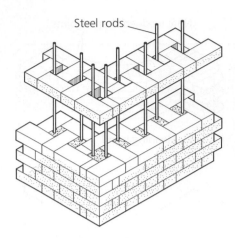

Steel rods

Fig 4.97 Quetta bond

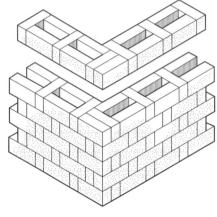

Fig 4.98 Rat-trap bond

Quetta Bond

While not used very often in this country, this bond has been used a great deal in countries subject to earth tremors. The front and back elevation of the wall is similar to Flemish bond but, from the plan, it will be seen that it is not built in a sectional way as illustrated in Figure 4.97 the transverse joints do not cross the full thickness of the wall: 46.25 × 102.5 mm recesses are formed along the length of the wall and continue through its full height. In these recesses, steel rods are placed and packed round with concrete or mortar as the work proceeds. This forms a series of slender vertical columns in and around the length of the wall and producing a reinforced brick wall without the use of special bricks.

Rat-Trap Bond

In rat-trap bond, the bricks are laid on their edges instead of on their usual beds and appear on the face in a way similar to Flemish bond. Figure 4.98 shows the bond. A space is formed between the front and back stretchers, which is usually left as a means of saving materials, or alternatively may be filled in with either a brick or concrete. The bond's use is limited to walls 215 mm thick, and therefore the bond can only be used for light structures and is normally confined to ornamental features.

Strength and Load Characteristics of the Various Bonds

Stretcher Bond

Although restricted to half-brick and cavity walls, possesses the ability to distribute loads over a maximum length of walling in a given number of courses.

Header Bond

Does not possess the above stated ability, but since it is adaptable to walls of one brick or more in thickness, the lack of longitudinal distribution is compensated for by transverse distribution according to the thickness of the wall.

English Bond

Presents a minimum of straight joints and therefore is very suitable for supporting heavy loads. Load distribution is effected both longitudinally and transversely.

Flemish Bond

Although sufficiently strong for most types of average work, is not as strong as English bond since it presents a number of unavoidable internal straight joints. The load distributing value of Flemish bond is good.

Garden Wall Bonds

These possess considerably large amounts of internal straight joints that consequently reduce the strength values. Load distribution is moderate.

Bonding of Blocks

When you have worked through this section, you will be able to:

- Bond blocks at corners and junctions
- Deal with broken bond
- Form and use indents in brick and block walls
- Know the position of expanding reinforcement or cavity wall ties in place of indents
- Block bond brickwork at junctions.

At the end of this section you should be fully conversant with the principles of bonding blockwork.

Setting Out the Bond

Blocks should be laid at half bond as far as possible. It will be found useful, when setting out blockwork, to run out the blocks dry first from one end of the wall to the other to ascertain the bond. There will usually be a cut piece of block required to complete the course the same as is found in brickwork. By beginning the next course from the opposite end of the wall from where you started, with a full block, and working back to the first corner, cutting will be curtailed to a minimum and a satisfactory bond found. This method should, however, not be carried to an extreme, a lap of 150 mm being the very least that should be used.

> REMEMBER
> A regular bond pattern should be maintained throughout the walls length, ensuring a minimum overlap of a quarter of block.

Position of Blockwork in a Contemporary House

1. Load bearing insulation blocks, on the internal leaf of the cavity wall.
2. Foundation blocks for cavity walls, 250 mm thick and upwards.
3. Load bearing specification, foundation blocks of the necessary thickness.
4. Load bearing blocks in various sizes from 100 mm to 250 mm.
5. Standard blocks in various sizes ranging from 75 mm to 250 mm.

Fig 4.99 **Section view of a house showing blockwork**
Source: CITB-ConstructionSkills.
Bricklaying Information Sheet, 1998.

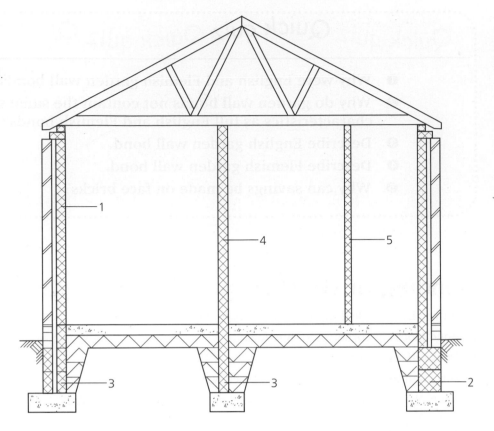

Bonding Block Corners

In order to maintain half bond at junctions and returns, a 100 mm cut block must be built in next to the return block as illustrated in Figure. 4.100.

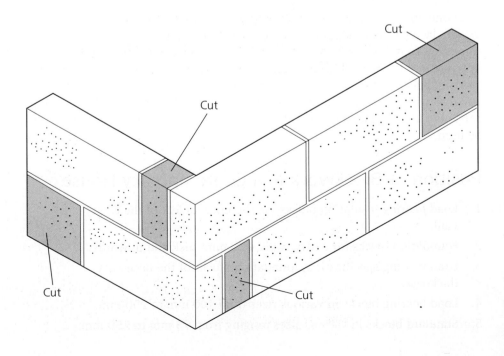

Fig 4.100 **Block return corner**

As with the details on half lap bonding explained previously in the rules of bonding, there are several ways one can choose to bond a blockwork corner. Figure 4.101 illustrates one method. This example uses a cut block on the second course at the corner. This results in a second cut at the stop end with a smaller cut on the first course.

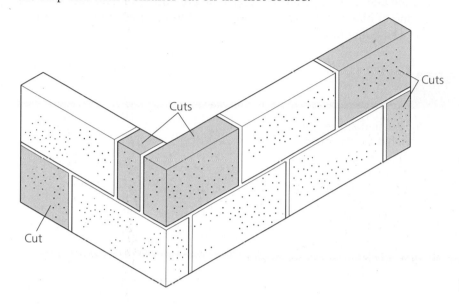

Fig 4.101 Alternative block corner

The illustrations show two methods, there are others; providing that one has kept to the principles of bonding, that is, no straight joints and bonded at the corners, these will be acceptable.

Figure 4.100 is probably the most used method of bonding a block corner, the cut blocks are shaded for emphasis. The most common width for blocks used in construction is 100 mm, the same width as the cut identified. The cut shown in Figure 4.100 acts, as it were, as a closer but if we increase the width of our blocks, what would be the result of this cut to the bonding arrangement?

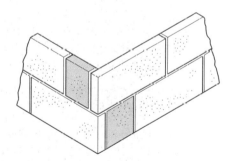

Fig 4.102 50 mm block corner

The answer of course would be that the cut would reduce in length. Figures 4.102 to 4.105 illustrate this point over a range of examples, from partition blocks measuring 50 mm wide to 215 mm load bearing blockwork. The length of the cut reduces as the block width increases. On the 215 mm block corner the proportions are that of a brick. That is, the width of the block is half of a block's length, so therefore, no cut is required.

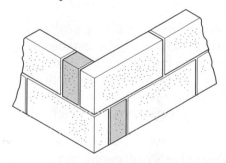

Fig 4.103 **100 mm block corner**

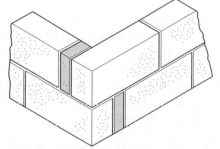

Fig 4.104 **150 mm block corner**

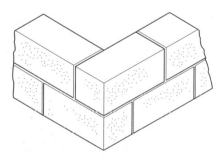

Fig 4.105 **215 mm block corner**

Bedding Blocks

The bedding of blocks is very similar to the bedding of a brick, the bed of the block is spread to receive the block and the complete cross joint placed on the block to be laid. The block should be rubbed into position along the bed and tapped firmly up to the previously laid block. The knocking of blocks should be minimized as it tends to disturb the whole of the wall being built.

Good Practice

When block laying on site the block manufacturer Celcon, advise that the following principles should be observed:

A regular bond pattern should be maintained, based on a minimum overlap of a quarter of a block.

Lintels should bear on to full blocks, wherever possible.

Cut blocks and coursing units should always be used for irregular or non-standard spaces; bricks, mortar or other dissimilar materials should never be used.

Blocks should be laid on a full bed of mortar, with 10 mm thick vertical and horizontal joints, 3 mm for the thin joint system. It is essential for the acoustic performance of party walls that all joints are fully filled.

When laying aircrete blocks a good plasticiser or the addition of lime will slow down the setting time of the mortar.

When laying dense concrete blocks a firm mortar consistency is required, that is not too wet.

When walls are to be externally rendered or internally plastered, the joints should be left recessed, except where the thin joint method is used.

Any movement joints and or bed joints reinforcement should be built-in as the work proceeds.

Blockwork should be protected from adverse weather during, and immediately after, laying has taken place.

Partition Walls in Blockwork

Walls enclosed within the external walls of a building for the purpose of dividing the internal space are known as partition walls and may be one of two classes, namely, loadbearing and non-loadbearing. Non-loadbearing partition walls are those used solely to divide up the floor area into rooms or spaces. It is therefore, only necessary that the base on which the partition rests shall be strong enough to carry the weight of the partition wall.

Blocks are ideally suited for the building of both loadbearing and non-loadbearing internal walls. The use of blocks creates a more robust partition, adding rigidity to the whole structure, making it less prone to damage than say wood and plasterboard studwork.

Preparation for and Building of Blockwork Partition Walls

External walls that are to receive partition walls must be so built that the eventual tying or bonding in of the partition may be easily carried out. It is therefore necessary that the position of all partition walls should be set out when the main walls have been started, in order that recesses may be formed into which the partitions will eventually be bonded. These recesses may take the form of indents, as shown in Figure 4.106 or continuous chases left out for the full wall height as illustrated in Figure 4.107, the latter method being considered the more satisfactory as no account has to be taken of the relationship between brick and block courses, especially if using the thin joint system

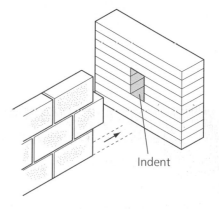

Fig 4.106 **Indent in the wall**

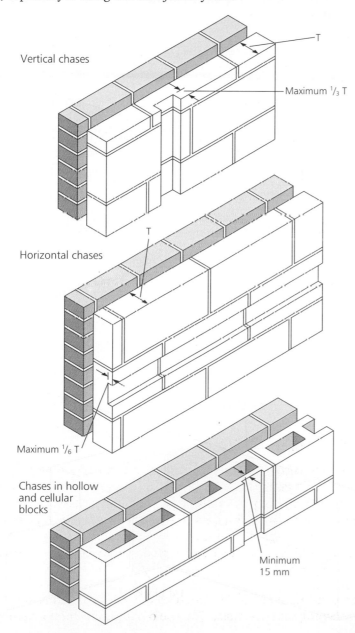

Fig 4.107 **Continuous chase in the wall**
Source:BDA

After the external walls and floors have been built, the positions of the partitions have to be carefully marked out and the various door frames erected in the required positions, after which the first courses of blocks are laid. Particular care should be taken to see that all frames are accurately placed, set vertical and true, and that the first course of blocks is in perfect alignment. The accuracy of all subsequent work depends upon the accuracy of the preliminary operations.

Junctions in Blockwork

As with returns in blockwork the minimum overlap on a T-junction should be quarter of a block. This is achieved by building in the 100 mm cut block on alternate courses as illustrated in Figure 4.108.

The degree of cutting of blocks will be determined by the position of the indent in relation to the blocks in the main wall, as illustrated in Figure 4.109.

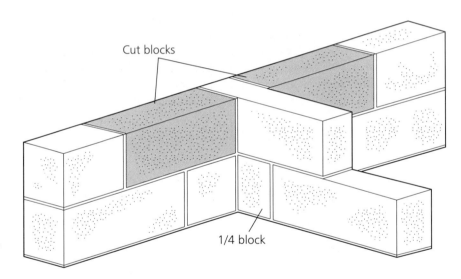

Cut blocks

1/4 block

Fig 4.108 **Junction position in centre of block in main wall**

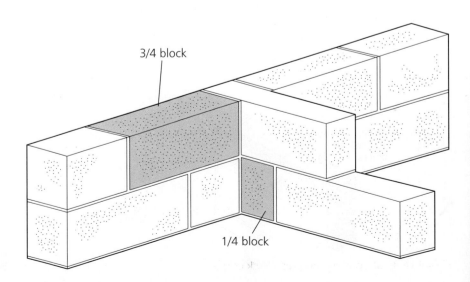

3/4 block

1/4 block

Fig 4.109 **Junction position off centre reduces the amount of cutting**

Therefore bonding junction walls in blocks is similar to bonding junctions in brickwork, and similar issues emerge. Figure 4.110 illustrates a half brick wall junction, showing two three-quarter bats over the tie brick. If we were to replicate this method for the width of block we are using, a weakness would be created at the junction.

If our junction is to be for a narrow partition wall, say 75 mm in thickness, the weakness would be exaggerated as there would be a near straight joint over the tie block. So the lap in this arrangement is not sufficient for this width of block at a junction. Therefore we require a larger lap over the tie block as illustrated in Figure 4.111.

We need therefore to think of other methods of bonding a half brick wall junction and see if anything can be learned for a blockwork example. Figure 4.112 shows an example of a full stretcher over the tie brick.

If we convert this solution into blocks it would appear as shown in Figure 4.113. For this width of block the bonding shown is far stronger than the previous example.

Providing straight joints are avoided it is not required to achieve a perfect half lap either side of the tie block. In the example shown a cut block is placed so as to enable half lap bond to be regained. If the junction is built in blocks 215 mm thick, the first method of bonding would be used, that is, two three-quarter length blocks over the tie block. Each width of block presents a different problem and must be solved accordingly.

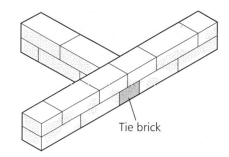
Fig 4.110 **Half brick wall junction showing two three-quarter bats over the tie brick**

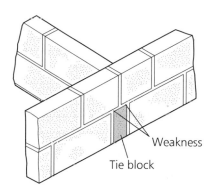
Fig 4.111 **T junction in partition wall 75 mm thick**

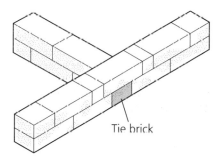
Fig 4.112 **Full stretcher over tie brick in junction wall**

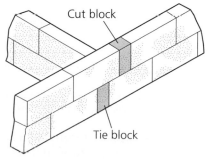
Fig 4.113 **Full block over tie block in junction wall**

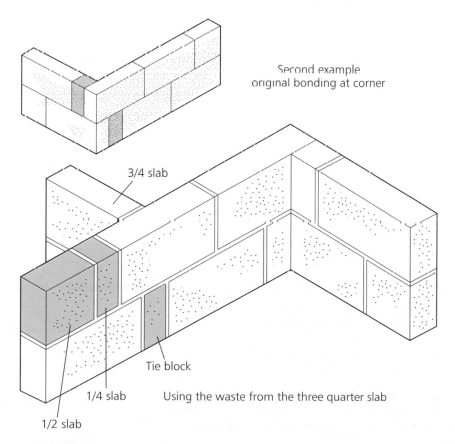
Fig 4.114 **First bonding method, block corner**

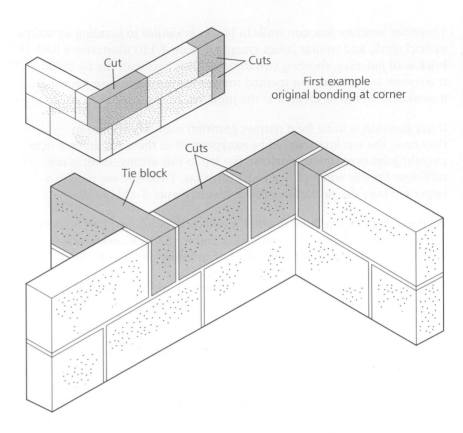

Fig 4.115 Second bonding method, block corner

Two other methods based on the examples above are shown in Figures 4.114 and 4.115. As you can see from the illustration, the example is based on the first corner arrangement (Figure 4.100) and is more economical with the use of cuts, therefore saving time and money.

The second method is again adapted from the original corner arrangement (see Figure 4.101). You can see that the half block and quarter block, which is shaded for recognition are laid next to each other for reasons of economy. The half block would be left over from another half block and the quarter block is the waste piece from the top course on the abutting wall. If the blockwork is to be plastered or covered in some way, then this practice is perfectly acceptable.

Good Practice

It is important that maximum strength of the junction is obtained, therefore care must be taken in the building of indents.

Ensure that the line of indents are vertical and that the width of each indent permits two 10 mm cross joints as illustrated in Figure 4.116.

Where blocks are of differing materials it is good practice to ensure that the junction is formed by using mesh reinforcement or wall ties. This avoids the possibility of different shrinkage or movement within the blocks as illustrated in Figure 4.117.

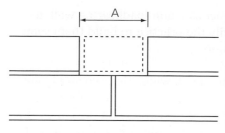

For **indents** or **block bonding** the overall width must allow for a joint either side of the brick or block to be tied into the main wall

Dimension (A) is the overall width for the indents or block bonding

Note: It is essential that full joints are acheived when tying-in

Fig 4.116 **Indents showing cut out**

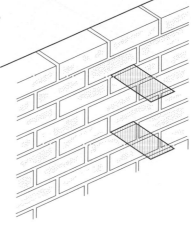

Fig 4.117 **Bonding using mesh or tie wires for the bond**

Block Indents

Indents in blockwork can be formed to allow for additional walls to be tied in at a later stage of construction. The indenting of blockwork may be necessary to provide ease of access for the loading out of materials or free passage for operatives.

Methods of Constructing Indents in Blockwork

In order to overcome straight joints at the junctions of block and brick walls, gaps, to the size of the blocks being used, are left in the block or brickwork. These gaps coincide with the position and courses of block wall as illustrated in Figure 4.18 and are called indents. On a construction site the indents are formed as the block or brickwork proceeds.

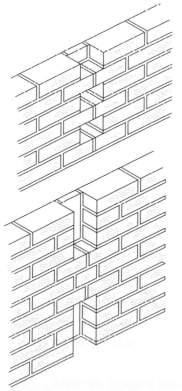

Types of tying-in methods
Method 1
Indents provided in alternate courses.

Method 1
Block bonding – especially suitable for tying-in blockwork.

Indents are provided three courses high.

Note: A thin section of brick bedded at the rear of the tying-in position, helps to ensure a full joint when the partition wall is built.

Fig 4.118 **Gaps or indents in the wall**
Source: CITB-ConstructionSkills. Training Workbook, 1994.

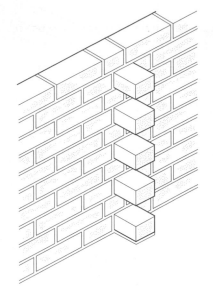

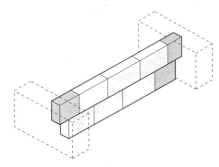

Fig 4.119 Toothing

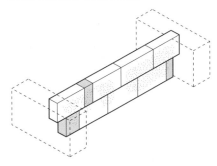

Fig 4.120 Block wall where tie blocks bond without undue cuts

Fig 4.121 Block wall where small cut has been introduced on second course

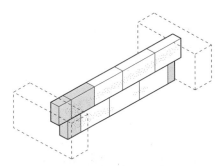

Fig 4.122 Block wall with two cuts on second course

If the block or brickwork is going to act as a non-loadbearing wall, a partition wall for example, it is usually the practice to build them some time later in the construction programme.

In Figure 4.118 the indent is just half a brick wide, plus two cross joints either side of the half bat. This is just enough room to fit a block 100 mm wide. If the indent were any wider it would cause a great deal of cutting to the brickwork, entailing making good afterwards. Providing the indent is in the correct position there should be little problem in laying a block there at a later stage of construction.

In certain circumstances, as an alternative to indents, toothing is formed using whole bricks that are built in as work proceeds and project half a brick in the future wall position as illustrated in Figure 4.119.

Bonding to an Indent

The bonding of the blockwork is straightforward enough. In the illustrations shown the indents are formed to coincide with the second course of blocks. There are three methods shown of bonding this length of walling. There is little to choose between the three examples shown, but the experienced bricklayer should always be aware of the bond when tying in to indents. In Figure 4.120 the tie blocks bond without any undue cuts to the blocks.

In Figure 4.121, because the courses have been reversed, a small cut has been introduced on the second course.

Figure 4.122 shows two cuts on the second course, which is a little wasteful of blocks. Always think ahead. Ask yourself the question, how am I going to tie into the block or brickwork using a minimum of cut blocks thereby reducing time and wastage of materials?

The use of indents is not only confined solely to the bonding of brick and block walls together. Indents are also used in the case of blockwork, for example, if a bricklayer is building a block wall that has a junction, it may not be convenient to build the adjoining wall at the same time as the main wall. In this instance the bricklayer will leave indents for completion of the work at a later stage.

Points to note ⯈ ■ Broken bond can be located centrally or moved to one end of the block wall.

■ Cuts used in blockwork can be smaller than one half of a full block.

■ To maintain strength in block walls try to keep half lap wherever possible.

■ Indents to accept tie blocks are used in conjunction with courses of bricks.

■ Indents should be wide enough to accept the width of a block plus 20 mm.

■ An alternative to indents is expanded metal strips or tie wires.

✓ Good Practice

In all work of this type, it must be remembered that success depends partly upon close adhesion between the mortar and the existing work. Every endeavour must be made to achieve this by clearing all brick dust away from newly cut indents and thoroughly wetting them before commencing to build, and also by forcing the mortar used in against the top of the indent. Particular care should be given to the task last mentioned and wherever possible, grout should be poured into the indent, this is easily carried out when increasing the thickness of walls.

Block Bonding Applicable to Both Brick and Blockwork Walls

It is a rule of bonding that bricks and blocks should overlap those beneath them by at least 46.25 mm, along the length of a wall and 102.5 mm across the thickness, but under certain conditions, this is not always possible and it becomes necessary to adopt an alternative. This alternative is known as block bonding and, as the name suggests, it means that the bonding is carried out in blocks of several courses instead of separate ones, as shown in Figure 4.123. The use of block bonding is generally confined to alteration work requiring the lengthening, the widening or the addition of walls to existing work.

Lengthening Walls by Block Bonding

To lengthen an existing wall and still maintain the general face bond, it would be necessary to cut recesses termed indents in every alternate course which, in effect, means the cutting out of the header and closer, as shown in Figure 4.124.

This method is difficult and, with certain types of bricks and mortars, time consuming. It can also without due care result in the surrounding brickwork being damaged, necessitating replacement, costing time and money. Consequently it is only used where the continuation of the face bond is essential, and even then only the front 102.5 mm of the brickwork is removed in this fashion.

Block bonding is the method generally used under such circumstances, that is, indents three courses in height are cut through the full thickness of the wall as illustrated in Figure 4.125. A similar method is used when it is necessary to brick up an existing door opening to form one continuous wall, for it will be easily understood that, if no ties were made between the new brickwork and the old, a much weaker wall would result with the junctions between the walls forming a likely place for cracks to appear in any plasterwork that it may later receive.

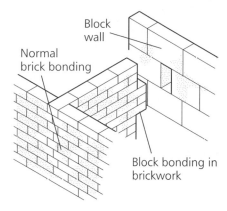

Fig 4.123 **Block bonding**

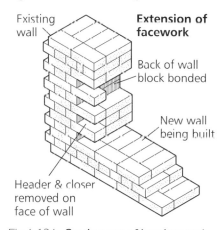

Fig 4.124 **Cutting out of headers and stretchers for indents**

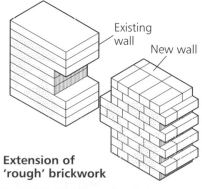

Fig 4.125 **Block bonding**

Cross Wall Construction

Alteration work often requires the division of large areas by means of additional brick and block walls, and these must be tied or bonded into the main walls. To do this, indents are formed in the main walls into which the new walls are to be bonded. For the reasons already given, it is not necessary or desirable to tie in every alternate course, therefore block bonding is used. The recesses are normally three courses in height, to receive a block course, and 102.5 mm deep, and of a width equal to the new wall plus 20 mm to allow for a cross joint either side.

Figure 4.126 shows the existing wall with the indents cut out and the form which the new wall must take. The latter wall is shown pulled apart to indicate more clearly the construction methods used.

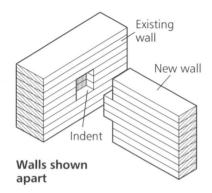

Existing wall

New wall

Indent

Walls shown apart

Fig 4.126 Existing wall with indents cut out

Block Bonding Used in Widening Walls

For various reasons, walls often need to be increased in thickness and, where the purpose of this increase is to add to the stability of the wall, adequate provision must be made to bond the new work into the old. There are two accepted methods of carrying out this type of work.

1. The use of indents built in as work proceeds.

2. The use of continuous chases built in as work proceeds.

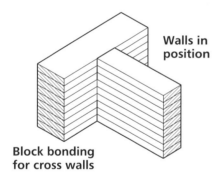

Walls in position

Block bonding for cross walls

Fig 4.127 Same wall built into its proper position

Storage of Blocks

Blocks should be unloaded on to a dry, level surface, and should be covered to protect them from bad weather. Blocks that have become wet should be allowed to dry out before use to reduce the risk of drying shrinkage in the completed blockwork

As a general rule, on hard standing, packs of blocks with or without pallets should be stored no more than three high. On uneven ground and on site, stacking should be normally restricted to a maximum of two packs high.

Quick quiz Quick quiz Quick quiz Quick quiz Quick quiz

❶ Describe half lap.

❷ Describe quarter lap.

❸ What is the difference between a queen closer and three quarter bat?

❹ Name one of the main functions of a brick wall.

❺ Why should brickwork be bonded?

Practical Skills   4.5

Use of Hand Tools

To explain the use of the majority of tools mentioned on pages 114–126, I will illustrate briefly the building of a small section of walling, dealing with each tool as it is required.

Using the Laying Trowel

In the process of laying bricks, the brick trowel is used to perform a series of operations, during which the trowel is seldom put down or changed from one hand to the other. It is the usual practice to give the mortar a final mixing after it has been placed on the board by drawing it down from the heap with the back of the trowel, an action which breaks down any lumpy particles that may still exist.

Correct Grip

This and all subsequent operations require free and easy manipulation of the trowel from the wrist and it is, therefore essential to master thoroughly the correct handling of the trowel. Figure. 4.128 illustrates the correct grip about the handle, showing clearly the thumb resting on the ferrule; only with the thumb in this position is it possible to acquire the required degree of dexterity.

Picking Up Mortar Correctly

Picking up the mortar from the board is a technique only developed by repeated practice, but the success of this first step depends on the ease and simplicity with which later operations may be carried out.

Method

From the mortar heap on the board and using the trowel knife fashion, a portion of the mortar is cut away and drawn towards the front of the board in the form of a roll about 220 mm long. The amount cut away will depend on the nature of the work but, for the student, it is advisable to only cut away sufficient mortar to lay one brick. Figure 4.128 shows the position of the mortar on the trowel before lifting, the mortar being

Fig 4.128 **Mortar on trowel before lifting**

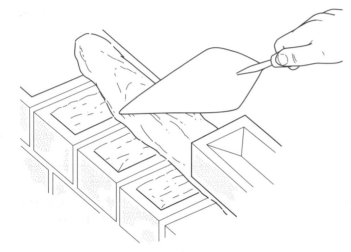

Fig 4.129 **Spreading mortar on a wall**

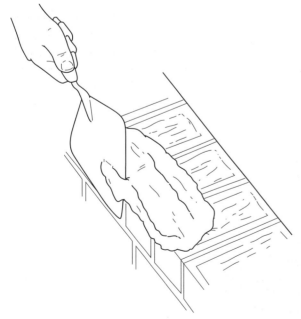

Fig 4.130 **Cutting off surplus mortar**

brought into this position by a sharp drive of the trowel. Then with the blade almost flat against the board its point is kept behind the roll from the beginning to the end of the movement.

Placing Mortar on the Wall

The mortar from this position is placed about 25 to 50 mm back from the face of the wall and is followed by a pushing movement with the back of the trowel which spreads the mortar out in a layer approximately 15 mm thick, as shown in Figure 4.129.

By subsequently drawing the point of the trowel through the centre of the layer, a mortar bed suitable to receive the brick is formed. A brick laid on mortar prepared in this manner will first rest on the two outer edges of the mortar and when rubbed down to its correct level will not only squeeze mortar from the front and back of the brick but will also squeeze it into the hollow left in the centre of the mortar bed.

Cutting Off Surplus Mortar

Before and after laying a brick, a certain amount of mortar will project beyond the face of the wall, and this must be removed. Figure 4.130 shows the position of the trowel for these operations, during which care must be taken to prevent any contact between the mortar and the face of the brick.

The surplus mortar, if kept on the trowel, is usually enough to form a cross joint which can be placed on the brick that is going to be laid next, as illustrated in Figure 4.131 or directly on to the brick that has already been placed on the wall, as illustrated in Figure 4.132

With either method, a wedge shaped joint filling, with its thicker part at the front of the brick, must be formed to ensure a solid cross-joint on the face of the wall between the bricks.

Further Uses of the Brick Trowel

Other operations carried out with the brick trowel are:

■ Tapping the brick down into position, a practice that should be avoided, it being better to rub the brick down to the correct level

■ Smoothing or ironing of face joints as the work is built, this is dealt with in further detail in the section on pointing

■ Filling or flushing up the internal vertical joints when a course is completed.

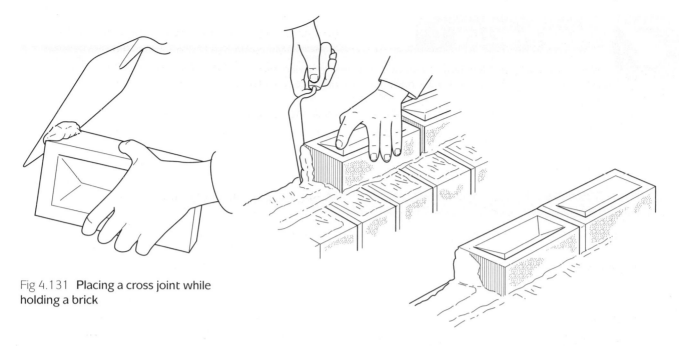

Fig 4.131 Placing a cross joint while holding a brick

Fig 4.132 Placing a cross joint while brick is on wall

Levelling a Corner

When a corner brick is laid it should initially be checked for height or gauge. The top of each course being kept level with the marks on the gauge rod. The brick should then be checked for level, and finally to see that it is vertically over the bricks below it, this procedure is known as plumbing. For the purpose of levelling, a one metre level may be used, although, for one brick, it is usually more convenient to use the shorter boat level.

Plumbing a Corner

For plumbing purposes the level is kept tightly against the bottom brick with the foot as shown in Figure 4.133 and held firmly with the left hand, leaving the right hand free to tap the bricks with the trowel into the correct position. This last task may be reduced to a minimum if, when first laying a corner brick, it is positioned as nearly as possible to its correct position by sighting vertically down the corner.

In order to plumb a corner after the full height of the spirit level has been reached, the level should only be raised enough to reach each subsequent course. This leaves the greater part of the level against the wall, which reduces the degree of error to a minimum. It is also important to note that the position of the level should be approximately 50 mm back from the corner of the wall, with the level being held as plumb as possible.

Fig 4.133 Plumbing up a corner

key terms

Level – Method of checking the horizontal courses of brickwork.

Plumbing – Method for checking the verticality of brickwork.

For plumbing the first two or three courses of a corner, it is usual to use the level, as the work proceeds, regular use of the level will ensure a greater degree of accuracy in the work.

Good Practice

When plumbing and levelling it can be tempting to strike the level with the trowel or even brick hammer, this practice should never be used as it merely damages the level with little or no effect on the brickwork. Always remember it is not the level that is wrong but the brick – so tap the brick not the level.

Work-based Evidence Required

- **Selection of resources associated with own work**

- Materials, components and fixings
- Tools and equipment.

To meet this requirement obtain photographs of yourself carrying out brickwork activities, such as building in a window frame to a cavity wall. You could also obtain a witness testimony from your supervisor stating that your selection of resources for the tasks was satisfactory. File and record in the usual way.

Running in Facework

Assuming that a corner has been built at each end of the wall, the bricks between them may be tested for alignment along the top and face of the wall with a straight edge as shown in Figure 4.134 or, where the distance is too great for a straight edge, with line and pins. In this method a line would be stretched from the top of one brick to the top of the brick at the other end of the wall, the line being held in position by inserting the pins into a suitable perpend. The bricks are now laid so that their top edges just coincide with the inside of the line as shown in Figure 4.135. The use of a tingle, shown in Figure 4.151 is dealt with on pages 199–200.

Tips for Maintaining the Quality of Workmanship

The quality of workmanship on site can have an overriding effect on the weather resistance of brickwork.

> Points to note ▸ ■ Cuts used in blockwork can be smaller than one half of a full block.

- Bricks should be laid on a full bed of mortar
- All cross joints and collar joints should be fully filled
- Immediately after the brick is laid, excess mortar should be struck off the external face of the work and off the internal faces of the leaves of cavity walls

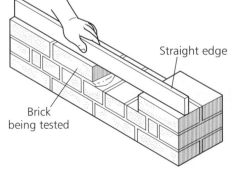

Straight edge

Brick being tested

Fig 4.134 **Testing the wall for alignment with a straight edge**

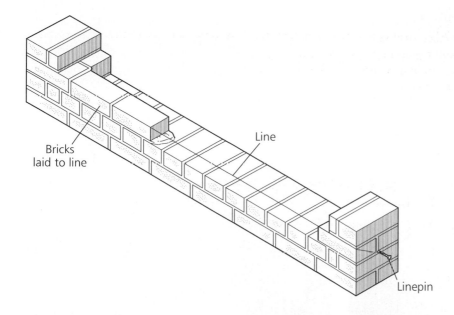

Fig 4.135 **Use of lines and pins**

- Care should be taken to ensure that mortar is not scraped on to the exposed face of the brick
- Unless otherwise specified, frogged bricks should be laid frog up and the frogs should be filled with mortar completely.

Sequence of Constructing Walling

This section is concerned with the correct sequence of constructing walling in brickwork. It deals with the building of short walls, of long lengths of walling with return ends, and with openings for doors and windows.

Work-based Evidence Required

- **Erecting masonry in brick and block and/or local materials to contractor's working instructions**

To meet the requirements for:
- Cavity wall structures
- Blockwork structures
- Solid wall structures
- Door and window openings

Obtain photographs of yourself building a straight solid wall, showing damp proof course and insulation in place and building a cavity wall with a return showing a door and window opening and a frame in position.

When the photographs have been developed place them on a photographic evidence sheet, and get your supervisor to authenticate them by signing and dating them. Place the evidence in your work-based evidence portfolio, when next in college and map and record it against the syllabus. Figures 4.136 to 4.139 show a bricklayer carrying out the actions mentioned above as an example of the type of evidence required.

Fig 4.136 Bricklayer building a straight solid wall, showing dpc

Fig 4.137 Bricklayer building a cavity wall showing insulation

Fig 4.138 Bricklayer building a solid wall with a return including a frame

Fig 4.139 Bricklayer builing a cavity wall with a return including an opening

Procedure for Building Short Walls

Before commencing to build, certain preparations as described in the following are necessary in order that the work may be carried out in the simplest and most efficient manner.

Mortar Board

The mortar board should be placed centrally and at a convenient distance from the proposed position of the wall, usually about 600 mm, as illustrated in Figure 4.140. It is important that the grain of the board is placed in the direction in which the mortar will be picked up, this is usually parallel to the length of the wall. The board should be raised from the ground on either bricks or blocks, to minimize the amount of bending required.

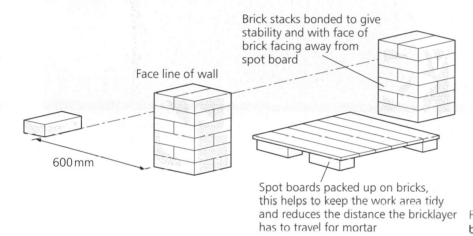

Brick stacks bonded to give stability and with face of brick facing away from spot board

Face line of wall

600 mm

Spot boards packed up on bricks, this helps to keep the work area tidy and reduces the distance the bricklayer has to travel for mortar

Fig 4.140 Mortar board in place with bricks to each side

Bricks and Mortar

Bricks should be placed on each side of the board in roughly bonded stacks about twelve to fourteen bricks high as illustrated in Figure 4.140, On the back corner of a board, a bucket of water should be placed in order to wet the board, after which the setting out proper may begin.

Work-based Evidence Required

■ Work skills to measure, mark out, lay, position and secure

To meet this requirement, obtain photographs of yourself transferring a level from say one corner of the building to a corner position using a straight edge and level or a cowley level and then transferring a datum height to a corner position with an optical level.

When the photographs have been developed place them on a photographic evidence sheet, and get your supervisor to authenticate them by signing and dating them. Place the evidence in your work-based evidence portfolio, when next in college and map and record it against the syllabus. Figures 4.141 to 4.143 show a bricklayer carrying out the actions mentioned above as an example of the type of evidence required.

Fig 4.141 **Bricklayer transferring a level with a straight edge and a level**

Fig 4.142 **Bricklayer transferring a level using a cowley level**

Fig 4.143 **Bricklayer transferring a datum point using an optical level**
Source: STosh

Setting Out the Wall

To set out the base of the wall, a thin layer of mortar, known as a screed, is spread on to the concrete foundation after plumbing down from the ranging lines, usually set above the work as illustrated in Figure 4.144. On the screed a straight line is marked with the point of the trowel to indicate the front of the wall.

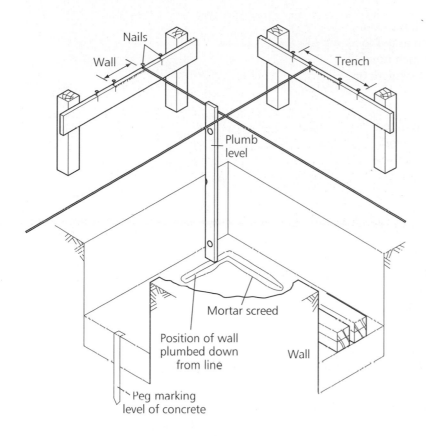

Fig 4.144 **Plumbing down from ranging lines to screed**

The required length of the wall is then measured off, and from each end further screeds are spread approximately at right angles to the face of the wall. A small building square is then placed in the correct position along the line representing the front of the wall and each end of the wall marked as illustrated in Figure 4.145.

For half-brick walls, one-brick walls and cavity walls, no further setting out would be required, but for thicker walls it would be necessary to mark out the back of the wall. This is achieved by laying a further screed and marking a back line parallel to the face of the wall at the required distance.

It can be used in your workshop training in conjunction with a **thin mortar screed** spread on the floor into which cuts are made with the trowel blade

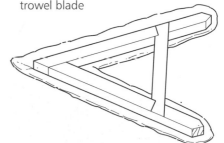

Fig 4.145 **Squaring screed lines and forming a right angle**

Work-based Evidence Required

- **Completion of own work within the estimated, allocated time to meet the needs of other occupations and/or client**

To meet this requirement, ask your supervisor to fill out a witness testimony sheet for you describing what work programme deadlines you met. For example, you might have been asked to complete a section of walling for say lunch time on Thursday, or to have finished the blockwork on a gable end by, say, Friday.

When you have received the signed and dated witness testimony sheet, place it in your work-based evidence portfolio, when next in college and map and record it against the syllabus.

Wetting Bricks

Most types of bricks should be thoroughly wetted before being laid in order to remove dust and dirt, and to ensure close adhesion between bricks and mortar by preventing the rapid absorption of the water from the mortar.

Note: Engineering or any other type of dense brick would not fall into this category and would not need to be wetted.

Building Corners

Corners should initially be built to a suitable height before the main length of wall is commenced. The building of a corner is really the construction of a small section of the whole wall to which the remainder of the wall will be aligned. In many ways its construction will follow the method described for short lengths of wall with the obvious exception that one end must be toothed, racked back, or part toothed and part racked back so that the rest of the wall may be easily and accurately built in.

It is good practice, when commencing to build corners, to check the first course for alignment by temporarily stringing a line along the top edge of brickwork from one end to the other. In order to ensure accuracy and correct alignment, as the work proceeds, the last brick of each course should be plumbed from the brickwork below and a straight edge occasionally held diagonally across the face of the work.

Since levelling from one corner to the other is difficult owing to the greatly increased distance between them, some other method must be made to fulfil the same purpose. For this reason, pegs, known as datum pegs, are fixed at the base of each corner, as illustrated in Figure 4.146, the tops of the pegs being levelled by means of an optical level around the building.

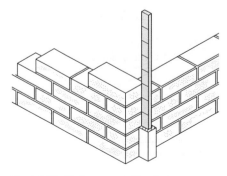

Fig 4.146 **Datum pegs fixed at corners**
Source: CITB-ConstructionSkills. Training Workbook, 1994.

As each corner brick is laid, it is checked for height by means of a gauge or storey rod, these being lengths of timber marked off into 75 mm divisions, see key terms. If the work is to be built correctly to gauge, and the same gauge rod used for each corner, the brick courses will be level throughout the height of the wall. Important levels such as the damp proof course, window sill and lintel levels, may be easily marked on the storey rod. These will serve as a precaution against their inclusion, or provision for their inclusion, being overlooked as the work progresses. After the corners have been built to ten or twelve courses, the walls between may be built, lines being used to ensure the correct level and alignment of each course as the work proceeds.

Laying the Corner Brick

The corner bricks should first be laid and tested for gauge, level and plumb as described previously, The corners are then raised as illustrated in Figure 4.147.

The bricks in between the corners are next to be laid, each brick being tested for alignment along their top and face. Assuming the bond has been previously worked out, it will be found more convenient to begin laying from the left-hand end of the wall wherever possible, and to complete the face of the work before commencing the back – as illustrated in Figure 4.148.

Procedure for Building Long Lengths of Walling

The method in preparing for and building a long section of walling is merely an extension of the method previously described for short lengths of wall, apart from the use of the tingle plate as described below.

Use of the Tingle Plate

Where there is a considerable distance between the two corners, it is often found difficult to pull the lines sufficiently tight and a noticeable sag in the line occurs. To alleviate this and to give support to the line, tingle plates are used at one or more points along the length of the wall. The level of the brick upon which the tingle plate rests is obtained by sighting along the line after the tingle plate has been approximately placed in position. Or more usually by gauging up from a datum peg in a way similar to that used for corners as illustrated in Figures 4.149 and 4.150. Also, a good quality nylon bricklaying line must be used, these are extremely strong and minimize sagging.

Once the level of the brick has been fixed, the tingle plate is set into position by weighting down with a brick or bat and in this way the centre or low parts of the line are raised to the correct level. A suitable place for the tingle brick would be on the reveals of door or window openings. Figure 4.151 shows one half of a partly built wall with the shape of the corners clearly outlined, the tingle plate in position near the centre of the wall, and the line in position ready for the next course to be laid.

In very high walls, it is wise to check regularly the height of each corner with a steel tape extended down to the first datum peg.

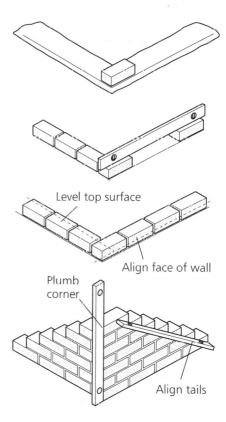

Level top surface

Align face of wall

Plumb corner

Align tails

Fig 4.147 **Corner being raised**

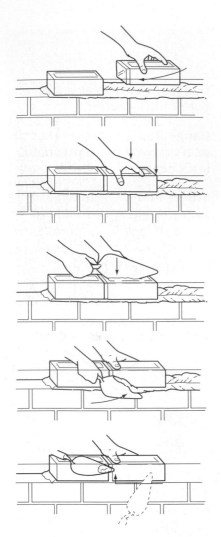

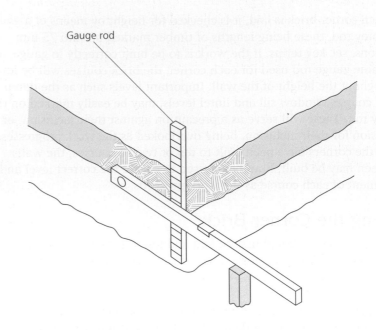

Fig 4.150 **Gauging from a datum peg**

Fig 4.148 **Running in between corners**

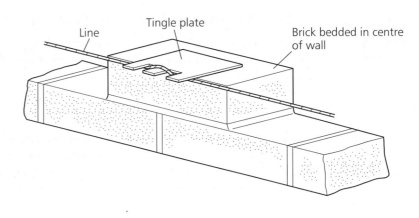

Line

Tingle plate

Brick bedded in centre of wall

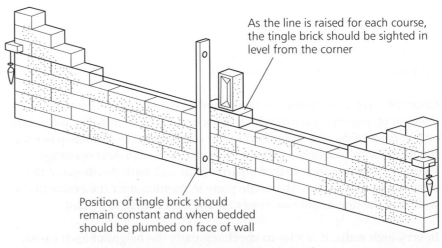

As the line is raised for each course, the tingle brick should be sighted in level from the corner

Position of tingle brick should remain constant and when bedded should be plumbed on face of wall

Fig 4.149 **Gauging**

Fig 4.151 **Tingle plate positioned for the next course to be laid**

Work-based Evidence Required

■ The use and maintainance of hand tools, portable power tools and ancillary equipment

To meet this requirement, obtain photographs of yourself organizing your own bricklaying work. For example, if you are building a cavity wall show on your photographs yourself at the work area which will include; mortar boards, brick stacks and the tools that you will be using. For equipment you could provide a photograph of yourself obtaining mortar from a mixer or silo, or cutting blocks with an angle grinder and so on. You could then show evidence of maintaining the above, for example, photographs of you cleaning your hand tools, cement mixer and portable power tools.

When the photographs have been developed place them on a photographic evidence sheet, and get your supervisor to authenticate them by signing and dating them. Place the evidence in your work-based evidence portfolio, when next in college and map and record it against the syllabus. Figures 4.152 and 4.153 show a bricklayer at his work station clearly illustrating his organization of the tasks required and obtaining mortar from a silo.

Fig 4.152 **Bricklayer at his work station showing mortar boards, brick stacks and tools**

Fig 4.153 **Bricklayer obtaining mortar from a silo**

Forming Openings for Doors and Windows

Door and window openings usually occur in a long wall, and the bond must be set out to reflect these openings at the outset so that, when the actual doors and windows are reached, there will be no noticeable change in the bonding of the brickwork. In setting out foundations, it is the usual practice to build the footings and brickwork below ground level with a different brick from the remainder of the wall. Owing to the usual variations in brick sizes, the bond of bricks to suit the various openings is not considered until the brickwork is just below ground level. Which in normal circumstances, is two courses below the damp proof course or 150 mm. When this level is reached, the position of the reveals is clearly marked, and a stretcher placed on the pier side of each mark (see bricks marked 6 in Figure 4.154).

key terms

Datum – A fixed reference point from which levels are set out.

Reveal – The area of walling at the side of an opening which is at right angles to the general face of the wall.

Sill – The lower horizontal edge of an opening.

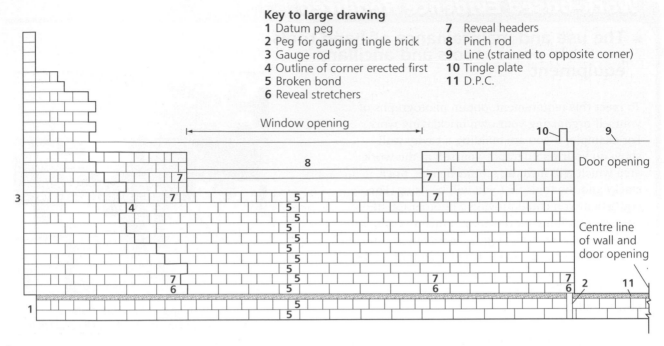

Key to large drawing
1 Datum peg
2 Peg for gauging tingle brick
3 Gauge rod
4 Outline of corner erected first
5 Broken bond
6 Reveal stretchers
7 Reveal headers
8 Pinch rod
9 Line (strained to opposite corner)
10 Tingle plate
11 D.P.C.

Window opening

Door opening

Centre line of wall and door opening

Fig 4.154 **Large wall**

The brickwork is then filled in between these bricks, any broken bonding that might occur being placed as centrally as possible (see bricks marked 5 in Figure 4.154).

After the stretcher course has been laid, the header course is set out to provide a quarter lap in the usual way. The bond is then maintained until the window openings are reached, care being taken to keep the reveal stretchers in a vertical line, by plumbing up the cross joints as the work proceeds. When the sill level is reached, the only adjustment required is to form the correct bond for the piers, by moving the headers marked with a 7 in Figure 4.154 from their original position to the reveal line, and insert a closer to fill the quarter of a brick gap left.

Reveal Bricks

It is general site practice to ensure that the reveal brick is the same as the brick on the corner in the same course, that is, if the corner brick is a stretcher, then all the reveal bricks should be stretchers in that particular course. Although this format is usually worked to, it may sometimes be disregarded to avoid an undue amount of broken bond, particularly when dealing with Flemish bond (see section about broken bond).

Window and Door Frames

If the window and door frames are on site and available for use, it is generally considered good practice to place them in the correct position and build them in as the work proceeds. If the frames for whatever reason are not available, it will be necessary to ensure that the openings are built a little larger than the frames so that the latter may be easily placed in position. For this purpose, a piece of batten is cut equal in length to the width of the frame plus a reasonable tolerance. This device is known as a pinch rod and it should be placed between the window or door reveals as they are set out and subsequently inserted at regular intervals to ensure that no cramping of the width dimensions takes place.

Setting Out of Mortar Boards

Mortar boards will be required at each end of the wall and at approximately two metre intervals between, they will also be required along the back of the wall where it is cavity walling or one and a half brick walling. The bricks should be placed on each side of the boards as before. During cavity wall construction the blockwork is built to bandstand height, then all mortar boards are transferred to the face brickwork side and so on.

Quick quiz Quick quiz Quick quiz Quick quiz Quick quiz

❶ When loading out, how far should your bricks and mortar board be away from the wall?

❷ What is a gauge?

❸ What is a vertical mortar joint called?

❹ How many millimetres are there in one metre?

❺ What is the main reason for bonding brickwork?

Jointing and Pointing

4.6

Joint Profiles

Note: When the joint finish is formed as the work proceeds the operation is termed jointing, but when deferred until a later stage it is termed pointing. Pointing will be dealt with later on in this section.

Mortar Joint Profiles

Definition – Joint profile is the shape of a mortar joint finish.

Thought should be given to the mortar joint profile, which will not only affect appearance but also the efficiency in repelling water. The efficient

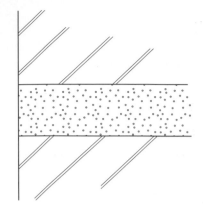

Fig 4.155 Flush joint

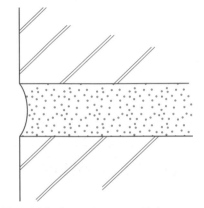

Fig 4.156 Curved recessed joint

shedding of water by mortar joints is essential for long term performance. Brick or blockwork that remains wet is more susceptible to frost and sulfate attack. The choice of joint profile should therefore be based on performance criteria, with aesthetic considerations being secondary.

Weather struck and bucket handle joints assist rainwater run-off, yet give some definition, and so are often considered an optimum solution. Recessed joints create shading that will emphasize the bricks, whilst flush joints have the reverse affect. Special joints may require special jointing tools.

Joint Finishes

Flush Joint

This joint gives maximum bearing area for the brick as illustrated in Figure 4.155 and is often favoured when coarse textured bricks are used. With some brick types the finish may appear a little irregular. This is suitable for moderate and sheltered exposures.

Curved Recessed or Bucket Handle Joint

This type of joint gives an improved appearance over a flush joint, as shown in Figure 4.156 with little reduction in strength. Owing to the compression of the joint and the superior bond, it has good weather resistance and is suitable for all grades of exposure.

Work-based Evidence Required

■ Forming Jointing and Pointing Finishes

To meet this requirement, obtain a photograph of yourself forming both a jointed and pointed finish to a mortar joint, remember they are different to each other. When the photograph has been developed place it on a photographic evidence sheet, then get your supervisor to authenticate it by signing and dating it. Place the sheet in your work-based evidence portfolio, when next in college and map and record it against the syllabus. Figure 4.157 shows a bricklayer forming a joint finish as an example of the type of evidence required.

Fig 4.157 Bricklayer forming a joint finish

Struck, Weathered or Weather struck Joint

This type of joint produces a contrasting effect of light and shade on the brickwork. Such joints, when correctly formed as illustrated in Figure 4.158 have excellent strength and weather resistance and are suitable for all grades of exposure.

Square Recessed or Raked Joint

This type of joint can produce interesting articulated joints, as illustrated in Figure 4.159 but weather resistance and strength will be considerably less than with other joint profiles. Use only with frost resistant bricks in sheltered exposure conditions. The recess should not exceed 3 or 4 mm and is not recommended with full fill cavity insulation.

Struck Joint

Used mainly on inspection chambers as illustrated in Figure 4.160 where the joint has to be formed overhand from outside the chamber.

Not suitable for external use as the base of the joint will hold water.

Pointing of Walls

Definition – Pointing is the process of finishing a mortar joint by raking out the jointing mortar before it has set hard, typically to a depth of 15 mm, and filling with additional mortar, to create a specific finish.

Repointing is the raking out of old mortar and replacing it with new.

This is not to be confused with:

Jointing: forming the finished surface profile of a mortar joint by tooling or raking as the work proceeds, without pointing.

Pointing

Pointing is the term applied to the process of raking out the joints in brickwork and refilling them with a mortar of a different character from that used in the body of the wall. The original object being to protect the bedding material of the brick and consequently the bricks also from the effects of the weather. In more recent times it has been used as a means of varying the appearance of the brickwork.

There are several types of pointing, and these may be carried out in a variety of colours by means of coloured cements and dyes and the use of different sands, the combination making possible an almost unlimited range of finishes.

The type of pointing adopted largely depends on the choice of the architect, particularly when appearance is the primary object, but it can be generally stated that :

For bricks of regular shape with sharp arrises, a smooth weathered type of pointing should be used as being effective and efficient.

For textured bricks of irregular shape, a pointing with a rough textured finish should be used.

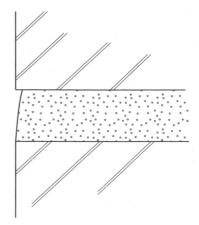

Fig 4.158   Weather struck joint

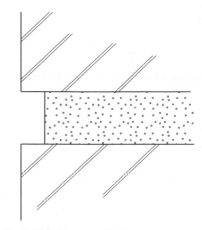

Fig 4.159   Recessed joint

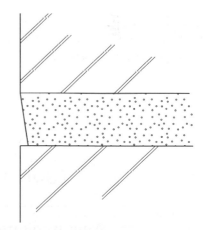

Fig 4.160   Struck joint

Finishes for Pointing

In addition to the insertion of jointing material after the original joint has been raked out, there are many finishes that may be applied to the joints during the process of building. A disadvantage of this method is the difficulty of maintaining an even colour throughout the whole work. This is due to possible variations in the colour and texture of the sand used and to a lesser degree the difficulty of ensuring constant proportions. An advantage of this method of finishing a joint is the fact that the finish is part of the bedding material. For this reason there is no possibility of the mortar becoming loose and leaving the wall, as sometimes happens in the case of pointing filled into raked joints.

Materials for Pointing

The selection of the aggregate and the matrix will depend on the type of pointing and the finish required. However, the mortar used should not be excessively strong in comparison with the brick, as there is then a tendency for the brick to wear away and leave the joints projecting.

Mixing

To mix a mortar that may be easily used, all the materials should be passed through a fine sieve and be well mixed in a dry state before any water is added. Since for pointing, the mortar is taken up on the back of a hawk, it is desirable to have it much stiffer than ordinary mortar. Therefore, a smaller amount of water is required and the mortar is brought to the correct consistency by beating the materials well together with the back of a shovel. It must also be remembered that an excess of water tends to render the joints porous.

Aggregates for Pointing

The aggregates for nearly all pointing mortars is commonly known as coarse stuff, which is a mixture of sand and lime to which cement and water are added to make mortar. The sand should be soft, that is, soft to the touch and above all clean. Since sand may vary in colour according to the amount of iron oxide it contains, it is important to set aside enough to complete the pointing of the whole job.

key terms

Hawk – A tool to hold the mortar when pointing.

Consistence – The degree of firmness with which the particles of mortar cohere.

Quick quiz Quick quiz Quick quiz Quick quiz Quick quiz

1. What is jointing brickwork?
2. State two reasons for jointing brickwork.
3. Draw and name five types of joint finish.
4. What is pointing brickwork?
5. State a suitable mortar mix for pointing.

Purpose and Positions of Movement Joints

4.7

Definition – A movement joint is a continuous horizontal or vertical joint in brickwork filled with compressible material to accommodate movement due to moisture, thermal or structural effects.

As a general rule, in long runs of continuous brickwork, movement joints should be provided at intervals not greater than 9 m. The width of joint should be 1 mm per metre run of brickwork. Therefore if we were to have movement joints every 10 m then the width of the joint would be 10 mm.

Movement in Brickwork

Movement of brickwork should be considered at the design stage. The main source of movement in brickwork dealt with in this section relates to moisture and temperature. Other factors may relate to loading and creep and in certain situations, it may be necessary to consider the effects of chemical action, ground movement and settlement.

In general, movement of brickwork that is reversible are caused by temperature changes and these can be calculated, by reference to the coefficient of thermal expansion, as indicated in British Standard 5628: Part Three or any one of numerous design guides produced by brick manufacturers and others. However, irreversible expansion of brickwork caused by the absorption of water can be larger and continue, albeit at a reducing rate, for a period of many years.

The movement properties of common building materials including brickwork are set out in Figure 4.161.

Moisture movement and thermal properties of common building materials

	Reversible moisture movement %	Irreversible moisture movement %	Coefficient of thermal expansion per °C $\times 10^{-6}$
Timber	± (0.5 – 2.5)†		6 – 70†
Steel (depending on type)			10 – 18 (depending on type)
Concrete	± (0.02 – 0.10)	(0.03 – 0.08)	7 – 14 (depending on type)
BRICK AND BLOCK			
Dense concrete aggregate concrete products	± (0.02 – 0.10)	– (0.02 – 0.06)	6 – 12
Lightweight aggregate concrete (autoclaved) products	± (0.03 – 0.06)	8 – 12	
Aerated (autoclaved) products	± (0.02 – 0.03)	– (0.05 – 0.09)	8
Calcium silicate bricks	± (0.01 – 00.05)	– (0.01 – 0.04)	8 – 14
Clay bricks	± (0.02)	+ (0.02 – 0.07)	5 – 8

Note: + expansion – shrinkage † depending on direction measured

Fig 4.161 **Chart showing movement properties of building materials**
Source: Ibstock

205

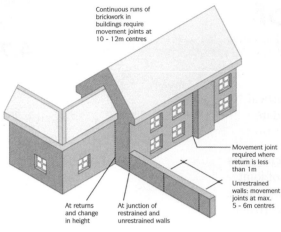

Continuous runs of brickwork in buildings require movement joints at 10 - 12m centres

Movement joint required where return is less than 1m

Unrestrained walls: movement joints at max. 5 - 6m centres

At returns and change in height

At junction of restrained and unrestrained walls

Positioning of Movement Joints

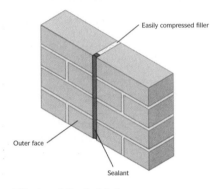

Easily compressed filler

Outer face

Sealant

Filled and Sealed Joints

Fig 4.162 Drawing showing spacing and thickness of movement joints
Source: Ibstock

The spacing and thickness of movement joints is related to the detailed design, length and height of brickwork, together with any requirements for structural restraint as shown in Figure 4.162.

A design guide for normal walling of reasonable height is that the joint width should be at least equal to the joint spacing plus an allowance of say 30 per cent to allow for compression of the filler material and the performance of the appropriate sealants.

Therefore movement joints at 10 m centres will need to be approximately 13 mm wide and the distance between movement joints should ideally be never more than 12 m. The majority of brickwork is set out for a 5 to 6 m grid, so for design purposes it is a normal rule that movement joints should be placed at 10 to 12 m centres. Movement also takes place at corners and not just in straight runs of walling. It is therefore important to include all continuous walling in any design assessment.

Unrestrained or lightly restrained walls such as, parapets and small freestanding walls should be given double the above amount of movement provision. In these cases, the distance between movement joints should be at 5 to 6 m centres, with coping and capping at half these distances.

Present research suggests (see BS 5628: Part 3) that the vertical movement of unrestrained walls is of the same order as horizontal movement. The standard also recommends suitable compressible materials such as foam rubbers and cellular polythene and the use of sealants such as low modulas silicone, which are suitable for the sealing of movement joints. The same standard also advises on unsuitable materials, for example fibreboard. Further guidance on the selection of sealants is given in British Standard 6213.

Clay and concrete bricks and blocks have different movement characteristics, these differences being both in size and direction. They should not be bonded together but separated by either a vertical or horizontal movement joint or by a slip plane.

Reinforcement in Relation to Movement

Forces at Work on Brickwork

Brickwork like concrete is at its strongest when in compression. The forces set up by reversible movement, irreversible movement or simply by changes in section due to door or window openings, can induce tensile forces, resulting in cracking occurring to the masonry. Such effects may be weakened or controlled by bed joint reinforcement, which can accommodate the tensile forces and help bond adjacent courses together as a whole.

Stitching rods may be inserted and grouted into the holes contained in some bricks to both locate and support the bricks over door and window openings. The rods should be made from stainless steel and used in accordance with a structural engineer's specification.

Proprietary Fixings

Innovative brickwork detailing, particularly corbelling, or where the bearing for successive courses in 102.5 mm brickwork is less than 70 mm, may require proprietary channels, cranked or special shape ties and angle supports fixed back to a reinforced concrete structure. The use of a Styrene Butadiene Rubber additive may also be used where bricks are to be bedded on stainless steel angles.

Quick quiz Quick quiz Quick quiz Quick quiz Quick quiz

❶ **In what pattern should wall ties be placed?**

❷ **What is the maximum spacing of wall ties, horizontally and vertically?**

❸ **When is brickwork at its strongest?**

❹ **Name two sources of movement in brickwork.**

❺ **What is a slip plane?**

Reinforcement Items 4.8

Definition – Light metal reinforcement is available in both roll and strip form. Laid in the mortar of bed joints as the wall is built it helps prevent cracking by distributing the high stresses that can occur from point loads.

Position

The mesh is laid on a course of bricks or blocks leaving about 25 mm clearance from the face of the work. If it is necessary to join two pieces of mesh, make an overlap of at least 75 mm. Mortar is then spread in the usual way for the next course, embedding the reinforcement completely between the courses. Mesh reinforcement needs to be placed on every third course for best effect.

Requirements

Reinforcement mesh is an expanded steel mesh supplied in the form of a coil for easy handling. It can be used as an anti-crack reinforcement

Fig 4.163 **Horizontal wall**
reinforcement
Source: Catnic

in the design and construction of brick and blockwork as shown in
Figure 4.163.

A range of widths are available to meet the majority of brick and
blockwork applications. For example, you would choose 64 mm strip for
a 102.5 mm wall thickness.

Reinforcement is used for a variety of applications in all types of building
situations. It can be used for the overall reinforcement of solid or cavity
walls. It may also be used in other high stress areas such as retaining
walls for tanks and reservoirs, as well as buildings on reclaimed land
that may be subject to settlement. (N.B. The product illustrated in
Fig. 4.163 is anti-crack only.)

PROTECT WORK

In this section you will learn about protecting work against damage from
general workplace activities, other occupations and adverse weather
conditions.

When you have completed this section you will be able to :
- comply with organizational procedures to minimize the risk of
  damage to the work and surrounding area.

Know and understand :
- how to protect work from damage and the purpose of protection.

This section will now cover protecting work.

Effects of Weather Conditions on Walling Construction

Exposure of Brickwork

A major factor influencing the performance of brick and blockwork is the degree to which it becomes wet. Good design aims to minimize water penetration, as excessive wetting can lead to frost or sulphate attack and staining or corrosion of non-stainless steel wall ties or reinforcement. Use of the appropriate damp proof course materials in the correct positions will also significantly reduce walls becoming wet.

The exposure of the site and of different parts of the building will have a bearing on the choice of both bricks and the mortar mix. The degree of exposure of the site is classified either in terms of the local spell indices, or in calculations referring to the British Standards as shown in Figure 4.164.

Factors affecting rain penetration of cavity walls

Factor affecting rain penetration	Increasing probability of rain penetration in the direction of the arrow			
Applied external finish	Cladding	Rendering	Other (e.g. masonry paint, water repellent)	
Mortar composition	Cement: lime: sand	Cement: sand plus plasticizer		
Mortar joint finish and profile	Bucket handle, weathered.	Flush	Recessed, tooled	Recessed, untooled
Air space (clear cavity)	Over 50 mm	50 mm		None
Insulation	None	Partial filling with 50 mm air space	Filled with type A insulant (50 mm cavity)	Filled with type B insulant (50 mm cavity)

Fig 4.164 Factors showing degrees of exposure
Source: Ibstock

Protection of Brick and Blockwork

All newly built brick and blockwork and brick, and blockwork under construction, must be protected adequately from rain, snow and frost. In most cases this is achieved by covering the top of the wall as shown in Figure 4.165 with a water resistant material. However, problems can arise in some situations, for example in brickwork facing to concrete construction, where rain may frequently run off the concrete in quantity and penetrate behind the facing brickwork.

In this situation a water resisting material is usually fixed to the vertical surface of the concrete and draped over and clear of the brickwork, the material being lifted as work proceeds.

Every opportunity must be made to allow the brick and blockwork to dry out when conditions permit. To encourage drying out, the covering material should be supported clear of the face of the wall, either by

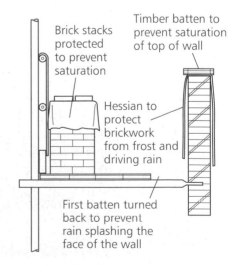

Brick stacks protected to prevent saturation

Timber batten to prevent saturation of top of wall

Hessian to protect brickwork from frost and driving rain

First batten turned back to prevent rain splashing the face of the wall

Fig 4.165 Protection of a wall

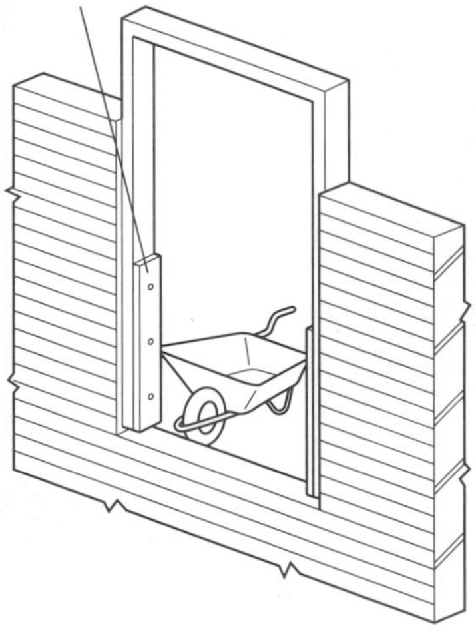

Timber battens to
protect door frame
from accidental knocks

Fig 4.166 **Protection of frames**
Source: CITB-ConstructionSkills, Training
Workbook, 1994.

laying it over a wooden framework or over projecting bricks, so that
ventilation can take place beneath the cover.

Hessian is frequently used as an insulating layer in sunny weather,
but it is useless if it becomes wet. Apart from the loss of its value as
insulation, Hessian, which is wet, will frequently cause serious staining
and efflorescence of the brickwork. It must therefore, be covered
with plastic or other waterproof materials in adverse conditions.
Mortar splashing and staining of brickwork will also occur in wet
weather unless the inner scaffold board is turned back when work
is left for the day.

Where site traffic is to pass close to buildings, protection should be
provided to avoid damage through splashing and impact. The internal
face of door frames should also be protected to prevent damage from
wheelbarrows as they pass through as illustrated in Figure 4.166.

Work-based Evidence Required

- ## Protection of the work and its surrounding area from damage.

To meet this requirement, obtain photographs of
the construction site where you are working,
showing the security fencing or hoarding erected
around the perimeter. For evidence of protecting
brickwork you could have a photograph, taken at
the end of the day showing walling sheeted over
to protect it from the weather. Similarly materials
such as bricks could be shown placed on pallets
sheeted up from the rain. For equipment it could
be a photograph of setting out levels and tripods
being placed in a secure site hut.

Fig 4.167 **Site showing security fencing**
Source: Celcon

When the photographs have been developed place
them on a photographic evidence sheet, and get
your supervisor to authenticate them by signing
and dating them. Place the evidence in your work
based evidence portfolio, when next in college
and map and record it against the syllabus.
Figures 4.167 to 4.170 show a bricklayer carrying
out the actions mentioned above as an example of
the type of evidence required.

Fig 4.168 **Walling showing protective sheeting**

4

Fig 4.169 Bricks on pallets sheeted over against the weather

Fig 4.170 Equipment being locked in a site hut

Exposure of Brick and Blockwork

Certain parts of the country have been designated areas of severe exposure. The meteorological criteria for these areas are defined below.

Meteorological Criteria

- Average annual frost incidence more than 60 days
- Average annual rainfall more than 1000 mm
- Elevation of the site more than 90 m above sea level.

Areas of Severe Exposure

Areas of the United Kingdom where the criteria for severe exposure apply are indicated on the map shown in Figure 4.171.

These areas are identified on the table by their postcode districts, although in only a few instances does a whole postcode district lie within an area of severe exposure.

Areas that are exposed to wind driven rain are illustrated on the map shown in Figure 4.172.

Exposure Within Brick and Blockwork Construction

The exposure category of tall buildings and those located on high ground should be classified as one grade more severe than would appear to be

key terms

Hessian – A rough textured sacking type material, much used in brickwork for the covering of walling.

Efflorescence – A white powdery deposit on the face of the brickwork due to the drying out of soluble salts washed from the bricks following excessive wetting.

Brickwork

Areas of Severe exposure

Areas of the United Kingdom where the meteorological criteria for severe exposure apply are indicated in the map below. These areas are identified in Table 1 by their postcode districts, although in only a few instances does a whole postcode district lie within an area of severe exposure.

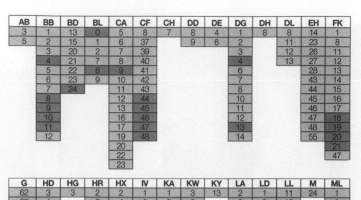

AB	BB	BD	BL	CA	CF	CH	DD	DE	DG	DH	DL	EH	FK
3	1	13	0	5	8	7	8	4	1	8	8	14	1
5	2	15	1	6	37		9	6	2		11	23	8
	3	20	2	7	39				3		12	26	11
	4	21	7	8	40				4		13	27	12
	5	22	8	9	41				6			28	13
	6	23	9	10	42				7			43	14
	7	24		11	43				8			44	15
	8			12	44				10			45	16
	9			13	45				11			46	17
	10			16	46				12			47	18
	11			17	47				13			48	19
	12			19	48				14			55	20
				20									21
				22									47
				23									

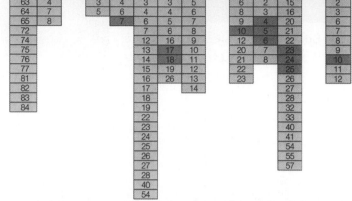

G	HD	HG	HR	HX	IV	KA	KW	KY	LA	LD	LL	M	ML
62	3	3	2	2	1	1	3	13	2	1	11	24	1
63	4		3	3	3	3	5		6	2	15		2
64	7		5	4	4	4	6		8	3	16		3
65	8			5	6	5	7		9	4	20		6
72				7	7	6	8		10	5	21		7
74					12	16	9		12	6	22		8
75					13	17	10		20	7	23		9
76					14	18	11		21	8	24		10
77					15	19	12		22		25		11
81					16	26	13		23		26		12
82					17		14				27		
83					18						28		
84					19						32		
					22						33		
					23						40		
					24						41		
					25						54		
					26						55		
					27						57		
					28								
					40								
					54								

NE	NP	OL	PA	PH	PH	S	SA	SK	ST	SY	TD	TS	YO
19	1	1	23	1	22	6	9	6	10	10	1	9	6
46	2	2	24	2	23	10	10	10	13	16	2		18
47	3	3	25	3	25	11	11	11		17	5		21
48	4	4	26	4	26	30	13	12		18	8		22
49	5	5	27	5	30		19	13		19	11		
66	6	6	32	6	31		20	14		20	71		
71	7	7	33	7	32		32	15		21			
	8	8	34	8	33		33	16		22			
	44	9	35	9	34		39	17		23			
		10	36	10	35		40			24			
		11	37	11	36		44			25			
		12	38	15	37		48						
		13	40	16	38								
		14	41	17	39								
		15		18	40								
		16		19	41								
				20									

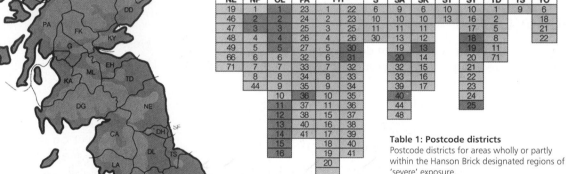

Table 1: Postcode districts

Postcode districts for areas wholly or partly within the Hanson Brick designated regions of 'severe' exposure.

- partly within
- wholly within

N — Areas of 'Normal' Exposure where the meteorological critera do not apply.

S — Areas of 'Severe' Exposure where the meteorological critera do apply. For identification of these areas, by postcode district see Table 1.

Fig 4.171 **Map showing areas of exposure**
Source: Hanson

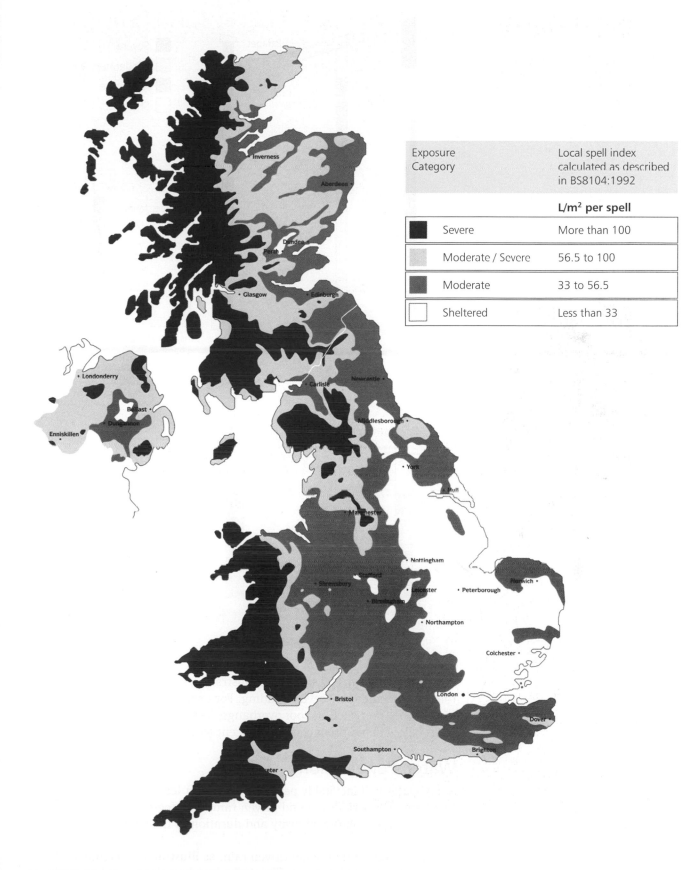

Exposure Category		Local spell index calculated as described in BS8104:1992
		L/m² per spell
	Severe	More than 100
	Moderate / Severe	56.5 to 100
	Moderate	33 to 56.5
	Sheltered	Less than 33

Fig 4.172 **Map showing areas of wind-driven rain**
Source: Ibstock

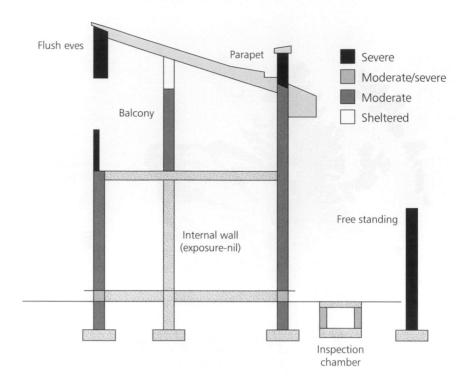

Fig 4.173 **High risk areas of buildings for exposure risks 1**
Source: Ibstock

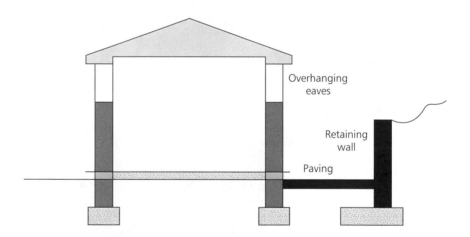

Fig 4.174 **High risk areas of buildings for exposure risks 2**
Source: Ibstock

required. Figures 4.173 and 4.174 illustrate certain parts of a building that may need a more severe grading. For example, parapet walling, tops of walls not protected by roof overhangs, freestanding wall and areas of walls below damp proof courses adjacent to ground level.

Water Penetration

Some water will inevitably penetrate the outer leaf of brickwork when there are long periods of wind-driven rain. The degree of penetration depends largely on the intensity and duration of the wind and rain.

During periods of light wind-driven rain, as illustrated in Figure 4.175 damp patches usually appear first at the joints on the cavity face of the brickwork. When the rain stops they will dry out.

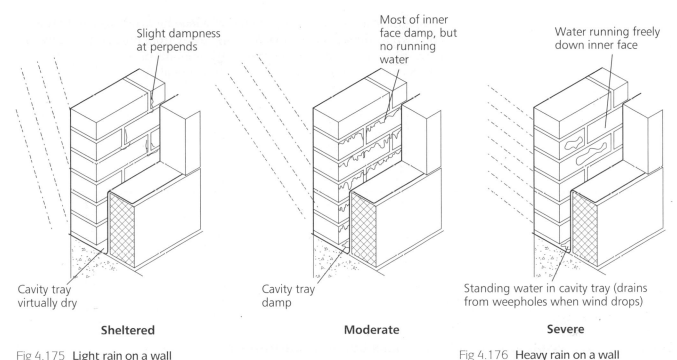

Sheltered

Fig 4.175 Light rain on a wall

Moderate

Severe

Fig 4.176 Heavy rain on a wall

After longer or more intense periods of wind-driven rain, the entire face of the wall may become wet and eventually water may run freely down the inner face of the wall, as illustrated in Figure 4.176.

Design Considerations

It is important to design the individual elements of a building with an eye for the prevention of future defects as shown in Figure 4.177. For sites of severe exposure, special details may be necessary, but in many cases simply following good practice guidelines will help to minimize any future problems.

One of the main factors to take into account in the British climate is water penetration from above and below the building. In addition to the aspects already mentioned, other factors, such as structural stability and the lack of movement joint provision, may have a bearing on the weather resistance capabilities of brick and blockwork. For example, moisture penetration through cracks in the brickwork.

Design Detailing

Certain design features will increase the vulnerability of brick and blockwork and the risk of it becoming wet, with consequent risk of frost damage. In these examples more durable bricks and mortar mixes are required, this choice may then have to be applied to the whole building.

Exclusion of Water

Good design contributes greatly in reducing the risk of water penetration. The wetting of walls can be reduced by ensuring that water

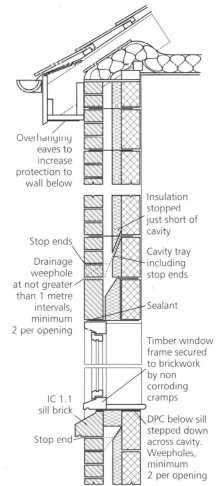

Fig 4.177 Eaves and window section

is thrown clear of the wall by the use of adequate overhangs and drips and by providing drainage to take water away from brick and blockwork. Large areas of glazing can produce large amounts of surface run-off, which can cause excessive wetting and the possibility of water penetrating the masonry below.

Where walls are to remain wet for long periods, as in Figure 4.183 above, consideration should be given to the use of stronger mortar mixes or sulphate resisting cement.

Quick quiz Quick quiz Quick quiz Quick quiz Quick quiz

❶ What do we use Hessian for?

❷ What are weep holes?

❸ What do you call a damp proof membrane which is fitted to the top surface of a lintel?

❹ What can happen if bricks become saturated?

❺ What is efflorescence?

RESOURCES

In this section you will learn about materials, components and equipment relating to types, quantity, quality and sizes of standard and specialist:

■ Bricks, blocks, mortars, frames, insulation, damp-proof barriers, lintels, fixings and ties

■ Hand and powered tools and equipment.

When you have completed this section you will be able to:

■ Select the required quantity and quality of resources for the methods of work

■ Interpret the given information relating to the work and resources to confirm its relevance

Know and understand:

■ The characteristics, quality, uses, limitations and defects associated with the resources and how defects should be rectified

■ How the resources should be used and how any problems associated with the resources are reported

■ The organizational procedures to select resources, why they have been developed and how they are used.

This section will now cover resources relating to the above.

Positioning of Wall and Insulation Ties

4.9

Wall Ties

Wall ties should be made of plastic or metal, preferably stainless steel. They are built into the two leaves of a cavity wall to link them together and thus make the wall stronger. They also act as a restraint fixing to tie cladding to a backing and also to tie insulation to the inner leaf of the cavity wall by means of retaining clips.

Density and Positioning of Ties

For walls in which both leaves of masonry are 90 mm or thicker, ties should be used at not less than 2.5 per square m, which equates to 900 mm horizontal × 450 mm vertical centres. This spacing may be varied when required by the Building Regulations. Wall ties should be evenly distributed over the wall area, except around openings, and should preferably be staggered.

Extra wall ties are required to the slope of the gable wall. Vertically: ties need to be placed at minimum 300 mm. Horizontally: ties need to be placed within 300 to 400 mm from the roofline. The actual measurement will depend on the angle of the roof slope. Distance from the slope: ties need to be placed within 225 mm of the verge as shown in Figure 4.178.

In cases where insulation board is incorporated within the cavity and restrained by ties with insulation retaining clips, it may be necessary to reduce the horizontal spacing of the ties to 600 mm. At vertical edges of an opening, unreturned or unbonded edges, and vertical expansion joints, additional ties should be used at a rate of one per 300 mm height, located not more than 225 mm from the edge of the masonry. A typical wall tie layout is shown in Figure 4.179.

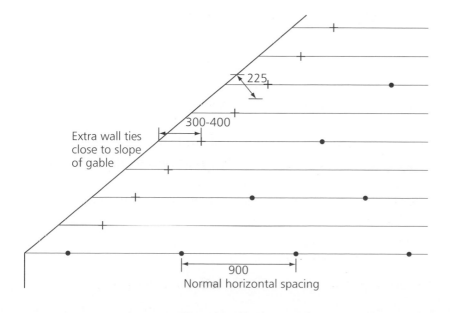

225

300-400

Extra wall ties close to slope of gable

900
Normal horizontal spacing

Fig 4.178 **Ties in a gable wall**

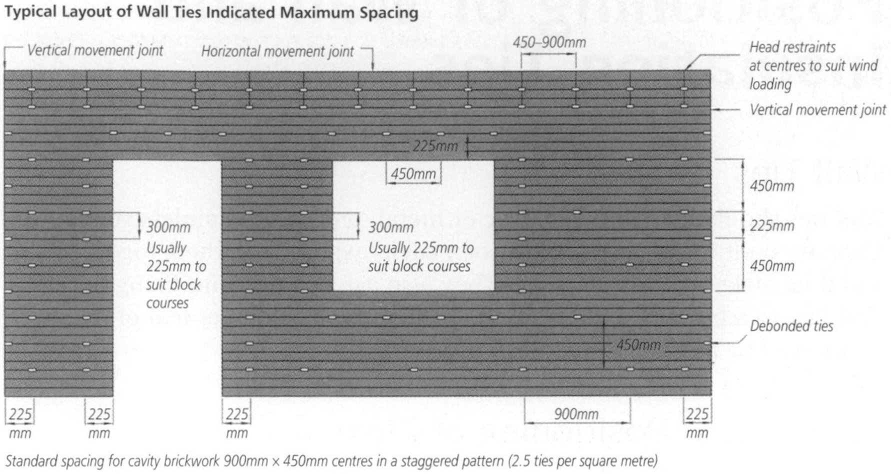

Typical Layout of Wall Ties Indicated Maximum Spacing

Fig 4.179 **Wall tie layout**
Source: Ancon Building Products

Standard spacing for cavity brickwork 900mm × 450mm centres in a staggered pattern (2.5 ties per square metre)

Embedment | Cavity width | Embedment

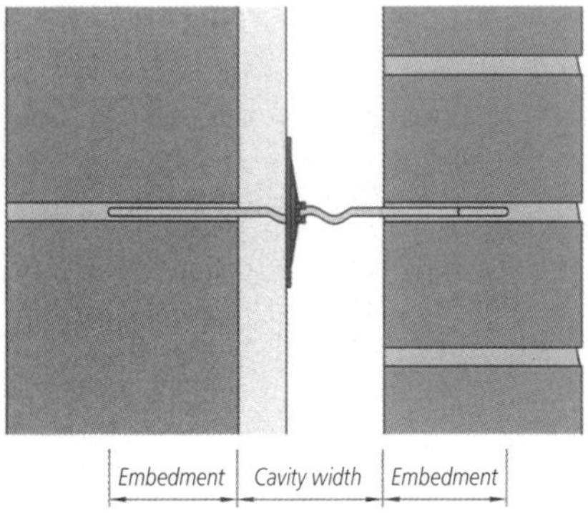

Embedment of Wall Ties

Fig 4.180 **Section of cavity showing correct embedment depths for wall ties**
Source: Ancon Building Products

Cavity Width (mm)	Length of Wall Tie (mm)	DD140-2 Wall Tie
50–75	200	HRT4/RT2/ST1
76–100	225	HRT4/RT2/ST1
101–125	250	ST1
126–150	275	SD1
150	300*	ST1

* These wall ties can be used in 126–150 mm cavities if they are embedded further into the inner level.

Fig 4.181 **Recommended lengths of wall tie for various cavity widths**
Source: Ancon Building Products

Length of Tie and Embedment

Wall ties should be of the correct length to ensure they are correctly embedded in the masonry. The tie should have a minimum embedment of 50 mm in each leaf of the wall but also take site tolerances into account for both cavity width and centring of the tie. For this reason it is suggested by manufacturers that tie lengths which achieve an embedment of between 62.5 mm and 75 mm should be used as illustrated in Figure 4.180.

The recommended lengths of wall tie to suit various cavity widths for use in masonry to masonry walls are shown in Figure 4.181.

REMEMBER In a main wall, ties are required every six courses of brickwork or every two block courses.

There are extra wall ties at openings.

If one leaf of masonry is less than 90 mm thick, the maximum spacing of ties is 450 mm.

Cavity Wall Ties

Application – For traditional brick and blockwork walls. They come in three types:

1. Heavy duty wall tie for buildings of any height.

2. General purpose wall tie for buildings not greater than 15 m in height.

3. Light duty wall tie for buildings not greater than 10 m in height.

Good Practice

Wall ties are an important element in the stability of cavity walls. The correct selection, spacing and installation of ties is essential to avoid damp penetration and the distortion or cracking of brickwork.

Many factors including cavity width, type and height of buildings, and location must all be considered in the selection of ties.

Vertical Movement Joints

Debonding sleeves are used on plain-ended wall ties, at vertical movement joints. The tie will restrain the masonry against lateral wind loads but the sleeve will allow the masonry to expand or contract. Debonding sleeves should be installed with a 10 mm gap at the end to allow for the expansion of masonry as shown in Figure 4.182.

Vertical movement joints
Debonding sleeves are used on plain-ended wall ties, at vertical movement joints. The tie will restrain the masonry against lateral wind loads but the sleeve will allow the masonry to expand or contract. Debonding sleeves should be installed with a 10 mm gap at the end to allow for expansion of the masonry.

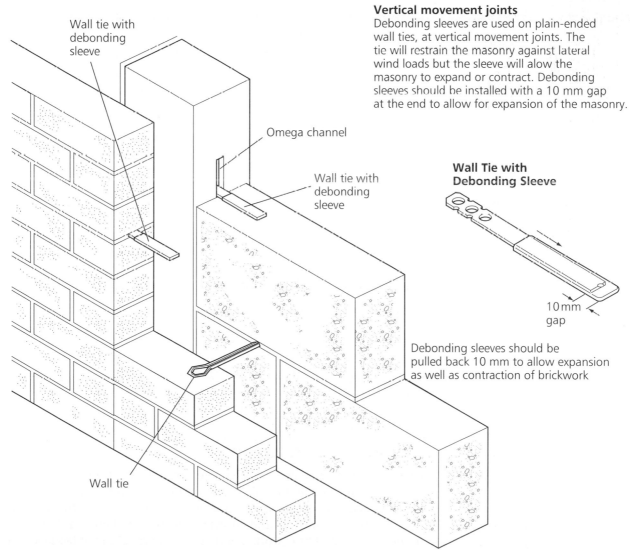

Wall Tie with Debonding Sleeve

10 mm gap

Debonding sleeves should be pulled back 10 mm to allow expansion as well as contraction of brickwork

Fig 4.182 Debonding sleeve at a vertical movement joint

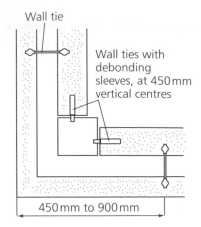

Fig 4.183 **Movement joint at an external corner**

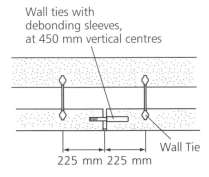

Fig 4.185 **Movement joint in cavity walling**

Further examples of fixings to vertical movement joints are as follows:

- External corner with fully bonded brickwork as shown in Figure 4.183
- Intermediate column with vertical movement joints in both brickwork and blockwork as shown in Figure 4.184
- Cavity wall with vertical movement joint in the brickwork as shown in Figure 4.185.

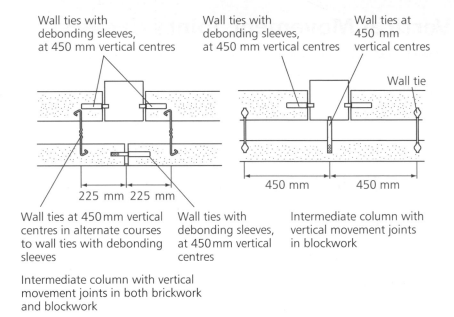

Fig 4.184 **Movement joint in brick and blockwork**

Hammer-in Ties for Multiple Cavity Widths

Hammer-in ties are used to fix masonry cladding to concrete. Use of the hammer-in tie can reduce the variety of tie lengths required on site and speed the rate of building. Hammer-in ties are available in a standard length of 310 mm that suits all cavities up to 150 mm wide and, unlike conventional frame cramps. They do not need a mechanical fixing.

Method of Installation

Once the plug is installed in the concrete, the hammer–in tie is inserted into a special installation tool, leaving it threaded and exposed. The tool is hammered until it is flush with the concrete, locating the thread in the plug. Using the same tool and ensuring adequate embedment is achieved in the outer leaf of brickwork, the tie is bent parallel to the brickwork as shown in Figure 4.186.

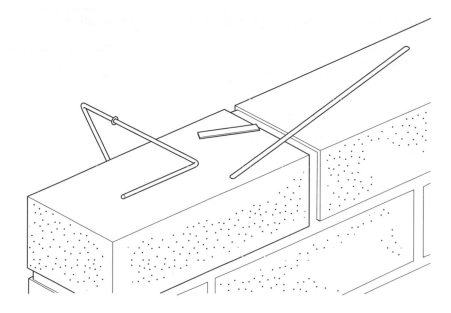

Fig 4.186 **Hammer-in tie**

Good Practice

Wall ties should be pressed down in, and surrounded by, fresh mortar.

To ensure cavity wall ties are effective at tying the leaves of masonry together they should be installed as the inner leaf is built and not simply pushed into a joint.

Ties should be installed with a slight fall to the outer leaf, never towards the inner leaf, as this could provide a path for moisture to cross the cavity.

The drip part of the tie should point downwards and be positioned near the centre of the open cavity.

Installed ties should be clear of mortar droppings to allow the drip to function and prevent water from crossing to the inner leaf of the wall.

Masonry Frame Tie

This is a tie for fixing timber door and window frames to brickwork.

Application – A screw-in tie used to join timber door and window frames to brickwork (see Figure 4.187).

The maximum vertical spacings of frame ties for most types of buildings in the UK with a maximum brickwork height of 15 m is illustrated in the chart shown in Figure 4.188.

Fig 4.187 **Masonry frame tie**

Maximum vertical spacing of Frame Ties for most buildings in the UK with a maximum brickwork height of 15 metres

Main Front and Rear Elevations with most Windows

Maximum Width of Frame (mm)	900	1200	1500	1800	2100	2400	2700	3000
Towns and cities	450	450	300	300	225	225	160	150
Open country	450	375	300	225	225	150	150	150

Note: The area of doors and windows in the wall is more than half the area of doors and windows in the other walls.

Side Elevations with few Windows

Maximum Width of Frame (mm)	900	1200	1500	1800	2100	2400	2700	3000
Towns and cities	450	300	225	225	150	150	150	75
Open country	375	225	225	15	150	75	75	75

Note: The area of doors and windows in the wall is more than half the area of doors and windows in the other walls.

Fig 4.188 Chart showing vertical spacings of frame ties
Source: Ancon

Ties for Tying Masonry to Steel Frames.

The tie spacing are based on 25/14 channel at 600 mm horizontal centres (see Figure 4.189).

Application – Channel and cavity wall ties for use in the construction of steel framed buildings. Self-drilling screws fix through the channel and the insulation material into the steel as shown in Figure 4.190.

Universal Wall Starter Systems

Application – For joining new walls to existing masonry as shown in Figure 4.191.

Wall starter systems come with all the necessary fixings in order to join a single skin of masonry 2.4 m high to an existing wall. They are suitable for:

■ Brickwork and blockwork
■ Imperial and metric masonry units

Tie Spacing Based on 25/14 Channel at 600 mm Horizontal Centres

Wind Zone Brickwork	Vertical Tie Spacing (mm) for Maximum Height of		
	15 m	25 m	40 m
A	450	450	300
B	450	300	225
C	450	225	225

Fig 4.189 Chart showing spacings of ties   Note: Wind zones are taken from DD140: Part 2 and are for towns and cities.

Fig 4.190 **Steel to masonry tie**

- Single leaf and cavity walls
- Internal and external use
- Wall widths from 60 mm to 250 mm
- Masonry up to eight metres in height, when connected together.

Wall starter systems are ideal for the building of conservatories, extensions and garden walls.

Starter Tie

Application – For joining new walls to existing masonry. This is a screw-in tie supplied with an 8 mm nylon plug for joining up masonry to existing walls without the need for jointing as shown in Figure 4.192. They are ideal for the building of conservatories, extensions and garden walls.

Cavity Starter Tie

Application – For the building of a new inner leaf of blockwork. A screw-in tie that simplifies the building of an inner leaf of blockwork within an existing structure. They come supplied with an 8 mm nylon plug.

Fig 4.191 Universal wall starter system

Fig 4.192 Starter tie

Quick quiz Quick quiz Quick quiz Quick quiz Quick quiz

❶ What is a horizontal mortar joint called?

❷ What are proprietary wall connectors made from?

❸ How are proprietary wall connectors fixed in place?

❹ Why are wall ties used?

❺ Draw two different types of wall tie and name them.

Types of Wall and Insulation Ties   4.10

Definition – A component, made of metal or plastic, either built into the two leaves of a cavity wall to link them, or used as a restraint fixing, to tie cladding to a backing.

To give stability to all types of cavity walls the inner and outer leaves must be tied together. This is achieved by using a metal or plastic wall tie that spans the cavity and is bedded firmly at right angles in both outer and inner leaves of the wall. A drip can be found in the middle of each wall tie. This helps to keep water or moisture away from the inner leaf.

Note: Proposed changes in the Building Regulations Part A, recommend that only stainless steel wall ties should be used in external cavity walls.

The Architect or designer will decide the distance between wall ties. He or she may consider:

■ How strong the wall needs to be

■ Where any insulation boards may be placed

■ The Building Regulations

■ The Masonry Code of Practice.

It is not always possible for the architect or designer to give the position of every tie placed in a wall. In some situations the bricklayer needs to make common sense decisions.

The distance between the wall ties is measured both horizontally and vertically. The Building Regulations and the Masonry Code of Practice recommends different maximum spacings, as you can see from the diagram shown in Figure 4.185.

There are a wide variety of wall ties available. The range of ties described below are the most commonly available and the most frequently used.

Heavy Duty Tie

Designed for traditional cavity wall construction, these ties combine ease of use with the expected safety and security standards. The ties can be easily built into brick or blockwork during construction, are smooth, without sharp edges and are designed to resist the collection of mortar (see Figure 4.193).

This type of tie may be positioned centrally or offset in the cavity provided that they are embedded a minimum of 50 mm on both leaves of masonry.

Housing Tie

A cavity tie suitable for use in the construction of houses not greater than 10 m in height (see Figure 4.194).

General Purpose Tie

Designed for fixing masonry to masonry in cavity walls of domestic houses and small commercial buildings up to three storeys in height not exceeding 15 m. The ties are suitable for cavity widths of 50 mm when installed at a density of 2.5 ties per square m (see Figure 4.195).

Strip ties are also available for fixing masonry to timber framing in dwellings of up to four storeys, up to a maximum height of 12 m. The ties are sufficiently flexible so as not to cause cavity growth as a result of the reduction of moisture content in the timber and settlement of the frame structure.

Insulation Retainers

Designed for retaining rigid board or mineral wool and fibreglass insulation material against the inner leaf of the cavity wall. Intended for use with wire and strip ties, they are however, flexible enough to use with most systems. The retainers are clipped on to the ties and the flat face of the disc pushed against the surface of the insulation (see Figure 4.196).

Length (mm)	Cavity (mm)
200	50-75
225	76-100
250	101-125
300	126-150

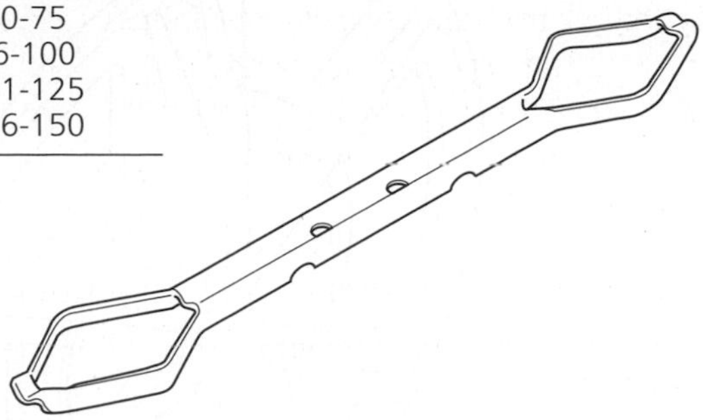

Application
Cavity wall tie suitable for use in the
construction of buildings of any height

Fig 4.193 **Heavy duty tie**

Length (mm)	Cavity (mm)
200	50-75
225	76-100

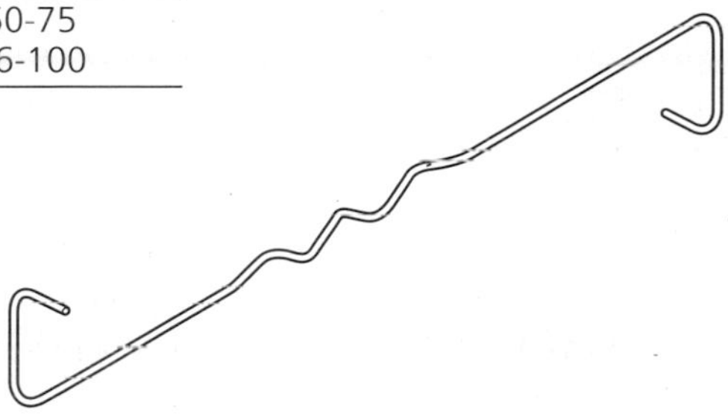

Application
Cavity wall tie suitable for use in the
construction of houses not greater than
10 metres in height

Fig 4.194 **Housing tie**

Length (mm)	Cavity (mm)
200	50-75
225	76-100

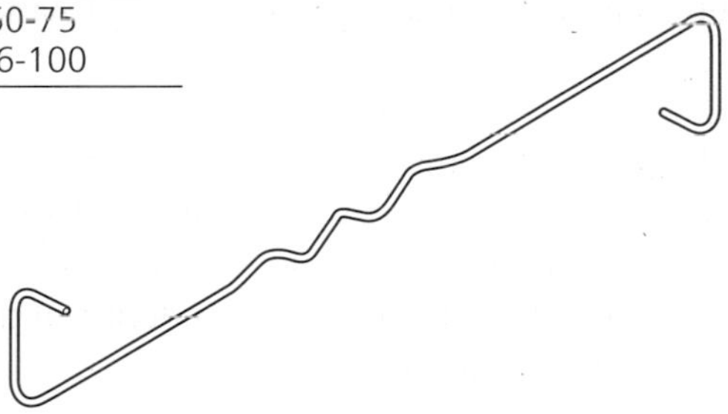

Application
Cavity wall tie suitable for use in the
construction of houses and small
commercial developments not greater
than 15 metres in height

Fig 4.195 **General purpose tie**

Fig 4.196 Insulation retaining clip

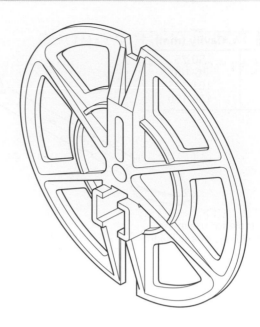

Fixing Devices for Frames 4.11

Door and Window Frames

There is a choice of procedure in the fixing methods used where door and window frames are concerned. They may be placed in position with temporary braces to hold them while the bricklayer carries out his work, or the brick or blockwork may be built and the frames put in afterwards.

In the former case, frame anchors are screwed to the frame and the fish tail ends built into the mortar joints. In the latter, wooden plugs are fixed into spaces between bricks, so as to provide a hold for screws or nails.

Internal door frames are usually left until the outer shell of the building and the joists are fixed into place. The internal door frames are then fixed and used as a guide for the position of partition walls. If the partition walls are built independently, a thinner door frame known as a lining is used.

Therefore frames may be fixed either:

- As the walling is being built, or
- After the walling has been completed.

Method for Fixing Frames During Construction

Door Linings or Casings

These are lightweight internal frames that can be fixed into position by nailing through the jambs into wooden pads, plastic plugs, fixing blocks or directly into the timber.

Fixing Blocks and Pads

Fixing blocks and pads are usually built into the door opening during construction by the bricklayer. Three or four blocks will be needed for each jamb.

Fixing a Door Frame

The door opening should be built with a clearance of approximately 20 mm so that the door linings fit loosely and can easily be plumbed and aligned with the walls.

As the door opening is built with clearance allowed, packing will need to be placed between the lining and the brick or blockwork. Plastic plugs can then be placed into the masonry and the lining plumbed in and squared.

The frame can now be placed into the opening and checked for plumb and level. It is good practice to make a temporary fixing at the top and bottom of each jamb, leaving the fixings protruding.

The frame should now be checked for accuracy and position. Any adjustment can be made before the frame is finally fixed.

Fixing Frames after Construction Has Taken Place

Fixing Devices for Blockwork

The cellular structure of aircrete blocks, comprising millions of non-connecting air cells provides a good fixing base without the problems normally associated with either dense materials, stud partitions or hollow partitions. However, care must be taken if satisfactory results are to be achieved. The correct length of nail or screw must be selected depending on whether standard blocks or the higher insulation blocks are used. In addition most of the fixing manufacturers have produced ranges of fixings especially to suit light or heavyweight fixings into blocks.

> Points to note
>
> **Fixings**: These may be screws, nails or patent fixing devices as previously described.
>
> **Methods of Fixing**: Should be neat and not spoil the appearance of the finished work.
>
> **Accuracy**: Care must be taken to make sure that all members are fixed plumb, level, square and straight.
>
> **Allowance**: Must be made when fixing members to unplastered walls. The plasterer will use the joiner's work as a guide to his finished plasterwork.

Fixings to Gable End Walls

To anchor pitched roofs and gable end walls, use 30 mm × 5 mm restraint straps which should extend under three rafters and be spaced at intervals no greater than 2 m (see Figure 4.197).

The steel straps in effect keep the gable end firm.

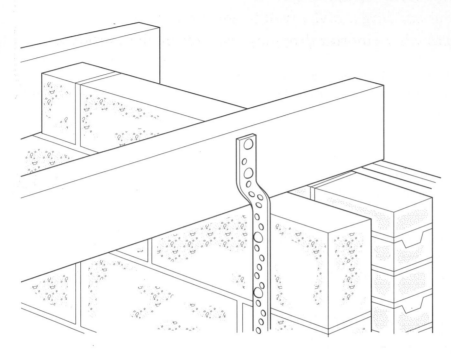

RESTRAINT STRAPS PROVIDE A SECURE ANCHOR IN ALMOST ANY SITUATION such as anchoring joists to walls, trussed rafters, flat roofs, pitched roofs and gable ends, etc.

Manufactured from
Pre-galvanized strip mild steel

Recommended fixings for horizontal straps   No. 12 x 50 mm plated wood screws or 3.35 mm diameter x 75 mm corrosion-resistant nails

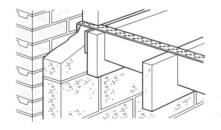 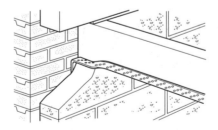 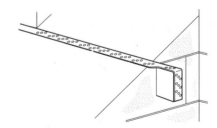

Floor level straps – joists parallel to wall. 30 mm x 5 mm restraint straps should be carried over 3 joists and spaced at intervals not exceeding 2 m

Floor level straps – joists perpendicular to wall. 30 mm x 5 mm restraint straps

Anchoring pitched roof and gable end, 30 mm x 5 mm restraint straps should extend under 3 rafters and be spaced at intervals not exceeding 2 m

 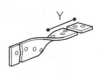 

H Type   T Type   F Type   L Type   LT Type

Fig 4.197 **Restraint straps anchoring a gable wall to rafters**

❶ Name three materials that wall ties are made from.

❷ What is the vertical spacing of wall ties around openings?

❸ What is the minimum size that wall ties should be bedded into each leaf of the cavity wall?

❹ Sketch one way of building a cavity wall below ground level.

❺ Name three places where mortar droppings can accumulate inside a cavity.

Lintels

4.12

Definition – A lintel is a structural member spanning an opening in a wall.

Lintels are introduced into the construction of a wall to bridge over an opening at a required level and support the wall above, thereby transferring its weight to the piers on which the lintel rests. The use of a lintel is the simplest method of carrying a load over an opening, the lintel being made of steel, reinforced concrete, stone or brick.

Lintels, when loaded, tend to bend and when the amount of bending reaches a certain limit fracture occurs; steel may be subjected to greater bending than brick, stone or plain concrete before fracturing. But the dimensions of a lintel have some effect upon the amount of bending; slender proportions will be attendant with excess bending. Since lintels must not noticeably defect, or bend, the proportions should be such as will provide sufficient stiffness or resistance to bending.

Types of Lintels

Steel Lintels

Domestic properties nowadays almost invariably use pre-fabricated steel lintels. These are manufactured in a great variety of shapes and sizes to suit the different designs of building. This type of lintel has great advantages in terms of lightness, strength and ease of use.

Cavity Wall Lintel

These are suitable for most domestic, small commercial developments and framed structures. They come supplied with insulation and metal lathing to provide a plaster key. Housing lintels require a separate dpc (see Figure 4.198).

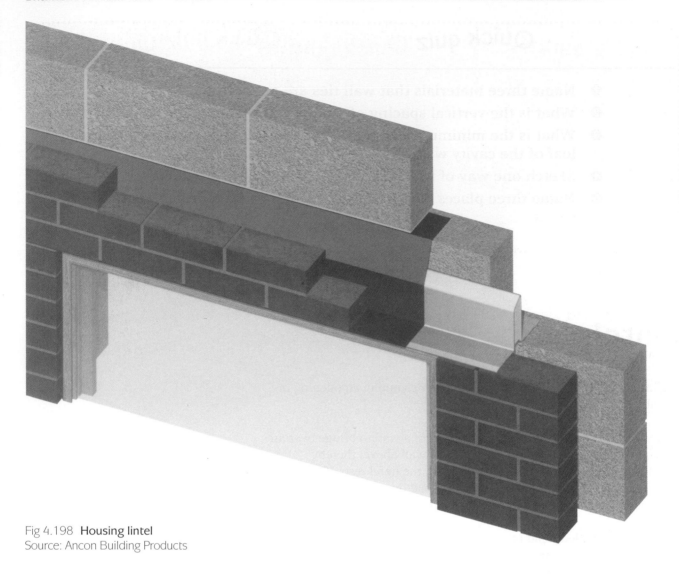

Fig 4.198 **Housing lintel**
Source: Ancon Building Products

Unilintels

Unilintels are designed for the heavy duty loading conditions often found in commercial developments and have the top flange built into the inner leaf. They come complete with metal lathing to provide a plaster key and can be used with a separate dpc (see Figure 4.199).

Single Wall Lintels and Angle Lintels

These lintels carry a single leaf, usually the external leaf, of a cavity wall. The lintel can be supplied with lips to either leg if required. These lintels require a separate dpc (see Figure. 4.200).

Eaves Lintels

Eaves lintels are built into the inner leaf at eaves level. Metal lathing is welded to the underside to provide a plaster key (see Figure 4.201).

Timber and Steel Frame Lintels

These lintels are designed to support the external brickwork over openings in timber or steel framed buildings. Timber frame lintels are

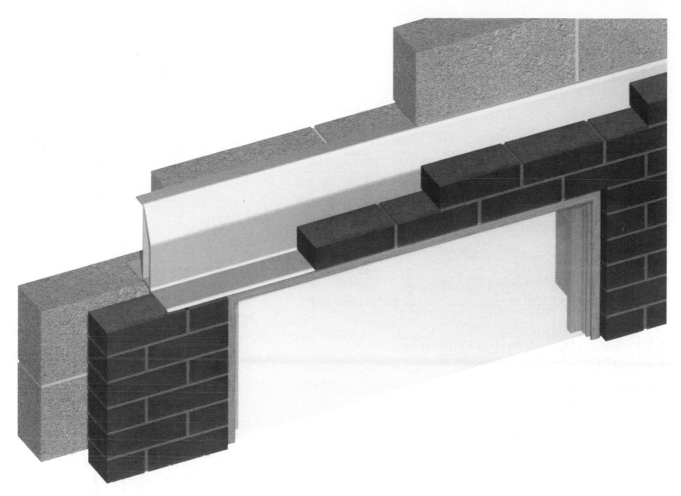

Fig 4.199 **Unilintel**
Source: Ancon Building Products

supplied with retaining clips and should be used with a separate dpc
(see Figure 4.202).

Custom Lintels

These lintels can be supplied for complex features such as corbels and
other architectural details. Special cranked, bay, corner and cantilevered
corners are available in addition to the following arch shapes: Segmental
arch, Semi-circular arch, Apex arch, Gothic arch, Flat top arch and
Double arch.

Most lintel manufacturers will offer advice on the most appropriate lintel
or alternative method of supporting masonry.

Requirements of Lintels

- A lintel has to carry weight as well as span a gap
- Anything that must carry weight has to be strong
- A lintel must also be durable if it is to form part of a building which is
  required to last

Single Leaf Lintels/Angle Lintels

These lintels carry a single leaf, usually the external leaf, of a cavity wall. The lintel can be supplied with lips to either leg if required. Single leaf lintels require a separate dpc.

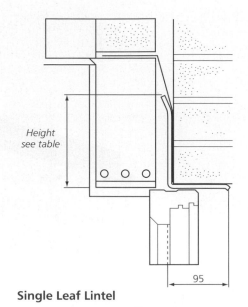

Single Leaf Lintel

Outer leaf (mm)	Ref.	Height (mm)	Gauge (mm)	1xx (cm^2)	2xx (cm^2)	Length (mm)	SWL (kN)
	SL31	95	3	50.7	7.2	750-1800	4
	SL41	95	4	66.5	9.5	750-2400	6
	SL32	150	3	175.4	17.1	750-2400	8
95-120	SL42	150	4	231.2	22.6	750-2400	12
						2550-3300	10
	SL33	200	3	379.7	29.1	750-2400	15
						2550-3300	12
	SL43	200	4	502.5	38.6	750-2400	20
						2550-3300	14
	SL53	200	5	622.3	48.0	750-1800	30
						1950-3300	26

Channel Lintels

Designed to fit solid walls up to 225 mm wide, the Channel Lintel can be supplied with welded metal lathing on any side to provide a plaster key.

Channel Lintel

Width 100 mm

Ref.	Height (mm)	Gauge (mm)	1xx (cm^2)	2xx (cm^2)	Length (mm)	SWL (kN)
SC322	155	3.0	328.4	37.3	750-1500	20
SC422	155	4.0	437.8	49.7	1650-2100	20
SC522	155	5.0	547.3	62.2	2250-3000	20
SC332	233	3.0	837.7	65.4	750-1500	20
SC432	233	4.0	1117.0	87.2	1650-2100	30
SC532	233	5.0	1396.2	109.1	2250-3000	40

RNote: Channel Lintels

These lintels have been tested using composite action with surrounding masonry to BS 5628, and should be suitably restrained during construction

Fig 4.200 Single leaf lintel and tables

- Corrosion must be avoided
- The appearance of the lintel must be considered
- A lintel must meet all relevant Building and Fire regulations.

Lintel Installation and Good Site Practice

As steel lintels are by far the most commonly used lintel used in the construction industry within the UK, it will be useful to describe the correct method of installation.

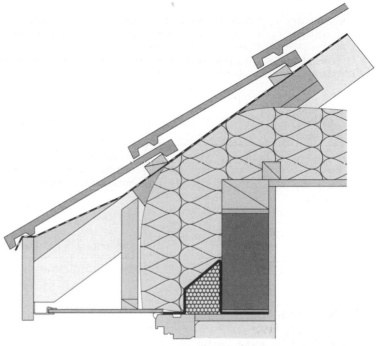

Fig 4.201 **Eaves lintel**
Source: Catnic

Provide for a nominal end bearing of 150 mm at each end of the lintel, as illustrated in Figure 4.203 in order to achieve the maximum safe working load.

Ensure that the lintel is fully bedded on bricklaying mortar.

Ensure that the lintel is level along its length.

In cavity walls, raise the inner and outer leaves supported by the lintel together.

Ensure that the lintel is level along its width, as illustrated in Figure 4.204.

Ensure that any masonry overhang does not exceed 25 mm.

Ensure that all wall dimensions are correct.

Masonry above lintels should be allowed to cure before applying floor or roof loads.

Isometric view of a typical timber and steel frame lintel over window

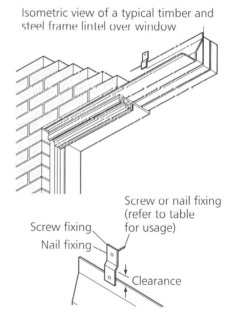

Screw or nail fixing
(refer to table for usage)

Screw fixing

Nail fixing

Clearance

Points to note Always install a separate damp proof course in severe exposure conditions.

Ensure that point loads are not applied directly to the flanges of lintels.

Locate the window or door frame so that the drip on the front of the lintel projects forward of the drip on the front of the frame.

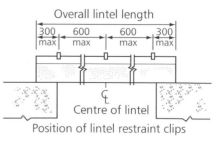

Overall lintel length

| 300 max | 600 max | 600 max | 300 max |

Centre of lintel

Position of lintel restraint clips

Fig 4.202 **Timber frame lintel**

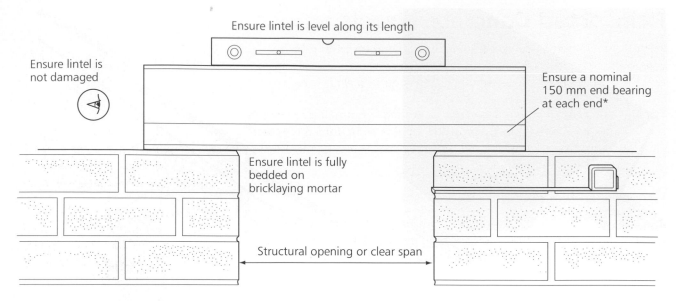

Ensure lintel is level along its length

Ensure lintel is not damaged

Ensure a nominal 150 mm end bearing at each end*

Ensure lintel is fully bedded on bricklaying mortar

Structural opening or clear span

Fig 4.203 **Lintel being installed**

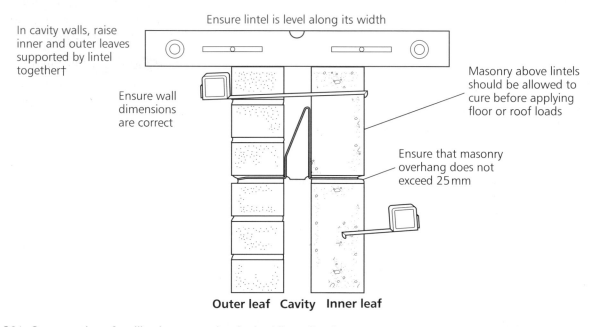

Ensure lintel is level along its width

In cavity walls, raise inner and outer leaves supported by lintel together†

Ensure wall dimensions are correct

Masonry above lintels should be allowed to cure before applying floor or roof loads

Ensure that masonry overhang does not exceed 25 mm

Outer leaf   Cavity   Inner leaf

Fig 4.204 **Cross-section of walling in preparation for bedding a lintel**

Lintel Installation and Poor Site Practices

Never use damaged lintels.

On no account cut down lintels from their manufactured lengths.

Do not apply point loads without prior consultation with a structural engineer.

Reinforced Concrete Lintels

The use of reinforced concrete lintels is very common within the construction industry. They have many advantages over other forms of lintel, chief of which is its adaptability to any desired shape or size.

A lintel supporting a load tends to sag, from this fact it will readily seen that the concrete in the upper part of the lintel is being forced together causing compression, while that on the lower part is being pulled apart or placed in a state of tension.

Rule

It is a rule that concrete, though strong in compression, is very weak in tension and, for this reason, steel rods are placed into the lower part of the lintel to absorb the tension and provide the needed strength. The number and size of the rods used, and the depth of the lintel, are dependent on the span and the load to be carried.

All concrete lintels are made by placing wet concrete in a timber or metal mould of the required size, the sides of the mould being removed when the concrete has set. This process is known as casting; there are two general methods, which are as follows:

Pre-casting

Lintels made this way are usually cast before building takes place, their size being limited, because of the difficulty in handling heavy and awkward loads. Advantage should be taken of this method wherever possible as it reduces any delays in the building process to a minimum.

Casting *in situ*

Lintels cast in the position they are to take in the building are said to be cast *in situ*, this being the favoured method used for all large lintels. Temporary form-work or timber or metal shuttering is erected in the required position, care being taken to ensure that it is rigid and will not distort as the concrete is placed into position.

Disadvantages

The main disadvantage of this form of construction is the necessity to leave sections of the work above the lintel unfinished until the concrete has set.

Rolled Steel Joist

Rolled steel joists are mainly used for commercial and industrial premises. They are manufactured in suitable sizes to suit the needs of commercial and industrial clients. RSJs have the strength and solidity required for industrial construction, and can be pre-drilled and bolted to other steel structures in a short space of time.

Stone Lintels

Stone lintels are confined usually to buildings built or faced with stone. They may be in one length, but more often are in three sections, assistance being given by a reinforced concrete lintel placed behind it. If the lintel is used on a brick clad building, then a relieving arch is usually placed over it to disperse the load.

Brick Lintels

Modern construction technology has introduced the use of the brick lintel or, as it is more commonly known, the soldier arch. The setting out and building of a soldier arch is an important part of the bricklayer's work for, although it consists only of bricks laid on end, it calls for great skill, to produce an arch that will not offend the eye.

A true arch is formed of a series of bricks that have been cut to a wedge shape which tend to tighten under load: it is therefore self-supporting. A soldier arch cannot be included under this heading as it must be provided with some form of support. Although, for small spans the adhesive and shear properties of a good mortar will often provide the necessary strength as for instance in a welsh arch (see Figure 4.205). It is more common, however, to support the underside of the arch upon a steel lintel built into the jambs.

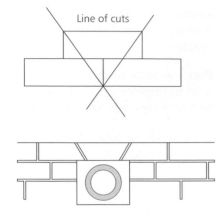

Line of cuts

Fig 4.205 **Welsh arch**
Source: CITB-ConstructionSkills. Training Workbook, 1994.

Quick quiz Quick quiz Quick quiz Quick quiz Quick quiz

❶ How do you know which is the top of a concrete lintel?

❷ Draw a sectional detail of a steel lintel bridging an opening.

❸ Describe the difference between a precast concrete lintel and one cast *in situ*.

❹ Why are steel rods cast into a concrete lintel?

❺ List three types of steel lintel.

Full and Partial Fill Insulation   4.13

Cavity insulation can be classified under two headings:

1. Full fill
2. Partial fill.

Both these methods satisfy the requirements of Approved Document L of the Building Regulations.

Full Fill Insulation

This can be achieved by building in insulation batts as work proceeds or by filling the cavity with foam or granules on completion of the work.

Care is required when considering a fully filled cavity since this can increase the likelihood of water penetration. When choosing an insulant for this application, reference should be made to the relevant British Standards.

Early consultation with a cavity fill manufacturer is advisable, particularly in relation to exposure of the site. Standards of workmanship and site supervision are crucial, as there is no residual cavity to prevent rain penetrating across to the inner leaf, as illustrated in Figure 4.206.

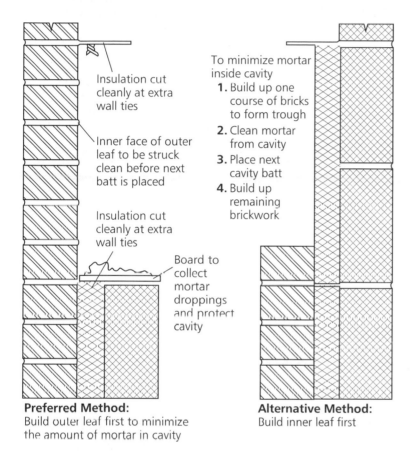

Insulation cut cleanly at extra wall ties

Inner face of outer leaf to be struck clean before next batt is placed

Insulation cut cleanly at extra wall ties

Board to collect mortar droppings and protect cavity

To minimize mortar inside cavity
1. Build up one course of bricks to form trough
2. Clean mortar from cavity
3. Place next cavity batt
4. Build up remaining brickwork

Preferred Method:
Build outer leaf first to minimize the amount of mortar in cavity

Alternative Method:
Build inner leaf first

Fig 4.206 **Full fill cavity**

Partial Fill Insulation

In partially filled cavity wall construction, a clear cavity of not less than 50 mm must be maintained in order to avoid bridging and to prevent the penetration of wind driven rain.

In order to accommodate the insulation and provide the required residual cavity, longer wall ties may be required together with special clips to fix the insulant securely to the inner leaf, as illustrated in Figure 4.207.

Insertion of an insulant within a cavity does not affect the durability of the external brickwork, but to reduce the risk of rain penetration to the internal skin, mortar joints should be completely filled, using only curved recessed or weather struck joints.

> Points to note

Complete filling of a normal 50 to 70 mm wall cavity with insulant can considerably increase the risk of rain penetration.

The type of insulant and the exposure of the site should be assessed carefully.

Consideration of increasing the cavity width may be appropriate in order to meet thermal and rain resistance requirements.

Fig 4.207 Partial fill cavity with wall restraint clips

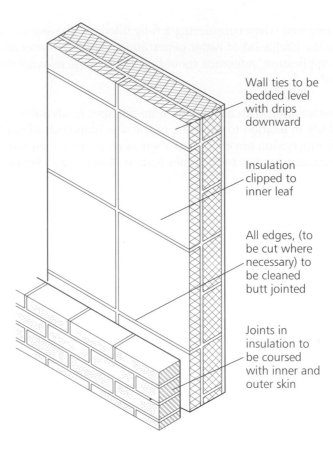

Wall ties to be bedded level with drips downward

Insulation clipped to inner leaf

All edges, (to be cut where necessary) to be cleaned butt jointed

Joints in insulation to be coursed with inner and outer skin

key terms

U value – The *U* value is a measurement of the heat loss through a wall, roof or floor. The lower the *U* Value the better the insulation.

K value – The *K* value, or thermal conductivity value, is used in calculating the *U* value of brickwork construction.

Thermal Conductivity – The measure of the ability of a material to transmit heat.

Elemental Method – The Elemental Method considers the performance of each aspect of the building individually.

Insulation Batt – Rectangular unit of rigid insulation material of uniform thickness used to partially fill the air space in a cavity wall.

Building Regulation Requirements

Approved Document L of the Building Regulations requires external cavity walls to give a *U* value of 0.35 W/m^2· *K* when using the Elemental Method of determination. This can easily be achieved with the range of insulants available. Examples of cavity wall construction with the resultant *U* values are shown in Figure 4.208.

One of the aims of the Building Regulations is to improve the energy efficiency of all new buildings and existing buildings, when they can be extended or altered. The key objectives can be summarized as follows:

■ Reduce carbon dioxide (CO_2) emissions

■ Improve design flexibility within the build process

■ Minimize technical risk

■ Avoid excessive cost.

Please Note: *U* Values and *K* values are rather abstract ideas and require explaining thoroughly by your tutor in order to be fully grasped.

THERMAL INSULATION

U-value	Outer Leaf (Brick Type & Density)	Cavity Insulation Examples	Inner Leaf – Type & Thermal Conductivity 'k' value)	Finish
0.27	Clay Facing Bricks up to and including 2000 kg/m^3	50 mm Clear Cavity	100 mm Lightweight block (0.11 k)	50 mm dry lining board on dabs (2.28 R)
0.28	Clay Facing Bricks up to and including 2000 kg/m^3	550 mm EPS Board (0.026 k) in 100 mm cavity	100 mm Lightweight block (0.11 k)	13 mm plasterboard on dabs
0.28	Clay Facing Bricks up to and including 2000 kg/m^3	50 mm Clear Cavity 48 mm Polyisocyanurate boards (0.019 k)	100 mm Medium density block (0.19 k)	13 mm plasterboard on dabs
0.28	Clay Facing Bricks up to and including 2000 kg/m^3	60 mm EPS (0.033 k) in 100 mm cavity	150 mm Lightweight block (0.11 k)	13 mm plasterboard on dabs
0.30	Clay Facing Bricks 1400 kg/m^3	50 mm Clear Cavity 50 mm Polyisocyanurate boards (0.019 k)	Handmade Facing (0.38 k)	Fair face
0.30	Clay Facing Bricks up to and including 2000 kg/m^3	50 mm Clear Cavity	100 mm Medium density block (0.19 k)	50 mm dry lining board on dabs (2.28 R)
0.30	Clay Facing Bricks up to and including 2000 kg/m^3	Bubble insulation in 60 mm Cavity NHBC require 75 mm	150 mm Lightweight block (0.11 k)	13 mm plasterboard on dabs
0.30	Stock Brick 1500 kg/m^3	50 mm Injected foam (0.018 k)	Clay Common (0.50 k)	13 mm plasterboard on dabs
0.32	Clay Facing Bricks up to and including 2000 kg/m^3	60 mm EPS board (0.033 k) in 100 mm cavity	100 mm Lightweight block (0.11 k)	13 mm plasterboard on dabs
0.33	Clay Facing Bricks up to and including 2000 kg/m^3	50 mm Epsx Board (0.032 k) in 100 mm cavity	100 mm Lightweight block (0.11 k)	13 mm plasterboard on dabs
0.34	Clay Facing Bricks 1400 kg/m^3	50 mm Clear Cavity 50 mm Insulation batts (0.024 k)	Handmade Facing (0.38 k)	Fair face
0.34	Clay Facing Bricks up to and including 2000 kg/m^3	Bubble insulation in 60 mm Cavity NHBC require 75 mm	100 mm Lightweight block (0.11 k)	13 mm plasterboard on dabs
0.34	Clay Facing Bricks up to and including 2000 kg/m^3	50 mm Clear Cavity 38 mm Polyisocyanurate boards (0.019 k)	100 mm Medium density block (0.19 k)	13 mm plasterboard on dabs
0.35	Clay Facing Bricks up to and including 2000 kg/m^3	50 mm Clear Cavity	100 mm Medium density block (0.17 k)	40 mm dry lining board on dabs (1.73R)
0.38	Clay Facing Bricks 1700 kg/m^3	75 mm Mineral Wool batts (0.036 k)	100 mm Heavyweight Block (1.12 k)	13 mm plasterboard on dabs
0.40	Handmade Facing 1400 kg/m^3	50 mm Clear Cavity 30 mm Phenolic foam boards (0.018 k)	Handmade Facing (0.38 k)	Fair Face
0.40	Stock Brick 1400 kg/m^3	50 mm Clear Cavity 50 mm cellular glass (0.048 k)	100 mm Lightweight block (0.11 k)	13 mm plasterboard on dabs
0.41	Clay Facing Bricks 1700 kg/m^3	65 mm Mineral Wool batts (0.036 k)	Clay Common (0.50 k)	13 mm plasterboard on dabs
0.42	Stock Brick 1500 kg/m^3	75 mm fibre boards (0.040k)	Clay Common (0.50 k)	13 mm plasterboard on dabs
0.43	Clay Facing Bricks 1600 kg/m^3	50 mm Clear Cavity	150 Lightweight Block (0.11 k)	13 mm plasterboard on dabs

Fig 4.208 **Cavity wall construction with resultant *U* valves**

Always maintain the specified cavity, placing insulation batts against the inner leaf and secure them with specially designated wall tie clips.

Where a clear airspace of a minimum of 50 mm is maintained, partial fill insulation does not increase the risk of rain penetration and can therefore be recommended.

Where cavity fill insulation is used the damp proof cavity tray must be provided with stop ends to prevent water running into the cavity and wetting the insulation.

Where batts butt up to reveals and lintel bearings they must be cut accurately to ensure no cold spots.

Where intermediate wall ties occur at reveals the batts can be cut to allow the tie to pass neatly through.

Batts must be closely jointed as condensation will form where gaps appear.

Note: Achieving good workmanship is essential when placing insulation materials.

The following points are offered for guidance when handling insulation boards of various types.

Always carry boards on edge – two men to a board.

Place boards down on their long edge before turning flat.

Use a platform or pallet to support boards when mechanically handling.

Do not carry boards horizontally.

Do not drag boards over each other.

Do not store boards outside unless on a level platform, clear of the ground and securely covered with an anchored polythene sheet or tarpaulin.

Sound Insulation

The sound insulation of a solid masonry wall is related principally to its weight. For cavity walls, sound insulation is additionally related to the width of the cavity insulation and the rigidity and spacing of wall ties.

It must be remembered that the smallest crack that provides an air passage will greatly reduce sound insulation. Good workmanship is necessary to ensure that all perpend joints are fully filled, that bricks are laid frog up and that plastering is of a high standard.

Of equal importance during the design stage is the reduction of flanking transmission and particular care is therefore necessary where floors are continued through separating walls and in detailing window and door openings.

Joints in Brick and Blockwork

All joints between bricks and blocks should be fully filled. Deep furrows in bed joints and tipped and tailed perpends will let additional water pass through the brick and blockwork and are not recommended.

Unless otherwise stated, mortar joints should be finished with a curved, recessed or weather struck joint. Jointing as the work proceeds is by far the best practice.

Quick quiz Quick quiz Quick quiz Quick quiz Quick quiz

❶ What is a *U* value?

❷ What are the two headings that cavity insulation can be classified under?

❸ Name three different types of full fill insulation.

❹ What type of full fill insulation does a bricklayer usually use?

❺ Which leaf of a cavity wall should partial fill batts be fixed to?

Positioning of Damp-proof Barriers ▦ 4.14

Frost rarely penetrates more than a few millimetres below the finished ground level, so neither bricks nor mortar are at risk from frost action below ground level.

The courses of the outer leaf of brickwork immediately above and below finished ground level are subject to more demanding conditions. If surface water is drained away from the brickwork in these conditions, then the majority of the facing bricks can be used with confidence.

The Building Regulations state that no wall or pier shall permit the passage of moisture from the ground to the inner surface of the building that would be harmfully affected by such moisture.

The horizontal DPC must be built in a full 150 mm above finished ground level. This is to prevent the surrounding ground building up and allowing the earth's moisture to bypass the DPC. Any damp proof membrane under adjoining floor slabs should be built into the

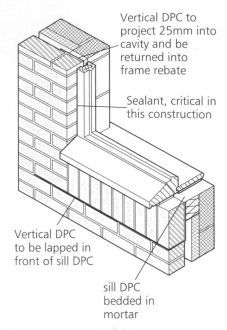

Vertical DPC to project 25mm into cavity and be returned into frame rebate

Sealant, critical in this construction

Vertical DPC to be lapped in front of sill DPC

sill DPC bedded in mortar

Fig 4.209 **Window opening with flush jambs**

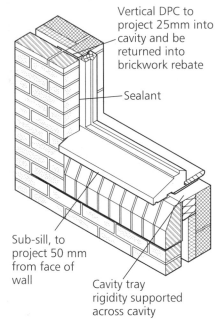

Vertical DPC to project 25mm into cavity and be returned into brickwork rebate

Sealant

Sub-sill, to project 50 mm from face of wall

Cavity tray rigidity supported across cavity

Fig 4.210 **Window with rebated jambs**

horizontal DPC. Where the DPC has to be joined on the length of the wall and at a junction, a minimum lap of 100 mm should be provided.

At ground level this can be achieved by building in a non-absorbent layer of material. This is called a damp proof course (DPC).

When it is not possible to drain surface water away from the brickwork, it is advisable to use a frost-resistant brick in the two courses above and the one below, finished ground level. This is necessary for the outer leaf only.

On sloping sites, the brickwork between ground level and the damp proof course may act as a retaining wall. To prevent water migrating into the brickwork, it is essential to apply water-proofing treatment to the face of the brickwork which comes into contact with the retained material.

The range of facing and common bricks produced by the majority of brick manufacturers can be used below the damp proof course and in foundations, with the exception of the examples just described. The bricks are not attacked by sulphates which may exist in the ground water or subsoil, so their durability under these conditions is not an issue.

Mortars, however, can be attacked by sulphates. When they are known, or thought, to occur in the ground water or subsoil, it is best not to use ordinary Portland cement. Instead it is good practice to use sulphate-resisting cement in a mortar not weaker than those shown in the section dealing with mortar mix proportions.

Damp proof courses and their location within certain features of a building are shown in Figures 4.209 to 4.212.

Placing Damp-proof Barriers

- Bed flexible damp proof barriers on fresh, smooth mortar
- Always lap damp proof barriers by a minimum of 100 mm
- Do not cover the exposed edge of damp proof barriers with mortar or render
- Do not allow damp proof barriers to project into cavities
- Always use the correct type of damp proof barrier for the type of job undertaken.

Bedding Damp Proof Courses

Care must be taken to ensure flexible DPCs do not get damaged during the building in process and when the load of the wall is placed on them.

The DPC should be sandwiched between two thin mortar beds, ensuring that there are no stones or debris in the mortar as this could puncture the DPC when the load of the wall is applied.

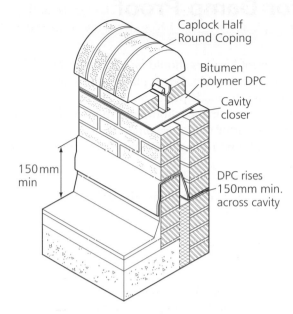

Caplock Half
Round Coping

Bitumen
polymer DPC

Cavity
closer

150 mm
min

DPC rises
150mm min.
across cavity

Fig 4.211 **Parapet wall**

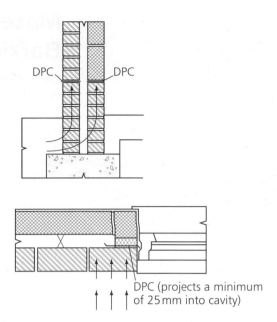

DPC   DPC

DPC (projects a minimum
of 25 mm into cavity)

Fig 4.212 **Rising and horizontal damp protection**

Damp-proof Barriers

4.15

Definition and purpose – A damp proof barrier is a continuous layer of damp resisting material, the chief object of which is to protect the super-structure of a building against dampness.

Most building materials are liable to be adversely affected by dampness, consequently, it is essential to provide a suitable means of damp prevention. In addition, the health of the occupants of a damp building may become seriously affected by the conditions that may arise out of dampness.

Prevention of Dampness

The damp proofing of a wall near its base is undertaken to prevent the rise of dampness, which may be drawn from the ground, into the brick or blockwork forming the foundation walling of the building. The placing of a suitable damp proof course horizontally in a wall at a level of 150 mm above the adjoining ground level usually fulfils the above requirements.

Since it is essential to protect floors and floor timbers against dampness, it may be found necessary to provide damp proof membranes at different levels and also in vertical positions around the building.

Materials for Damp Proof Barriers

Material for use in damp proof barriers should be permanently impervious to moisture and be durable. When placed in the wall it should be capable of resisting the loads put upon it. These loads which tend to cause crushing or other damage, should not induce the wall to develop a sliding action. The latter may arise when the damp proofing material has a smooth surface and the wall is subjected to horizontal or inclined thrusts.

Suitable damp proof barriers may be formed by the proper use of the following materials.

Lead-core Reinforced DPC

A lead-core reinforced damp proof course suitable for inclusion in brick, block, stone or concrete walls of both solid and cavity construction. The dpc is composed of a continuous core of lead reinforced with a tough, high quality Hessian. These layers are coated with a polymer modified bitumen and surfaced on both sides with a silica sand finish.

It can be used as a dpc in all masonry walls of both solid and cavity construction. It is particularly suitable for horizontal and cavity tray situations.

Pitch Polymer Damp Proof Course.

An extremely versatile, high performance, pitch polymer, damp proof course. When used alone or in conjunction with self-adhesive waterproof membrane, a continuous barrier against water and vapour can be formed.

Suitable for inclusion in brick, block stone or concrete walls of both solid and cavity construction and in horizontal, vertical, stepped and cavity tray situations, as well as in beam and block flooring.

Liquid Waterproofing Membrane

A rubberized bitumen emulsion that dries to form a durable elastic waterproof membrane for floors, walls and roofs. Usually formulated to be solvent free and to avoid the use of hazardous components such as flammable solvents and coal tar. Liquid waterproofing is a cold applied high performance membrane, which when fully dry forms an elastic coating able to accommodate minor structural movements.

Suitable for use on the following building materials :

Floors – concrete and sand and cement construction

Walls – brick, block and concrete

Roofs – Mastic asphalt, felt, fibre cement, corrugated iron, slates and so on.

Protection Board

Designed as an important tanking accessory for use with damp proof membranes to meet the tanking requirements of the specifier and contractor. Protection board is an acrylic lacquer coated tough, bitumen impregnated cellulose board, used for the protection of waterproof membranes against damage.

Designed to protect both self adhesive sheet waterproofing membranes in both horizontal and vertical applications

Self Adhesive Damp Proof Membrane

Tanking is a critical area of construction where if failure occurs, it can result in disruption in the use of the building and also expensive remedial work. This tough, self-adhesive waterproofing membrane system can be used on floors as a damp proof membrane and in solid concrete floors. It can also be used in basements as a vertical and horizontal membrane and in internal and external tanking situations.

Engineering Bricks

Two or more courses of engineering bricks suitably bonded and properly bedded in cement mortar.

The above forms of damp proof course materials may be divided into two groups according to their nature:

- Flexible
- Rigid.

The lead, pitch polymer, liquid membrane and self-adhesive membrane constitute the flexible type while the dry lining protection board and engineering bricks form the rigid type.

Flexibility is desirable where a damp proof course requires to be shaped into a given form and also where it is required to withstand, without fracture, the effect of settlement. Of the rigid type, those formed with such materials as engineering bricks bedded in suitable mortar are capable of withstanding intense pressure, while being extremely durable and practically impervious to moisture. In addition, it is possible to obtain a satisfactory key between the damp proof course and the brick or blockwork to prevent possible sliding action.

key terms

Tanking – Waterproofing horizontally and vertically, that is, in the form of a tank.

Quick quiz Quick quiz Quick quiz Quick quiz Quick quiz

❶ What do the letters DPC stand for?
❷ Name four types of flexible DPC.
❸ Name two types of rigid DPC.
❹ What is the minimum lap required when joining two pieces of DPC?
❺ Name three materials that DPC can be made from.

Information on Hand tools

For further information about bricklaying and other tools, why not visit the websites of the better known manufacturers and suppliers?

Information on Health and Safety

For further information on all aspects of health and safety not only for power tools but for all aspects of safety, contact the Health and Safety Executive.

Health and Safety Executive

www.hsebooks.co.uk

Health and Safety Executive priced and free publications are available by mail order from: HSE Books, PO Box 1999, Sudbury, Suffolk CO10 6FS. Telephone: 01787 881165; Fax: 01787 313995.

HSE priced publications are available from good booksellers or why not visit their website and order on-line.

Information on Power Tools

For further information about power tools, why not contact the websites of the better known manufacturers and suppliers?

Information on Mortar Mixing Machines

For further information about mortar mixing machines, why not visit the websites of the better known manufacturers and suppliers?

Information on Bricks

For further information about bricks and other associated products why not visit the websites of the better known manufacturers and suppliers? Or the following?

The Brick Development Association

www.brick.org.uk

Brick Information Service – 09068 615290.

The Brick Development Association provides a comprehensive range of advice and information on every aspect of brick construction. They are dedicated to promoting the use of brickwork in our environment in the most effective and attractive way. The brick Development Association also offers a comprehensive consultancy service supported by a wide range of publications and online advice either through professional experts on the phone or via their website.

Information on Blocks

For further information about blocks and other associated products, why not visit the websites of the better known manufacturers and suppliers? Or the following?

Concrete Block Association (CBA)

www.cba–blocks.org.uk

The CBA is the trade body that represents manufacturers of aggregate concrete building blocks in Great Britain. The CBA represents an industry of some 50 manufacturers producing around 60 million square metres of concrete blocks per year from over 100 block plants nationwide.

Information on the Thin Joint Blockwork System

For further information about the thin joint blockwork system, why not visit the websites of the better known manufacturers and suppliers?

Information on Mortars, Cements and Limes

For further information about mortars, cements and limes, why not visit the websites of the better known manufacturers and suppliers? Or the following?

Mortar Industry Association

www.mortar.org.uk

Information on Plasticizers and Accelerators

For further information about plasticizers and accelerators, why not visit the websites of the better known manufacturers and suppliers?

Information on Factory Produced Mortars

For further information on factory produced mortars and other associated products, why not visit the websites of the better known manufacturers and suppliers? Or the following?

Mortar Industry Association

www.mortar.org.uk

The Mortar Industry Association since its inception in 1971 has been providing independent advice and technical support to specifiers and users of mortars. Today the association is active in the fields of standardization, the provision of technical data and the implementation of best practice in brick and blockwork specification. The association welcomes enquiries and a range of technical literature will be supplied on request.

Information on Bonding of Brickwork

For further information about the bonding of brickwork, try and obtain the following books which you will find are of great value to your studies.

W G Nash wrote a number of books on brickwork notably his series *Brickwork One, Two* and *Three*. Probably the best book for the new student would be *Brickwork One*, which in many ways is an introduction to bricklaying. There is an excellent chapter on bonding which is detailed and very informative. Maybe after you have read *Brickwork One* you might want to move on to the other books in the series, they are well worth a visit. The books (like this one) are published by Nelson Thornes.

Nelson Thornes

www.nelsonthornes.com

Information on Specific Bonds in Brickwork

For further information on specific bonds in brickwork, contact some of the brick manufacturers. They all have technical departments whose job it is to advise and help those planning the design of brick buildings.

Information on the Bonding of Blockwork

For further information on the bonding of blockwork why not consult the following text books, which give valuable information on the topic.

Peter Roper has written a book on the subject of blockwork entitled, *A Practical Guide to Blockwork*. As you might expect the book covers every aspect of blockwork from how blocks are made, properties and performance to site practice. The book is highly informative and extremely comprehensive. The book is published by International Thomson Publishing Limited.

Arnold

www.arnoldpublishers.com

The Brick Development Association (BDA) Guide to Successful Brickwork is a book now in its second edition that is probably second to none in its coverage of the craft of brickwork. Written by various authors the book has a clear and informative style. There is a detailed section on blockwork, entitled Blockwork Inner Leaves, Walls and Partitions written by R. Daniel. The book is published by Arnold.

Brick Development Association

www.brick.org.uk

Nelson Thornes

www.nelsonthornes.com

Bricklaying by W. G. Nash is for beginners to the craft but again is highly informative, and has a very useful chapter on blockwork. The publisher is Nelson Thornes.

CBA

www.cba–blocks.org.uk

The Concrete Block Association (CBA) produces a comprehensive range of technical datasheets that are freely available. By visiting the CBA website you can view, download or order copies on-line.

Information on Setting Out of Brickwork

For more information about the setting out of brickwork, obtain from the library or your tutor the set of training workbooks produced by the Construction Industry Training Board (CITB). These workbooks give a step by step guide to the various operations involved in the setting out of walls and small buildings.

The workbooks are just one of over 400 aids to training published by the CITB. Others include videos, tape slide programmes, open learning packages, books, manuals, training support packages, work sheets and so on.

For a free copy of the catalogue listing all CITB publications contact: CITB Publications, Bircham Newton, Kings Lynn, Norfolk, PE31 6RH, Telephone. 01485 577800. Or visit their website at www.citb.co.uk

Information on Pointing and Jointing

For further information about pointing and jointing, the following books are both informative, interesting and extremely useful to the student of brickwork.

Books

The BDA Guide to Successful Brickwork (Various authors). Publisher: Arnold. A member of the Hodder Headline Group. London.

This book has an excellent section about pointing and repointing written by R. Baldwin, which goes much further than I am able to do here in its detail and informative content. The book itself is a must for all those interested in brickwork

Creative Brickwork (Terry Knight on behalf of the Brick Development Association). Publisher: Arnold as before.

The book has an excellent section about mortar joints and how their design and specification affects the appearance of brickwork. The book also covers the history of bricks in the UK.

Design decisions that affect appearance. Site practices as they affect the appearance of brickwork. Weathering of brickwork and brick manufacture. Again this book is a must for all students and lovers of brickwork.

Trade Literature

There are many brochures, booklets and leaflets available that are usually free, which deal with all aspects of brickwork including pointing and jointing. In the second part of this chapter I have listed a wide range of manufacturers and suppliers who will be more than happy to supply you with the information that you may require.

Information on Movement Joints

Information and detailed advice on movement joints based on British Standard 5628: part 3 and British Standard 6213 are available from The Stationery Office (TSO) bookshops. There is also a wide range of technical literature and advice available from brick manufactures.

TSO shops

www.tso.co.uk

TSO shops are the ideal place to purchase a large range of official, regulatory and specialist publications. If you require a copy of the Building Regulations, the latest Health and Safety Executives guidelines or simply some guidance TSO staff will help you to find exactly what you need. In addition to stocking their own titles, TSO shops also offer a large range of titles from other authoritative organizations. They are a main stockist for Health and Safety Executive (HSE) publications. TSO shops carry around 1000 HSE titles. If you require a title they do not have in stock they will order it for you.

TSO shops are also official distributors for the British Standards Institution and offer a print on demand service that enables them to provide any British Standard immediately.

TSO shops are located in six major cities across the UK, London, Birmingham, Manchester, Cardiff, Edinburgh and Belfast, each with a mail order operation ensuring that you can purchase and receive publications conveniently wherever you are.

Information on the Effects of Weather

For further information about the effects of the weather on walling construction, why not visit the websites of the better known manufacturers and suppliers?

Information on Steel Reinforcement

For further information about steel reinforcement mesh see British Standard 5628: Part 2: 2000. British Standards are available at The Stationery Office bookshops.

TSO bookshops
www.tso.co.uk

Information on Wall Ties and Restraint Fixings

For further information on wall ties and restraint fixings, why not visit the websites of the better known manufacturers and suppliers?

Information on Tie Wires and Associated Products

For further information about tie wires and other associated products, why not visit the websites of the better known manufacturers and suppliers?

Information on Lateral Support at Roof Level

For more information on lateral support at roof level see the Building Regulations which are available in your local library or college library. Alternatively they can be purchased individually or as a set from The Stationery Office bookshops.

The Stationery Office Bookshops
www.tso.co.uk

Information on Restraint Straps and Associated Products

For more information about restraint straps and other associated products, why not visit the websites of the better known manufacturers and suppliers?

Information on Lintels and Similar Products

For more information about lintels and similar products, why not visit the websites of the better known manufacturers and suppliers?

Information on Insulation and Insulating Products

For further information about insulation and insulating products, why not contact the following website or see the Building Regulations and relevant British Standards, which are available at The Stationery Office bookshops.

The Stationery Office Bookshops
www.tso.co.uk

Information on Damp Proof Barriers

For more information about damp proof barriers why not visit the websites of the better known manufacturers and suppliers? Or the following?

Building Research Establishment
www.bre.co.uk

For a range of technical information, not only on damp proof barriers but on every aspect of the built environment, contact the Building Research Establishment at the address below.

The Building Research Establishment, Garston, Watford, WD25 9XX.
Telephone: 01923 664000.

Chapter Five

Set Out Masonry Structures

NVQ Level 2   Unit No. VR 41   Set Out Masonry Structures

This unit is about:

- ❦ **Interpreting information**
- ❦ **Adopting safe and healthy working practices**
- ❦ **Selecting materials, components and equipment**
- ❦ **Setting out brickwork and blockwork and vernacular style structures on level ground.**

There are two sections in this chapter, resources and methods of work.

This chapter will now cover setting out for masonry structures.

Resources

5.1

In this section you will learn about materials, components and equipment relating to type, quantity, quality and sizes of standard and specialist:

- Levels, lines, profiles, tape measures, pegs, squares and fixings
- Hand tools and setting out equipment.

When you have completed this section you will be able to:

- Select the required quantity and quality of resources for the methods of work.

Know and understand:

- The characteristics, quality, uses, limitations and defects associated with the resources
- How the resources should be used and how any problems with the resources are reported
- The organizational procedures to select resources, why they have been developed and how they are used.

This section will now cover resources.

Setting Out Materials and Equipment

When you have worked through this section, you will be able to:

- Establish lines and levels for construction activities including setting up profiles boards and pegs, using appropriate equipment: tapes, rules, spirit levels, straight edges, lines and levelling instruments
- Record readings in an acceptable manner so that reference can be made to them at a later date
- Describe how deviations in position, alignment and level are identified and action taken to remedy such deviations.

Timber for Pegs and Profiles

Pegs

Wooden pegs are used in the setting out of buildings for a variety of reasons:

- To establish the corner points of a building
- To support profile boards
- To establish the level of concrete in a foundation trench
- As a datum peg.

All wooden pegs should be square in section. Sizes can range from 30 mm to 50 mm square, depending on the nature of the soil and the position in which the peg is to be placed.

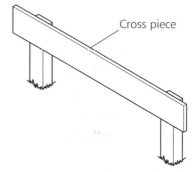

Fig 5.1 Pegs and profile board fixed

Profile Boards

Profile boards are used to indicate the position of walls and foundations. They are usually made from timber 100 mm × 50 mm in cross section. Pegs and profile boards are fixed together to construct profiles as shown in Figure 5.1

Method of Assembly

All profiles need to be of rigid construction. The pegs must be firmly placed in the ground.

Nails or screws used for fixing boards to pegs should be staggered diagonally on the board for maximum strength and left proud of the board as shown in Figure 5.2.

The length of the board used must be long enough to contain the information required, that is, wall and foundation widths as shown in Figure 5.3.

Two profiles are needed at each corner of a building as shown in Figure 5.4.

Profiles are also required for setting out any load bearing internal walls.

Ranging lines are then located on to the profiles, which trace out the alignment of walls and foundation trenches.

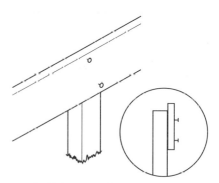

Fig 5.2 Fixing boards to pegs with screws or nails

| Points to note | For greater accuracy in setting out, it is important that all profile boards are at the same height.

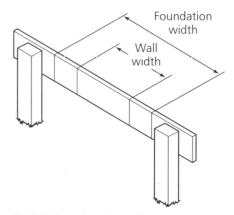

Fig 5.3 Boards with wall and foundation widths

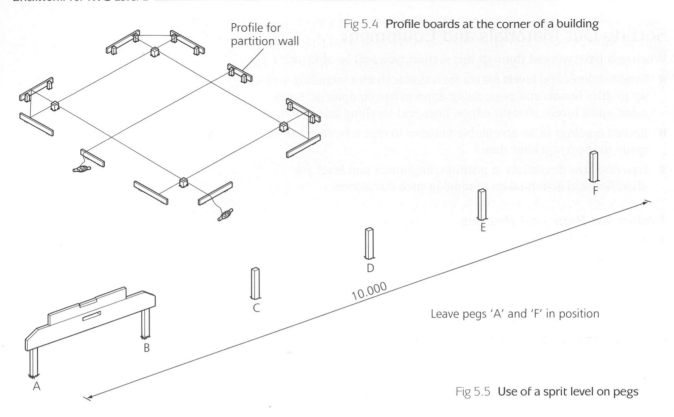

Profile for partition wall

Fig 5.4 **Profile boards at the corner of a building**

10.000

Leave pegs 'A' and 'F' in position

Fig 5.5 **Use of a sprit level on pegs**

The Builder's Square

When you have worked through this section, you will be able to:

■ Set out a right angle using a builder's square

■ Check for square

■ Measure and mark out corners on foundations and floors.

The builder's square is used for the setting out of right angles on site.

A builder's square is usually made from wood. It is braced to maintain its squareness and one side is longer than the other. When first made, a square's accuracy can be guaranteed, but on site after exposure to the weather and possibly misuse, its accuracy should not be relied upon.

Most builder's squares are made of 75 mm × 30 mm timber half jointed at the 90 degree angle with a diagonal brace, tenoned or dovetailed into the side length as illustrated in Figure 5.6.

When setting out with a builder's square, accuracy depends on lining up the ranging line with the side of the square. Greater accuracy can be achieved when the sides of the square are increased in length.

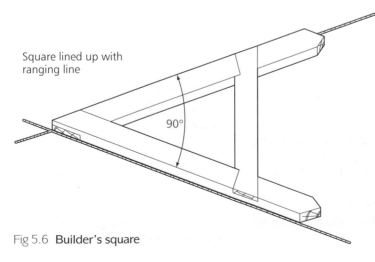

Square lined up with ranging line

90°

Fig 5.6 **Builder's square**

Work-based Evidence Required

■ **Work Skills Required to Measure, Mark Out, Level, Position and Secure**

Use and maintain:

■ Hand tools

■ Setting out equipment.

To meet this requirement, obtain a witness testimony sheet from your supervisor stating that you have used work skills to measure, mark out, level, position and secure a building, whilst using hand tools and setting out equipment.

When you have received the signed and dated witness testimony sheet from your supervisor, place them in your work-based evidence portfolio when next in college and map and record it against the syllabus.

Optical Setting Out Equipment

When you have worked through this section, you will be able to:

■ Set up optical levels and tripods

■ Book readings from optical levels

■ Use a levelling staff

■ Recognize the different types of optical level available.

Automatic Levels

Automatic telescope levels are a range of instruments each using the same basic principles of a telescope set on a tripod fixed on to a horizontal plane. The difference between the various automatic levels is the manner in which the telescope is levelled.

Key Parts of Automatic Levels

Telescope

The telescope is usually a tube with a large object lens at one end and a small eyepiece at the other. Between these two lenses are the focusing lenses. The function of the telescope is to magnify the image to ease reading (see Figure 5.7).

Diaphragm

This positions the cross hairs on the lens as shown in Figure 5.7.

Collimation Line

This is a line passing through the centre of the telescope. For an automatic level to be correct, the collimation line must be exactly horizontal.

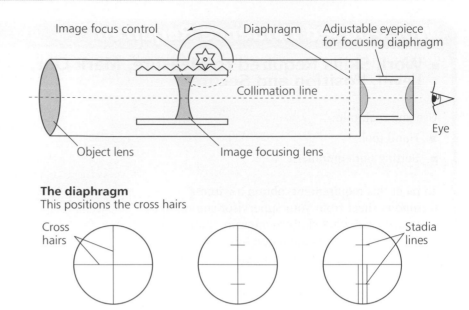

Fig 5.7 **Diaphragm and telescope**

Bubble Tube

Most instruments have a spirit level tube that is used to level the instrument.

Circular Bubble

The majority of automatic levels have a bubble level. This is to help in making the instrument approximately level.

Types of Level

Cowley Level

The Cowley automatic level is a simple self-levelling instrument widely used for general site levelling. The level consists of:

- A metal cased box containing a system of mirrors and prisms.
- A tripod with a central pin. The metal cased box is placed on to the pin, which then activates the level.
- A graduated staff consisting of a sliding target which moves up and down the staff. An arrow on the target gives the precise measurement on the graduated staff, as illustrated in Figure 5.8.

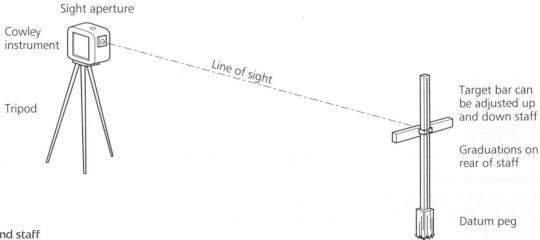

Fig 5.8 **Cowley level and staff**

Slope Attachment

A small optical attachment that enables the Cowley level to be used to set out gradients.

There are two models available with ranges of 1 in 10 to 1 in 50 and 1 in 60 to 1 in 250 respectively.

Optical Site Square

This is an optical instrument used for setting out right angles on site. The site square contains two telescopes set permanently at 90 degrees to each other. They can be adjusted vertically to enable fixing points to be located at convenient points.

A tripod with adjustable legs and a steel rod which allows the instrument to be set up over a fixed point, for example a saw mark on a profile or a nail in a peg as illustrated in Figure 5.10.

The site square will give a range from 2 to 90 m.

TRY THIS OUT

Using the Cowley Level

Equipment and materials required
- Cowley level and staff
- Bricks and mortar
- Brick trowel
- Notepad and pencil.

Method

Set the Cowley level up in the prescribed manner.

Bed two bricks at point A

Take a level reading of the bricks and note this down.

Bed two bricks at point B and C as illustrated in Figure 5.9.

Adjust the height of the bricks until they are level with point A

Competence check

Repeat procedure to as many levelling points as required by your tutor.

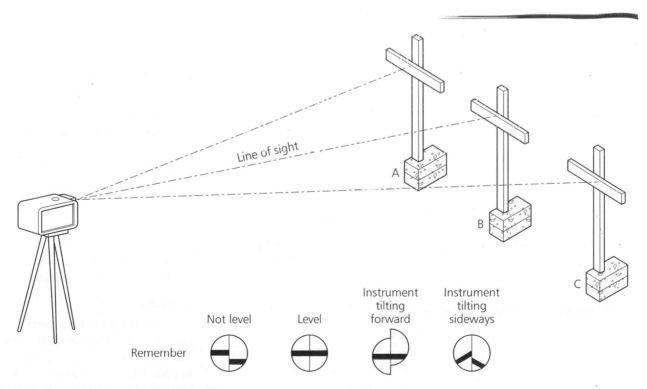

Fig 5.9 Levelling exercise using a Cowley level

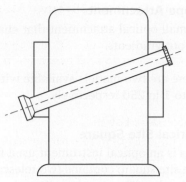

Telescopes at right
angles in plan

Telescopes tilt to give range
of sight between 2.0 m and 90.0 m

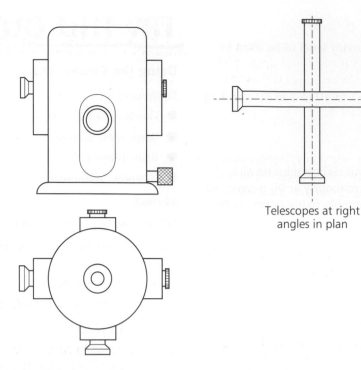

Fig 5.10 **Cowley site squares**

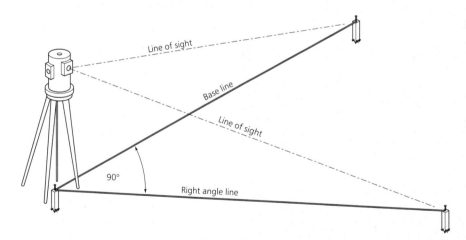

Fig 5.11 **Site square to form a right angle**

TRY THIS OUT

Setting Out a Right Angle

Equipment and materials required

- Site square and tripod
- Wooden pegs
- Nails
- Ranging line
- Note pad and pencil.

Method

Set out the base line of the building.

Set up the site square over the corner peg with a nail slightly protruding from the top of it.

Line the site square up with the base line.

Lock site square into position.

Reposition second ranging line so as to line up with right angled telescope as illustrated in Figure 5.11.

At this point both lines will be at right angles to the base line.

Competence check

Get your tutor to check your work to see if you have carried it out competently. It is important in your job as a bricklayer, that you are able to use simple setting out equipment effectively.

Electro-Magnetic Distance Measurement (EDM)

This instrument generates an electro-magnetic wave within or near to the visible spectrum, with a modulated wave superimposed upon it for phase comparison purposes. From the transmitter, set over the survey station, the signal is directed to a reflector that returns the signal back to the transmitter, measuring the distance as it does so.

Automatic Level

The majority of automatic levels have a locking clamp or friction stop and a slow motion screw to direct the telescope centrally on to the staff. Most have a horizontal circle graduated in degrees so that horizontal angles can be set out.

Laser Level

All the instruments described so far have been optical levels and require two people for their operation. The laser level is not an optical level and can be operated by only one person.

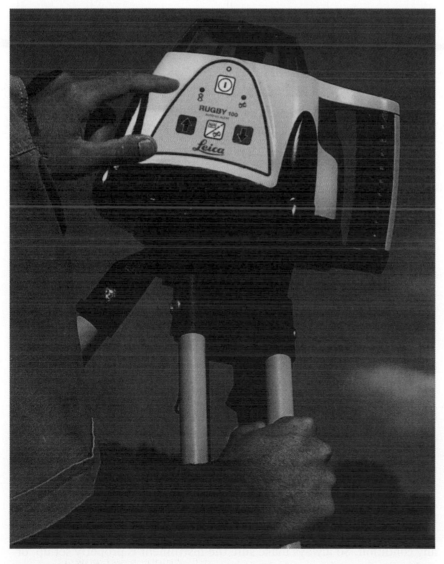

Fig 5.12 **Laser level**
Source: Leica

TRY THIS OUT

Setting up an Automatic Level

Equipment and materials required
● Automatic level and tripod
● Levelling staff
● Notepad and pencil.

Method

Attach the level to the tripod.

Using the footscrews centre the fish eye bubble.

Sight on to the staff.

Take a number of staff readings.

Competence check

Get your tutor to check your work to see if you are competent at this activity.

TRY THIS OUT

Setting up a Laser Level

Equipment and materials required
● Laser level and tripod
● Notepad and pencil.

Method

The level is set up using the fish eye bubble as for the automatic level.

The level is then turned on and a laser beam is sent out on a level plane. A special target receiver is then used to transfer this level to a target at the position where the level is to be taken and set out, as shown in Figure 5.12.

Competence check

Get your tutor to check your work to see if you are competent at this activity.

TRY THIS OUT

Taking Staff Readings

Equipment and materials required

- Staff and tripod
- Notepad and pencil.

Method

Practice taking staff readings by writing down the values of the readings from a levelling staff held by a colleague in various places in college or on site.

Competence check

Get your tutor or supervisor to check your work for accuracy. It is important that you become competent in this exercise, as mistakes can prove costly on site.

> *Points to note*

If you are responsible for the use of an instrument always check and check again. Do not take risks.

TRY THIS OUT

List the equipment you would use for each of the following setting out activities, as well as any other items of general equipment required.

- Linear measurement
- Angle measurement
- Line levels
- Plumbing and fixing verticals
- General equipment

Competence check

At the end of the exercise get your tutor to check your results.

Other Levelling Equipment

Tripod

Tripods support the level and are made of aluminium or wood. They should be set up as level as possible and at a height convenient to the user.

Levelling Staff

Levelling staffs are made in either aluminium or wood or glass fibre and may be telescopic or folding. They come in lengths of 3, 4 and 5 m. The common E-type face markings on the staff are shown in Figure 5.13.

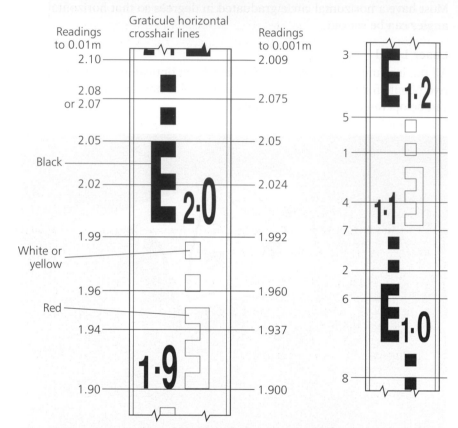

Fig 5.13 **Marking graduations on a staff**

The marks are 10 mm deep with spaces of 10 mm between. Different colours usually red and black are used for graduation marks in alternate metres.

Checking Instruments for Accuracy

Always be aware of the limitations of equipment and instruments. This applies to the control of dimensions as much as it does to the initial setting out.

Always test the equipment you are about to use to ensure their accuracy. Instruments are used on site, then go back to stores and in many cases are rarely checked. The instruments are then re-allocated and may be in any condition. So always make sure the instrument is properly set up, or make allowances for any faults or inaccuracies found. If a fault is discovered, return the instrument to stores for adjustment or repair.

Measuring Tapes

When you have worked through this section, you will be able to:

- Recognize the different types of tapes available
- Use tapes as an aid to setting out work for construction activities.

All measuring tapes should be manufactured in accordance with British Standard 4884 Measuring Instruments for Construction Works.

Steel Tapes

For maximum accuracy always use steel tapes. The majority of steel tapes are graduated into metres, centimetres and millimetres and can be read to the nearest millimetre. Tapes are usually available in lengths of 3, 5, 20, 30, 50 and 100 m.

Synthetic Tapes

Synthetic tapes are usually available in 20 and 30 m lengths. This type of tape is liable to stretch or shrink, and is therefore not as accurate as a steel tape.

TRY THIS OUT

You have been using a 30 m plastic tape on site, and you think it may have stretched in parts. How would you check it? Assume you do not have any other equipment available.

Competence check

Get your tutor or supervisor to check your answers.

✓ Good Practice

Care and Maintenance of Measuring tapes

Clean and lightly oil the tape at the end of each working day.

Do not leave tapes lying on the ground, they are liable to be damaged or to kink and break.

Always have the tape wound on its spool when not in use.

When using a tape for measuring purposes ensure it is carried by two people across the site and not dragged.

Do not allow site traffic to run over any measuring tape.

Ranging Lines

When you have worked through this section, you will be able to:

- Identify a ranging line
- Position a ranging line on to profiles for the face line of walls.

Definition – A ranging line is a stout line used for setting out purposes.

Ranging lines are produced in lengths known as shanks. A bricklayer would have two shanks on a pair of line pins, but for setting out purposes, four or five shanks would be required. The lines themselves are usually made from hemp or nylon. Although it can stretch more than hemp, nylon line will retain its tension when strung between pegs or profiles.

Fig 5.14 Spliced line

TRY THIS OUT

● Using a spirit level, draw a horizontal, straight line with a pencil or marker between two perpends on a wall you have built in the workshop.

● Get your tutor to check your work for accuracy.

key terms

Scale drawing – A drawing drawn in proportion to actual measurements – proportions must be the same.

Sectional drawing – An imaginary cut through part of a building to show in detail how it is constructed.

Abbreviations – Shortened words or phrases, e.g. bwk for brickwork.

Perimeter – The outer edge of any area.

Taut – Tightly pulled.

Temporary – For a short time only.

Transfer – To change over.

A right angle – A 90 degree angle.

Setting out – Marking out areas to exact measurements.

Plumb – True vertical.

Note: The term knot is sometimes used instead of shank when describing line.

If a line breaks, it should be spliced together as shown in Figure 5.14 and not knotted. The strand of line is opened up to allow the other end of line to pass through, when tension is applied the strands will tighten up to hold the ends together.

Spirit Levels and Straight Edges

When you have worked through this section, you will be able to:

■ use a spirit level and straight edge to transfer levels

Spirit Levels

A spirit level is a metal straight edge specially fitted with glass tubes containing a spirit and a bubble of air. These level tubes are set into the straight edge so that when the straight edge is placed across two points that are exactly level the air bubble will be exactly in the centre of the tube, this position being clearly marked with incised lines. In a similar way tubes are fitted to read correctly with the level held vertically.

To check the accuracy of a spirit level it is usual to reverse it in its length to see if the bubble remains in the same position. If not, it can be adjusted until it does.

Straight Edge

A straight edge is any piece of wood that has parallel sides which can then be used as a straight edge, but not accurately. A purpose made straight edge is preferable (see Figure 5.15).

When a straight edge is used, it should be reversed each time a level is taken. This will reduce any errors caused by a faulty level or in the straight edge itself.

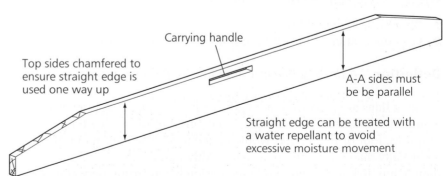

Carrying handle

Top sides chamfered to ensure straight edge is used one way up

A-A sides must be be parallel

Straight edge can be treated with a water repellant to avoid excessive moisture movement

Fig 5.15 **Purpose made straight edge**

❶ **What is EDM short for?**

❷ **Name three types of optical level.**

❸ **Explain how a spirit level can be checked for accuracy.**

❹ **Why should a spirit level and straight edge be reversed for alternate readings?**

Methods of Work 5.2

In this section you will learn about the application of knowledge for safe work practices, procedures, skills and transference of competence, relating to the areas of work and material used, to:

- Set out brick, traditional and thin joint block structures on level ground
- Construct corner profiles
- Transfer levels: spirit level, straight edge, water level and laser level
- Use hand tools and setting out equipment.

When you have completed this section you will be able to:

- Comply with the given contract information to carry out the work efficiently to the required specification.

Know and understand:

- How methods of work, to meet the specification, are carried out and problems reported.

This section will now cover methods of work.

Interpretation of Construction Drawings

When you have completed this section, you will be able to identify discrepancies and errors that may occur on drawings and other contract documents that affect the dimensional accuracy of the work. These include information that is:

- Dimensionally inaccurate
- Missing
- At variance with information in other documents.

Construction Drawings and Specifications

Construction or working drawings and written specifications must contain the information required for a construction team to be able to convert the design for a proposed building into a completed structure. In order for this to take place the following information should be included on the working drawings:

- Elevations
- External finishes to walls and roof
- Positions of window and door openings
- Scales
- Overall dimensions of the building
- Position of internal walls, room sizes, door and window openings
- Position of fitments, baths, sinks, toilets and so on

Scales

The sizes of buildings and construction sites means that drawings need to be scaled down from full size to sizes that will fit on a sheet of drawing paper. This is known as drawing to scale. A scale drawing is different from a sketch because every measurement in a scale drawing has to be in proportion to the real thing and must be exact.

Dimensions can be taken from a drawing by the use of a scale rule.

The main scales used in construction are:

Scale	Drawing is:
1 : 1	the same size as the object
1 : 5	5 times smaller than the object
1 : 10	10 times smaller than the object
1 : 50	50 times smaller than the object
1 : 100	100 times smaller than the object
1 : 500	500 times smaller than the object
1 : 12 500	12 500 times smaller than the object

Although imperial measurements are still used in some cases on site, the metric measurement is now accepted universally for drawings with a millimetre as the basic unit.

Section Drawings

Section drawings provide vertical dimensions and constructional details of foundations, floors, walls, roof, damp proof courses and membranes and the height of ground levels as shown in Figure 5.16a and b.

Location Drawings

This provides the position of the building in relation to the site and its surroundings. For example, adjoining buildings, roads, boundaries and so on, as shown in Figure 5.17. They also contain the following information:

- Provision of access
- Drainage and sewers
- North point
- Title panel
- Site address
- Scales used on working drawings
- Drawing number

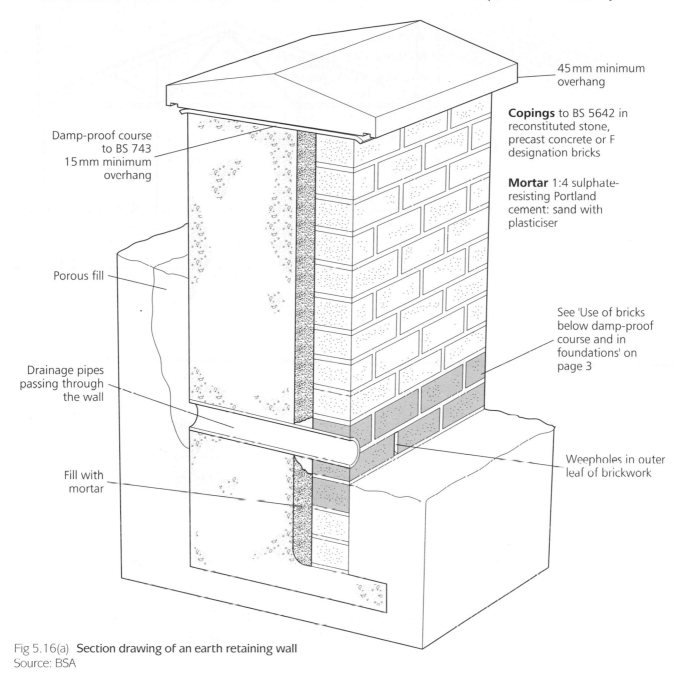

45 mm minimum overhang

Copings to BS 5642 in reconstituted stone, precast concrete or F designation bricks

Mortar 1:4 sulphate-resisting Portland cement: sand with plasticiser

Damp-proof course to BS 743 15 mm minimum overhang

Porous fill

Drainage pipes passing through the wall

Fill with mortar

See 'Use of bricks below damp-proof course and in foundations' on page 3

Weepholes in outer leaf of brickwork

Fig 5.16(a) **Section drawing of an earth retaining wall**
Source: BSA

- Client
- Date of drawing.

Note: Location drawings may be referred to as block plans and site plans.

Understanding Construction Drawings

The ability to read and understand construction drawings and sketches is an essential function of any bricklayer in the construction industry. As a student you must study this section carefully to fully understand the way working drawings are prepared. To develop the skill of interpreting working drawings and sketches you must practise reading sample drawings provided by your tutor at college and supervisor at work.

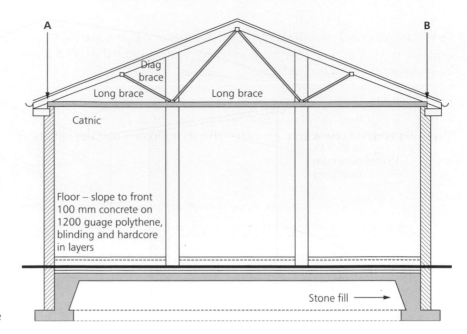

Fig 5.16(b) **Section drawing of a garage**

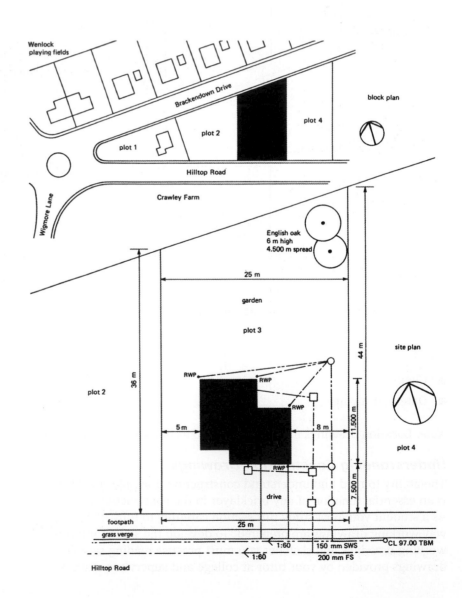

Fig 5.17 **Location plan**
Source: P. Brett

Construction drawings and sketches are pictures or diagrams used to describe the building specifications and procedures required to erect a building as shown in Figure 5.18.

Working drawings are usually prepared by architects or designers using manual draughting techniques and computer aided design software. These drawings along with the written specification describe the details of the building.

A plan shows different views, or elevations, of a room or a building

Rear elevation
(a view of the back)

Floor plans
(showing the walls and foundations)

Cross-section
(as if the building has been cut through)

Concrete tiles

Lateral restraints 30 × 25 galvanised straps to wall plates. 30 × 5 galvanised straps to end 2 rafters and end 2 ceiling joists, at max 2m spacing

30° roof, concrete tiles on 25 mm treated battens and felt and proprietary roof trusses to BS 5268 in max 600 metres properly braced with 100 × 50 bracings double nailed

1050

rwp

Diag brace

Long brace   Long brace

Catnic

Rear (To plot 17)

Right side (to home)

Floor – slope to front 100 mm concrete on 1200 guage polythene, blinding and hardcore in layers

rwp

Front standing

Left side (to plot 8)

600 x 200 footings at least 1m deep to solid ground to satisfaction of building inspector (ground is clay)

450   5118   450

600

Diagonal (walls) – 8.074m

4950

600

678   1936   790   1936   678

5668 o/a

rwd and gully   100

100
328
900 nominal
328

450

Catnic CN48 lintel ci angle

Catnic CN71F lintel

1170

Catnic CN71A lintels   450

2302
328

rwp and gully

100

328   2286   440   2286   328

Oakwood Lane Elton	
House for plot 7 detached garage [sheet 6 of 6]	
Robert S Green Architect	
3, Holly Lane, Elton Shropshire S74 1BX	
Telephone 01861 814871	
Sept 2003 Scale 1:50 : 1:100	Drawing: 1074/28/6

Front elevation
(a view of the front)

Floor plans
(showing the walls and foundations)

Fig 5.18 **Working drawings**
Source: BSA

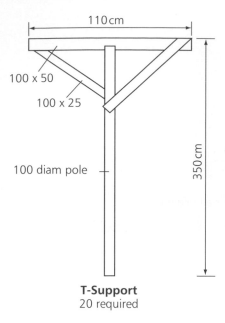

110cm

100 x 50

100 x 25

100 diam pole

350cm

T-Support
20 required

Fig 5.19 Sketch used to explain instructions

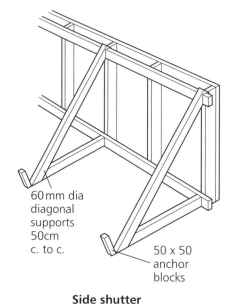

60mm dia diagonal supports 50cm c. to c.

50 x 50 anchor blocks

Side shutter

Fig 5.20 Detailed sketch that includes construction details

Sketches

Sketches are merely freehand pictures that can be drawn by anyone as a method of explaining specific instructions as shown in Figure 5.19.

In brickwork, sketches may be drawn by the bricklaying foreman to describe the size requirements of a building component or a construction procedure. Look at the sketch in Figure 5.20 and try to identify the construction details.

Scales Used in Construction Drawings

The scales used in construction or working drawings differ according to the type of information that is being shown. The most common are as follows.

Plans and Elevations

Plan and elevation drawings identify the positions occupied by the various areas within the building and identify the location of the main elements and components. Scales 1 : 200, 1 : 100 and 1 : 50 (see Figure 5.18).

Location Drawing

Location or site drawings show the position of the proposed building and the general layout of roads, services and drainage on the actual site. Scales 1 : 500 and 1 : 200 – see Figure 5.17.

Block Plans

Block plans identify the site in relation to the surrounding area. Scales 1 : 2500 and 1 : 1250 as shown in Figure 5.21.

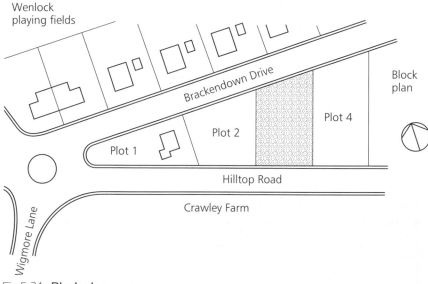

Wenlock playing fields

Brackendown Drive

Block plan

Plot 4

Plot 2

Plot 1

Hilltop Road

Crawley Farm

Wigmore Lane

Fig 5.21 Block plan

Assembly Drawings

Assembly drawings show in detail, the junctions between the various elements and components of a building. Scales 1 : 20, 1 : 10 and 1 : 5 as shown in Figure 5.22.

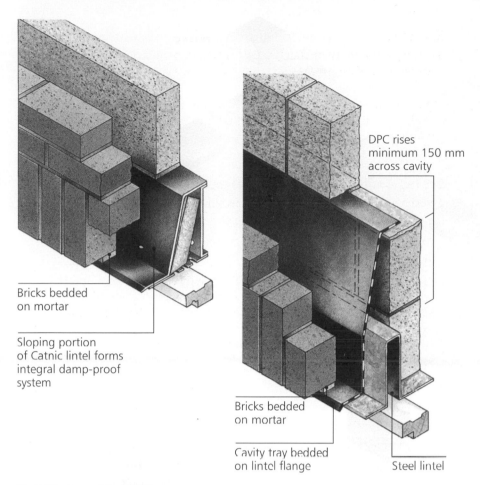

DPC rises
minimum 150 mm
across cavity

Bricks bedded
on mortar

Sloping portion
of Catnic lintel forms
integral damp-proof
system

Bricks bedded
on mortar

Cavity tray bedded
on lintel flange

Steel lintel

Fig 5.22 **Assembly drawing**
Source: Helfen

Component Drawings

Component range drawings are specific to the proposed building itself
and show the dimensions and layout of a standard range of components.
Scales 1 : 100, 1 : 50 and 1 : 20 as shown in Figure 5.23.

Detail Drawings

Detail drawings show all the information that is required in order to
manufacture a component. Scales 1 : 10, 1 : 5 and 1 : 1.

Symbols

Symbols or hatchings is the term that describes the marking on a cross
sectional drawing used to denote the material that the building is
constructed from. The symbols are official British Standards and can be
found in BS 1192, which controls drawing practice across all sections of
the building industry (see Figure 5.25).

Examples of Types of Symbols

- Brickwork
- Blockwork
- Concrete
- Stonework
- Hardcore

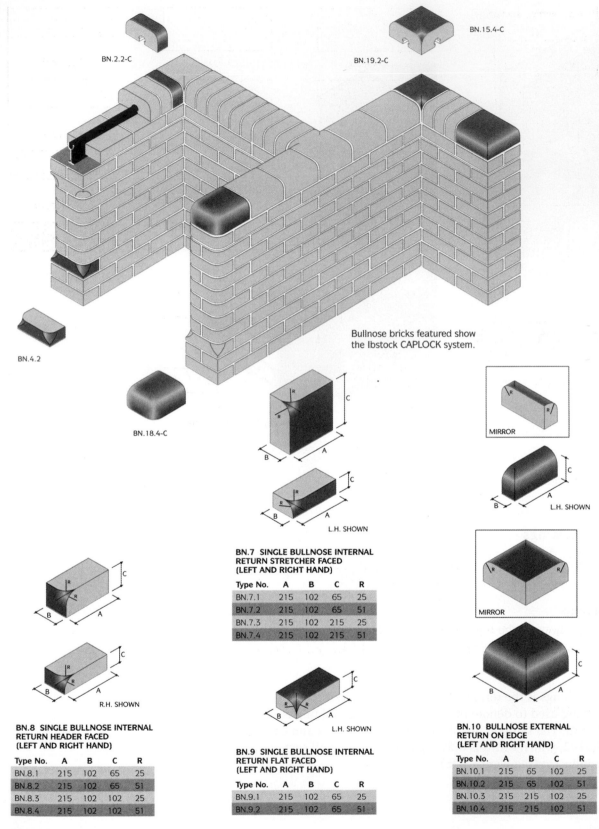

BN.2.2-C

BN.15.4-C

BN.19.2-C

BN.4.2

BN.18.4-C

Bullnose bricks featured show
the Ibstock CAPLOCK system.

MIRROR

L.H. SHOWN

L.H. SHOWN

MIRROR

**BN.7 SINGLE BULLNOSE INTERNAL
RETURN STRETCHER FACED
(LEFT AND RIGHT HAND)**

Type No.	A	B	C	R
BN.7.1	215	102	65	25
BN.7.2	215	102	65	51
BN.7.3	215	102	215	25
BN.7.4	215	102	215	51

R.H. SHOWN

L.H. SHOWN

**BN.8 SINGLE BULLNOSE INTERNAL
RETURN HEADER FACED
(LEFT AND RIGHT HAND)**

Type No.	A	B	C	R
BN.8.1	215	102	65	25
BN.8.2	215	102	65	51
BN.8.3	215	102	102	25
BN.8.4	215	102	102	51

**BN.9 SINGLE BULLNOSE INTERNAL
RETURN FLAT FACED
(LEFT AND RIGHT HAND)**

Type No.	A	B	C	R
BN.9.1	215	102	65	25
BN.9.2	215	102	65	51

**BN.10 BULLNOSE EXTERNAL
RETURN ON EDGE
(LEFT AND RIGHT HAND)**

Type No.	A	B	C	R
BN.10.1	215	65	102	25
BN.10.2	215	65	102	51
BN.10.3	215	215	102	25
BN.10.4	215	215	102	51

Fig 5.23 **Component drawing**
Source: Ibstock

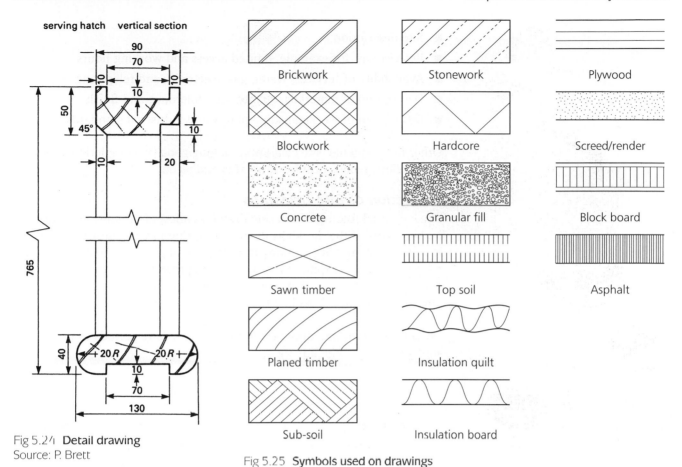

Fig 5.24 **Detail drawing**
Source: P. Brett

Fig 5.25 **Symbols used on drawings**

- Insulation
- Sub-soil.

The symbols illustrated in Figure 5.25 only represent a small sample of those that are used regularly on all standard site drawings.

Abbreviations

Because of the amount of detail shown on drawings, abbreviations are used for many of the materials or components used. Examples of these are:

- Brickwork – bwk
- Damp proof course – dpc
- Concrete – conc
- Foundations – fdn
- Insulation – insul
- Rainwater gully – rwg
- Soil and vent pipe – svp

Specifications

The specification is a detailed description of all the essential information and requirements that will affect the price of the work but cannot be shown on the drawings. Items included in the specification are:

- Site description
- Restrictions, for example, limited access and working hours
- Availability of services, water, gas, electricity and telephone
- Description of materials, quality, size, tolerance and finish
- Description of workmanship, quality and industrial standards.

Other requirements: site clearance, making good on completion, names of suppliers, names of sub-contractors and so on.

Protection of Site Drawings

The continual folding of working drawings allows fold lines to occur, making parts of the drawings illegible resulting in vital information being lost. To overcome this, working drawings should be fixed to a board and covered with a transparent film which also protects the drawing from dirt and poor weather. Another method would be to roll the drawings up after use and place them in a tube.

Do not leave working drawings in the open for long periods as the sunlight will quickly fade them.

Good Practice

Before using any working drawing it is essential that you have an understanding of them and what is required of the setting out process.

All intermediate dimensions should be added together and checked against overall dimensions as wall dimensions are not always shown on working drawings.

If you discover any errors in the working drawings inform your supervisor before carrying out any work.

The Basic Principles of Setting Out 5.3

When you have worked through this section, you will be able to check sources of information to ensure that they are up to date in respect of:

- Boundaries of operation
- Datum heights
- Levels of existing buildings and other fixed objects
- Dimensions, location and levels of existing work area
- Building line, frontage line and square line
- Variations between specified and actual work dimensions
- The personnel responsible for works.

Describe the roles and responsibilities of the contracting staff for dimensional quality control.

Setting Out

As a bricklayer it is unlikely that you have ever had the responsibility for surveying a large site or for setting out a project. But in the future you may well become a supervisor, then you may have the responsibility for controlling setting out operations and the accuracy of it.

This means checking the work carried out by other people and ensuring that it meets the needs indicated in the drawings. It also means knowing what to do when something is wrong. At the beginning of any contract there must be agreement on three important aspects of setting out operations, these are:

- What are the key levels and setting out points?
- Who is responsible for the various stages of setting out?
- What is the decision making procedure?

Usually the contractor checks that the information on the setting out drawing is correct. This drawing comes from the architect or designer.

The Objectives of Setting Out a Building

The objective when setting out a building is to provide lines and levels to an accuracy and in a way that ensures the building is built within the specified tolerances taking into account the building sequence and work programme.

Construction Surveys

Construction surveys are usually separated into two planes: the horizontal and the vertical. The horizontal allows you to develop a plan view — that is setting out work on the ground from a drawing (see Figure 5.26).

Work on the vertical plane is usually called levelling. This enables you to find the relative differences in elevation between two or more points, compared with say a setting out point with a known height such as a datum (see Figure 5.27).

Setting out and levelling are normally undertaken just before the building work begins. It may and usually does continue as well during the building process.

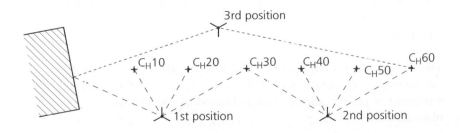

Fig 5.26 Horizontal setting out

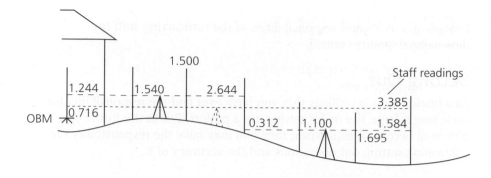

Fig 5.27 **Vertical setting out**

Reasons for Setting Out

- To identify the correct building, or site or field
- To place the work in the correct position on the site
- To place the building so that it faces the right way
- So that the building is the correct size and that the foundation and floors are all at the right level
- To ensure that all walls are truly plumb
- So that door and window openings in walls and floors are correctly positioned
- To ensure that separate buildings are correctly placed in relationship to each other.

Transferring Levels   5.4

When you have worked through this section, you will be able to:

- Use a spirit level and straight edge, water level and a laser level to transfer levels.

Levelling

Levelling may be defined as a method of expressing the relative heights of any number of points above or below, some plane of reference called the datum. The site datum is transferred from the nearest ordnance bench mark on to the site by means of transferring levels. Some examples of transferring levels are described below.

Water Level

A water level is a length of hose with a transparent tube set in each end. The hose is filled with water, a cap or cork being provided to prevent spilling. Care must be taken to see that no air is trapped when filling.

The level works on the principle that water finds its own level. It can be used over distances of 30 m or so, and is useful for marking a number of points quickly, especially around corners and obstructions.

TRY THIS OUT

Spirit Level and Straight Edge Transferring Levels

Equipment and materials required

● Spirit level and straight edge

● Wooden pegs

● Notepad and pencil.

Method

Starting from a temporary bench mark align the straight edge towards the intended datum point. Drive in a temporary peg at the full extent of the straight edge and level with the temporary bench mark. Finally check for level to ensure accuracy.

To ensure that the spirit level remains in the same position on the straight edge, mark the end of the spirit level A on to the straight edge. Repeat the process to extend the temporary levelling pegs until the final datum peg position is reached, as shown in Figure 5. 28.

For greater accuracy, reverse the spirit level and straight edge at each intermediate levelling stage. Ensure that the spirit level remains on the mark A as shown in Figure 5.29.

Competence check

Get your tutor to check if your work is accurate. It is important that you are competent in carrying out this activity.

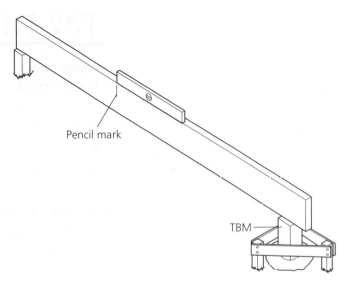

Pencil mark

TBM

Fig 5.28 **Correct use of spirit level with a straight edge**

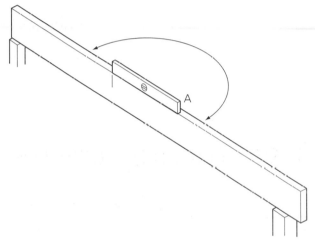

A

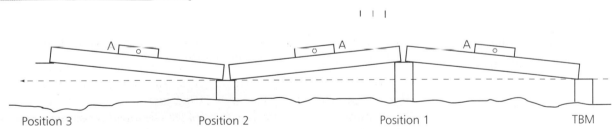

Position 3   Position 2   Position 1   TBM

Fig 5.29 **Marking straight edge for spirit level position**

TRY THIS OUT

Water Level
Transferring Levels

Equipment and materials required

● Water level

● Water

● Notepad and pencil.

Method

Filling instructions.

Connect the plastic hose to both tubes and, ensuring that both plastic valve caps are open, fill with water via one of the tubes.

When water is flowing freely from the tube at the opposite pipe end turn off the water source and close one end.

Shake out about ten centimetres of water from the open tube just enough to reduce the water level, then close the second end cap.

Fixing Points

Allow the water level to settle by venting both valve caps, ensuring that both tubes are held vertically and, when satisfied that their are no bubbles close the valve caps.

Take one of the tubes and fix to a nail or peg (your fixed point) at the start position. Then take the second tube to the finish point and set an approximate level. Remove both air vent caps and water will settle.

Move the second tube at the finish point either up or down as suits. Check reading, i.e. plus or minus, against a number on the tube. Look at the reading on the tube at the finish point and when this registers the same as the number reading on the tube at the fixed point you will know that the levels you are taking are correct.

Before moving to another site, ensure that both water level tube caps are closed.

Competence check

Get your tutor to check if your work is accurate. It is important that you are competent in carrying out this activity.

✓ Good Practice

Ensure that both filler caps and vents are closed securely. In cold weather, store away from frost and ice, if in doubt, drain the pipes. Do not use anti-freeze. Do not allow the plastic hose to become twisted or kinked.

TRY THIS OUT

Optical Level
Transferring Levels

Equipment and materials required

● Optical level and tripod

● Levelling staff

● Notepad and pencil.

Method

If required to find the difference in level between points A and B as shown in Figure 5.30 the optical level is set up approximately half way between points A and B. Staff readings are then taken at A and B as shown.

The difference in levels =
6.28 m – 3.46 m = 2.82 m.

Optical Level

Transferring levels using a spirit level and straight edge is only suitable for small buildings. Optical levelling is another method of transferring levels, and is suitable for greater distances.

Fig 5.30 **Difference in levels**

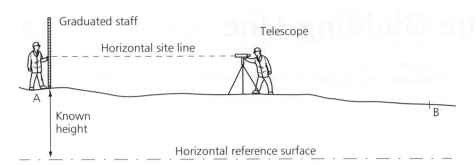

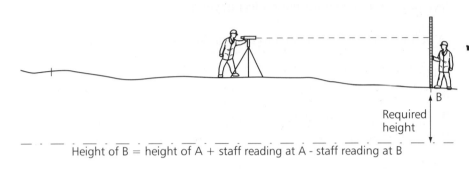

Height of B = height of A + staff reading at A - staff reading at B

Laser Level

The letters of LASER tell you what the equipment really does. They stand for Light Amplification by Stimulated Emission of Radiation. Most lasers used in the construction industry are of the helium–neon gas type that produces a polarized beam in the form of an intense red light.

Source: CITB – ConstructionSkills. Maintaining Dimensional Accuracy, 1994

Points to note ➤ An increased staff reading shows a fall, a decreased staff reading shows a rise.

TRY THIS OUT

Laser Level Transferring Levels

Equipment and materials required
● Laser level and tripod
● Notepad and pencil.

Method

Set the laser level up using the bubble level as for the automatic level.

Decide with your tutor, which levels are to be transferred.

Switch the level on, this results in a laser beam being sent out on a level plane.

A special target receiver is then used to transfer this level to a target at the position where the level is to be taken or set out.

Mark positions of transferred levels.

Competence check

Get your tutor to check if your work is accurate. It is important that you are competent in carrying out this activity.

Quick quiz Quick quiz Quick quiz Quick quiz Quick quiz

❶ **What scale is a block plan usually drawn to?**
❷ **What kind of hammer would you use for knocking in the wooden pegs when marking out a site?**

Purpose of the Building Line ▰▰▰ 5.5

When you have worked through this section, you will be able to:

■ Explain the purpose of the building line
■ Identify the buildings corners or site position.

The building line is a line fixed by the Local Authority planning department as a limit for building towards a road. It is the line that the face of the building must not project beyond.

A building line can be related to the building in different ways.

A building can be:

■ Angled to the building line
■ Behind the building line
■ On the building line.

In certain circumstances part of the building may be permitted to project beyond the building line, for example a porch.

Establishing the Building Line

Before any setting out work can be started, the position of the building line on the site must be determined. The building line is found from the block plan that refers only to the position of the building and gives no detailed information as to the building itself.

The position of the building line is usually indicated by a dimension from a fixed point such as an existing building or kerb line. This line is marked on the site by pegs of 30 mm × 30 mm timber driven into the ground at the extreme corners on the front of the building, nails or saw cuts being used to indicate the exact position on the tops of the pegs.

Step 1

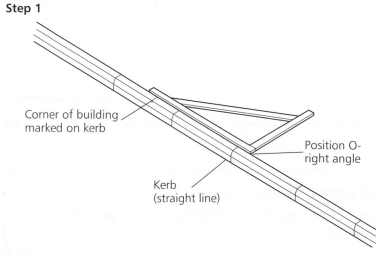

Corner of building marked on kerb

Kerb (straight line)

Position O- right angle

Fig 5.31 Builder's square against kerb

Method

When establishing the building line, dimensions are taken from points marked well beyond the position of the proposed building.

Dimensions are usually taken from the rear edge of the kerb.

The longest side of the builder's square is positioned against the rear edge of the kerb.

Place the builder's square well past the building's corner mark, as indicated on the roadside kerb as shown in Figure 5.31.

Step 2

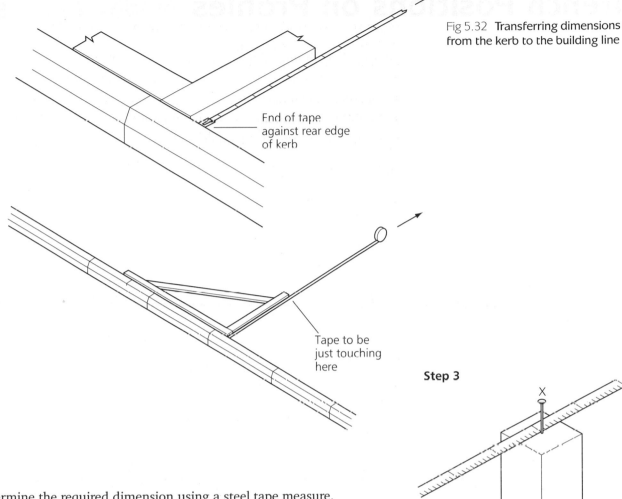

Fig 5.32 **Transferring dimensions from the kerb to the building line**

End of tape against rear edge of kerb

Tape to be just touching here

Step 3

Fig 5.33 **Peg with nail establishing correct position**

Determine the required dimension using a steel tape measure. The dimension is now transferred from the rear edge of the kerb to the building line as shown in Figure 5.32.

When the position is established drive in a wooden peg. The exact position being marked by a nail in the top of the peg as shown in Figure 5.33.

Good Practice

Always align the tape along the edge of the builder's square.

Always keep the tape taut.

Methods to Indicate Wall and Trench Positions on Profiles

5.6

After working through this section, you will be able to:

- Locate and position corners using profile ranging lines
- Measure and mark corners
- Establish dry bond arrangements for brickwork
- Explain the marks shown on profiles.

Profile Boards

In the initial stages of most building projects, you will probably observe pieces of timber board fixed in a pattern and placed in the ground. These boards and the ranging lines, which are attached to them, are called profiles because they represent the exact shape and dimensions of the building under construction.

Method

Profile boards are used with pegs to secure the ranging lines clear of the proposed excavation. As the boards are to carry precise markings of wall and trench positions and widths, it is good practice to use 75 mm × 30 mm planed timbers. The board may be fixed on the side or on top of the pegs as illustrated in Figure 5.34.

Setting Out With Profiles

In order to establish the position of the building after excavation begins, profiles are placed at points where they will not be disturbed later on. The usual position being approximately 1 m away beyond the projection of the foundation, as shown in Figure 5.35. Another method is to attach the boards or lines to existing buildings.

Ranging Lines

Between the profiles, a ranging line is strung over the points marked on the pegs and the points where it meets the profile boards should be carefully marked on the boards with nail or saw cuts, as previously described. This line represents the front line of the building or the building line; from it, the position of all other walls can be set out.

After these lines have been strung at right angles from the first two pegs to mark the position of the end walls as shown in Figure 5.36, the length of these walls should be measured off and pegs fixed to the mark the back corners of the building.

Lines may now be strained across these pegs in both directions and their position permanently recorded on further profiles.

Cross Walls

The position of any cross walls should also be recorded in the same way, all marks on profiles being fixed by the use of nails or saw cuts. Apart

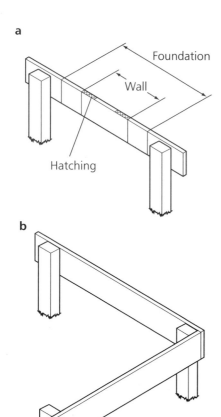

a

b

Fig 5.34 **Correct fixing of profile board to pegs**

Points to note

Never use pen or pencil marks on profile boards as these can easily weather away.

a

Profiles should be positioned approximately 1.000 m minimum away from the trench edge

Fig 5.35 **Profile board set back from building**

Spirit level

The cross pieces should be level

Future foundation excavation

b

Fig 5.36 **Procedures in setting out**

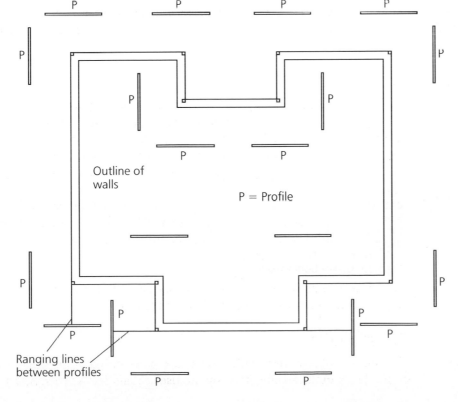

P = Profile

Outline of walls

Ranging lines between profiles

1 Peg out corners

2 Erect profiles

3 Strain lines across pegs and mark position on profiles

4 Mark out profiles and remove pegs

5 Strain lines between profiles as required

Marking wall line on profile

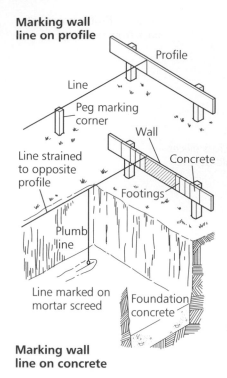

Fig 5.37 **Marked out profile board**

from the face line of each wall, the full width of the foundations should be clearly shown, including the wall thickness. Figure 5.37 shows a corner profile fully marked out as required for a one and a half brick wall with footing courses.

Excavation of the Foundations

With the ranging lines strung from profile to profile on the marks indicating the width of the concrete, the excavation of the foundations can begin. It will be necessary first to establish a datum level, from which other levels may be taken, for example the top of a damp proof course on an existing building and so on. The datum point is usually fixed on the top of a stout peg fixed into the ground and usually surrounded by concrete to avoid disturbance.

Excavation is now begun until the approximate level of the trench bottom is reached, when pegs are fixed into the ground to give the level at the top of foundation concrete. Care must be taken to see that the tops of the pegs are set at the required distance down from the top of the datum peg previously set up.

Boning Rods

To gauge the correct depth a boning rod is used. This is a gauge of the correct height with a cross piece fitted to make it appear like a tee square, as illustrated in Figure 5.38.

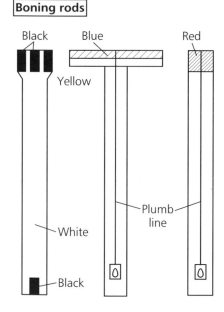

Fig 5.38 **Boning rods**

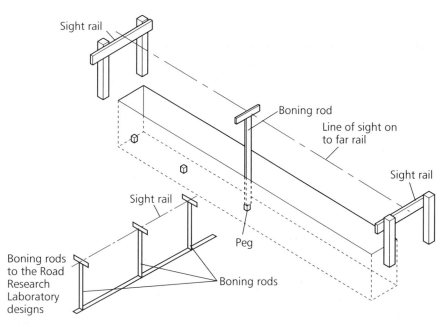

Fig 5.39 **Use of boning rods**

The end of the boning rod is placed upon a peg for testing, and the peg is driven into the ground until the crosshead is on a level with the profiles, which is easily seen by sighting across them, as shown in Figure 5.39. Excavation is now resumed until the bottom of the trench is at the required depth below the tops of the pegs, this being equal to the depth of the foundation concrete.

Levelling the Pegs

The pegs are left in the excavation to serve as a guide when levelling the concrete. To ensure that all these pegs are set with their tops at the same level, a long straight edge, approximately 3 m long, is used for levelling, in conjunction with a 1 m long spirit level. In order to reduce any inaccuracy to a minimum, the straight edge and level should be reversed each time a fresh level reading is taken.

Concrete for Foundations

On completion of the excavation, the foundation concrete may be placed into position and carefully levelled in with a straight edge to the heights indicated by the tops of the pegs.

Setting Out the Brickwork

After the concrete has been placed and set, the ranging lines should be fixed at the wall lines on the profiles. To transfer the position of the line to the bottom of the trench, a spirit level is required and this should be plumbed from the ranging line and its position marked on a mortar screed spread on the concrete. A mark is made at each end of the wall, being set out, as shown in Figure 5.40.

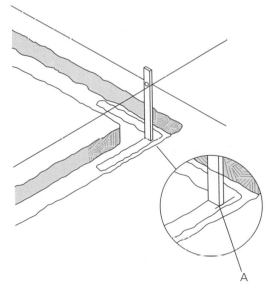

Position spirit level to the inside of the ranging line.

The spirit level must show upright.

The spirit level should have a minimal air gap to the line.

Use the upper bubble in the spirit level (nearest the line).

Mark wall position onto screed (A), using the tip of a brick trowel.

Fig 5.40 **Marking out screed from ranging lines**
Source: CITB-ConstructionSkills. Training Workbook, 1994.

In this way, the position of each corner may be marked out and the corners then built as previously described. It is good practice to check the wall lines again with ranging lines strung between the profiles before ground level is reached, so that any slight adjustment necessary may be made at this stage.

Setting Out Right Angles   5.7

When you have worked through this section, you will be able to:

- Use the builder's square, 3 : 4 : 5 and diagonal methods of forming and checking angles of 90 degrees
- Measure accurately and establish dimensions
- Mark angles clearly when using a chalk line.

Setting Out With a Builder's Square

Setting out with a builder's square can be used in conjunction with a thin mortar screed spread on the floor, in which indentations can be made with the blade of the trowel, or it can be used on a solid surface such as a concrete floor with a chalk flick line.

Method 1

Lay a thin screed of mortar on the floor and mark off a right angle with a builder's square using the point of a trowel as illustrated in Figure 5.41.

Using a tape, measure off 500 mm on both sides of the right angle as illustrated in Figure 5.42.

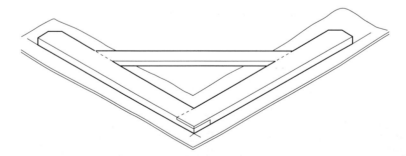

Fig 5.41 **Mortar screed marked with trowel**

Complete the screed by forming a square and mark off parallel lines at 500 mm and join them together as illustrated in Figure 5.43

To check the setting out for accuracy, measure the distance from corner to corner A – A and B – B. Both measurements should be the same, if the setting out is square, as illustrated in Figure 5.44.

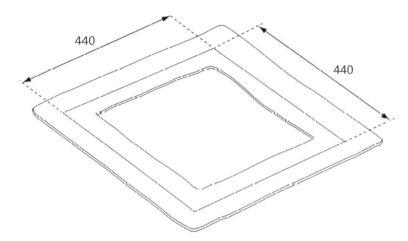

440   440

Fig 5.42 Measuring off sides for a right angle

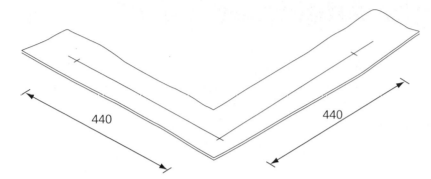

440

440

Fig 5.43 Forming a square by joining parallel lines

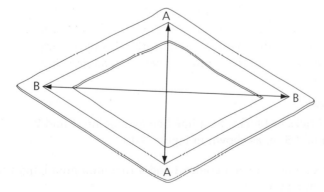

A

B   B

A

Fig 5.44 Checking diagonals to test

Method 2

This method involves setting out a right angle using the builder's square and a chalk flick line. The degree of accuracy will depend on lining up the chalk line with the edge of the square as shown in Figure 5.45.

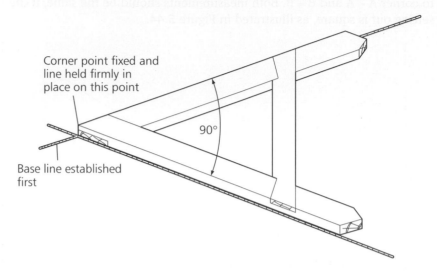

Corner point fixed and line held firmly in place on this point

90°

Base line established first

Fig 5.45 **Lining up a chalk line with the edge of a square**

A base line is established.

The corner point is fixed and the line held firmly in position at this point.

The chalk flick line is then pulled tight, lined up with the edge of the square and then raised slightly in the centre and let go (flicked). This will result in a chalk mark on the floor from which to work.

The 3 : 4 : 5 Method

What is the 3 : 4 : 5 method? A triangle constructed with sides to the ratio of 3 : 4 : 5 units will produce a right angle at A, as shown in Figure 5.46.

Therefore, a right angle can be produced using the 3 : 4 : 5 method. Where the drawings require setting out for walls longer than 5 m, the builder's square is not very accurate as it does not extend far enough along the ranging lines to ensure accuracy, as illustrated in Figure 5.47.

Therefore, for walls longer than 5 m, the use of the 3 : 4 : 5 method is preferred. You will need to know how to apply this principle in practice and set up a right-angled triangle with sides measuring 3 m, 4 m and 5 m. We now need to set out and check an angle using the 3 : 4 : 5 method.

Method

Using bricks or blocks, fix a line between points 1 and 2, a minimum length of 4.5 m, as shown in Figure 5.48.

Now fix a line between points 3 and 4 to a minimum length of 4 m, as shown in Figure 5.49.

Allow at least 50 cm between the line and the brick as shown in the illustration.

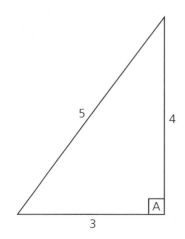

Fig 5.46 **Right angles using the 3 : 4 : 5 method**

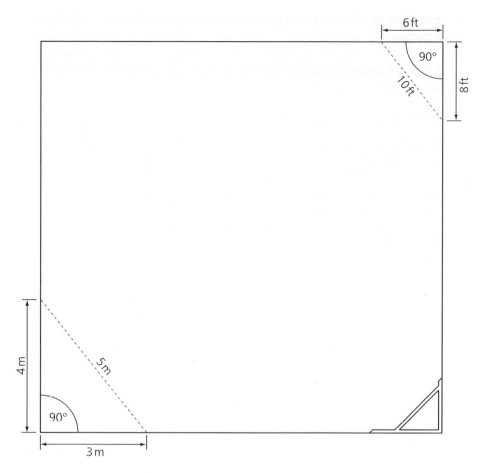

Fig 5.47 **Inaccuracy of builder's square over 5 m**

Note: You will need someone to help you with this.

From point A, measure and mark three metres on line A – B as shown in Figure 5.50.

Now from point A measure and mark out four metres on line A – C as shown in Figure 5.51.

Fig 5.48 **Marking out positions 1 and 2**

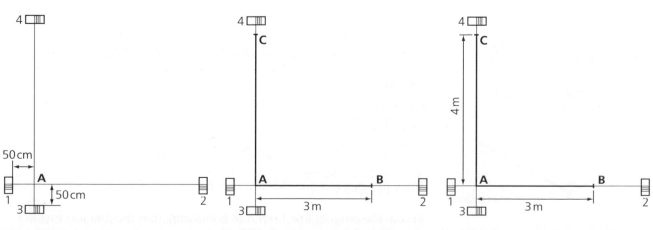

Fig 5.49 **Forming points 3 and 4**   Fig 5.50 **Setting out a right angle**   Fig 5.51 **Setting out a right angle**

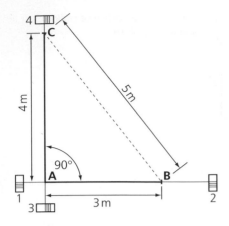

Fig 5.52 Checking the angle 1

Always check dimensions more than once.

You have now formed an angle. Now you must check for the 90 degree accuracy.

Carefully fix the tape at point B. move the other end of the tape across to point C and read the measurement, as shown in Figure 5.52.

Checking the Angle

If the measurement B – C is exactly 5 m, you have an accurate angle of 90 degrees.

If the measurement B – C is greater than 5 m the angle is more than 90 degrees. Correct the error by moving the tape which represents sides A – B inward to a position where measurement B – C is exactly 5 m, as illustrated in Figure 5.53.

If your measurement is less than 5 m, the angle is less than 90 degrees. Correct the error by moving the tape which represents side A – C outward, increasing the angle until the measurement B – C is 5 m, which is 90 degrees, as illustrated in Figure 5.54.

Competence Check

If you have any difficulty in forming the angle, ask your tutor for assistance.

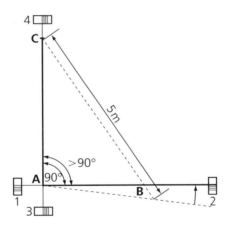

Fig 5.53 Checking the angle 2

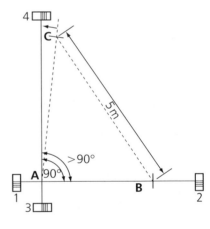

Fig 5.54 Checking the angle 3

Setting Out Corner Positions for a Building

Method

Identify the dimension for the side of the building, point F as illustrated in Figure 5.55.

Run a ranging line from point A through point D.

Drive in a peg at a suitable distance E beyond point F.

Secure the ranging line from A to E ensuring that the line just touches the nail in peg D as shown in Figure 5.55.

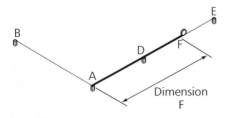

Fig 5.55 Setting out a right angle

Note: Always keep the tape taut for accurate dimensions.

Measure dimension F accurately.

Drive in peg F and locate exact position by a nail in the peg as shown in Figure 5.56.

Note: Ensure that the top of peg F is reasonably level with the tops of pegs A and B.

(Source: CITB – Construction Skills)

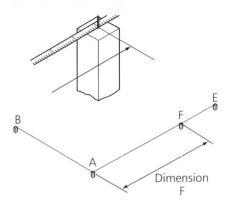

Fig 5.56 Locating position on a peg using a nail

Checking for Squareness

When you have completed marking and setting out right angles, they should be checked for squareness.

There are three methods of checking for squareness:

■ The 3 : 4 : 5 method
■ The builder's square method
■ The diagonal method.

The 3 : 4 : 5 method has already been explained. Another method is to use a large builder's square and check each angle for 90 degrees.

The Diagonal Method

To use the diagonal method of checking a corner for squareness proceed as follows:

Method

Using a tape, measure diagonally from corner point A to point H and from point E to point K, as shown in Figure 5.58.

If the measurements A H and E K are the same, your setting out is square.

If the measurements are not the same, the angles must then be checked for 90 degrees using a builder's square or the 3 : 4 : 5 method. Make the necessary changes and check diagonals again.

Competence Check

If the setting out is still not square, ask your tutor for assistance.

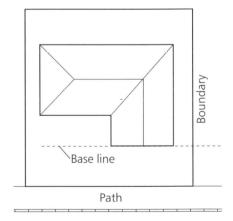

Base Line – The base line is set out on site from adjacent features such as boundaries, the centre of a road or kerb and is the front line of the building (see Figure 5.57).

Note: Do not confuse the base line with the building line.

Fig 5.57 **Base line**

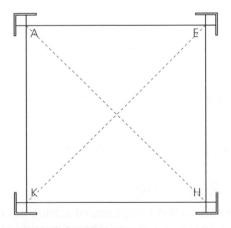

Fig 5.58 Diagonal method of checking a corner

Setting Out a Small Building 5.8

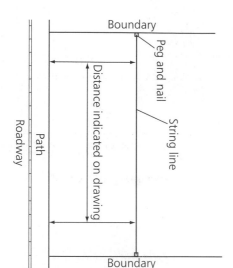

Fig 5.59 **Building line and boundaries of site**

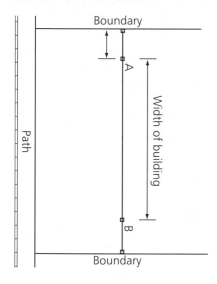

Fig 5.60 **Width of proposed building and boundary**

⟩ *Points to note* ⟩

For greater accuracy in setting out always use nails in the tops of pegs, to fix for example, the location of pegs A and B. Nails in the tops of pegs are also useful for holding the tape when checking dimensions.

When you have carried out this exercise you will be able to:

■ Position setting out lines to the building, frontage and right angles

■ Locate dimension positions

■ Check for square

■ Position ranging lines

■ Transfer datum points using a straight edge, spirit level and optical levels.

Equipment and Materials Required

30 m steel tape with 1 mm graduations

Ranging line

Timber pegs and profile boards

Builder's square

Straight edge

Spirit level

Optical level

Site square

Lump hammer and nails.

Method

Obtain a working drawing from your tutor. Refer to this drawing at all times, ensuring that you use the dimensions on it and no others. Do not use scaled measurements.

Determine the Building Line

Measure from any fixed point indicated on your drawing. The building line will be defined by the use of pegs with nails in the top and ranging line strung between them. Figure 5.59 shows the wooden pegs placed on the boundary of the site. This is an excellent place to afford protection to the pegs and to assist later when transferring the ranging lines to the profile boards.

Set Out External Corners

In order to set out the external front corners you will need to determine the measurement from one of the site boundaries. The boundaries will be shown on your working drawing usually on the block plan.

Method

Peg A is placed in position by measuring from the boundary of the site.

Peg B is placed in position by taking the width of the proposed building from the working drawing as shown in Figure 5.60.

Setting Out Right Angles

In the first part of this section you practised setting out right angles using the builder's square and an optical level. In this part of the section

290

you can choose either method for setting out. Figure 5.61 shows the working drawing with all four corners set out. Pegs A-B-C-D now establishes the corners of the building.

An alternative method of setting out right angles is to set out a right angle at point A and then complete the setting out by means of establishing parallel lines E-E and E-F, as shown in Figure 5.62.

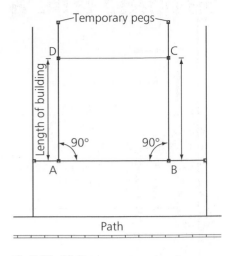

Fig 5.61 **All four corners set out**

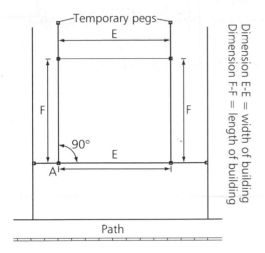

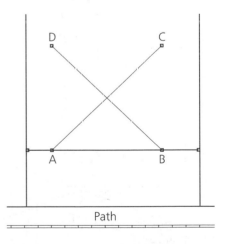

Fig 5.62 Setting out using parallel lines

Checking Diagonals

Before carrying out the operation of setting out the corners, check that your dimensions for width and length of the building are correct. Once you have done this you can check for squareness. To do this, measure the diagonals from A-C and B-D as shown in Figure 5.63. For the building to be square they should both be equal in length.

If the diagonal lengths are not the same, move pegs C and D the same distance parallel to the front line until the diagonals are equal. This task will be made easier if you use two tape measures.

Before going on to the next part of this setting out exercise make a final check on the overall dimensions.

Transferring Ranging Lines on to Profiles

The profile boards and pegs can now be erected in order to carry the ranging lines clear of the excavation. The profiles should be extended approximately 1 metre away from the excavation if you intend to hand dig them and some 5 m away if using a machine. Ensure you keep these distances the same for all four sides, as shown in Figure 5.64 this will assist you when you come to check the final dimensions.

The required setting out information, marked on each profile board is illustrated in Figure 5.65.

Fig 5.63 Checking of diagonals

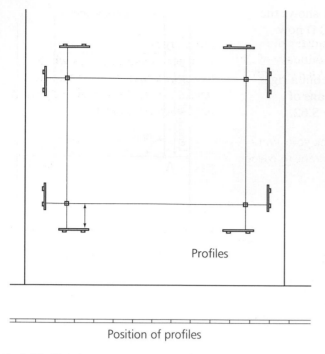

Profiles

Position of profiles

Fig 5.64 **Site showing layout of profile boards**

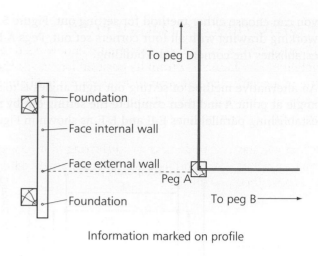

To peg D

Foundation

Face internal wall

Face external wall

Peg A

Foundation

To peg B →

Information marked on profile

Fig 5.65 **Profile board showing information markings**

Transferring External Dimensions

In order to transfer the external dimensions of the building from the pegs to the profiles, you must now extend the ranging lines through to the profile board and fix it on to a projecting nail as shown in Figure 5.66. The remainder of the marks on the profile board can be measured from the external wall of the building.

After setting out the external walls, profiles can now be erected for the internal walls by using a series of parallel lines from the original square. Excavation trenches can now be marked out by spray paint or a line of lime, sand or cement.

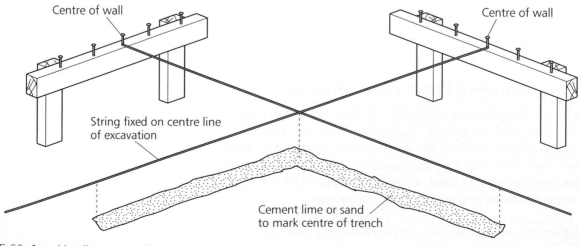

Centre of wall

Centre of wall

String fixed on centre line of excavation

Cement lime or sand to mark centre of trench

Fig 5.66 **Attaching lines to profiles**

Transferring the Datum Point

To complete the setting out operation you now need to transfer the height of the datum peg from its position just inside the boundary of the site to a position close to corner A, as shown in Figures 5.28 and 5.29. Carry out this task using a straight edge, spirit level and pegs as described previously.

When you have carried out the transferring of levels, check your work with an optical level and if correct transfer a new datum point to corner C as described previously.

> **Points to note** ⟩
>
> In order to reduce errors when using a straight edge and spirit level, reverse the straight edge and level each time of use.

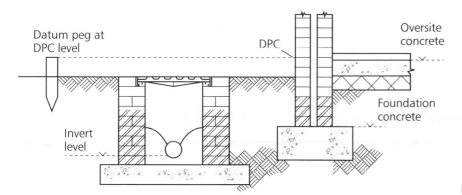

Fig 5.67 **Transfer of datum pegs**

Work-based Evidence Required

■ Setting out to contractors' working instructions

Set out to contractors' working instructions:

■ Regular shaped brick and block and/or vernacular style structures on level ground.

To meet this requirement, obtain a witness testimony sheet from your supervisor stating that you have set out to your supervisor's instructions a regular shaped brick and block structure.

When you have received the signed and dated witness testimony sheet from your supervisor, place them in your work-based evidence portfolio when next in college and map and record it against the syllabus.

Competence check
Inform your tutor when you have completed this setting out exercise and get him to assess it for competence.

Temporary Bench Marks (TBM) and Datum Points

5.9

When you have worked through this section, you will be able to:

■ Identify a temporary bench mark
■ Understand the purpose of a temporary bench mark
■ Understand the purpose of a datum.

TBM is the abbreviation for a temporary benchmark. A TBM is a known height point from which all other levels are taken.

The TBM can be related to an Ordnance Survey benchmark which is usually found on certain public buildings. On site the TBM can be surrounded by concrete for protection and a timber fence if additional protection is required, as shown in Figure 5.68. Identification of the TBM is often aided by painting it a bright colour.

All site levels are taken from the top of the TBM peg and, many other different site levels are related to the TBM.

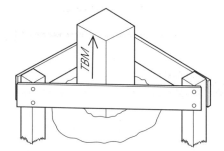

Fig 5.68 **TBM and protective fence**

Datum Points

A datum height is a level point established in relation to a TBM.

Datums are level reference points for various work activities, for example:

■ Damp proof courses
■ Invert levels
■ Oversite concrete
■ Foundations.

Site Datum

It is important to have a fixed point on site to which all other levels can be related. This is known as the site datum, it is located at a convenient height, usually damp proof course level. The datum itself must be related to some other fixed point, usually an ordnance survey benchmark, or some other clearly visible point such as a kerb edge or frame cover. Ordnance benchmarks are transferred to the site by means of a series of levels using an optical level and staff.

The site datum is marked by a peg or steel post, concreted into the ground to protect it and located at a convenient point, usually near the site office.

| Points to note | Ordnance Survey benchmarks (OBM) appear on numerous public buildings, usually incised into walls as shown in Figure 5.69.

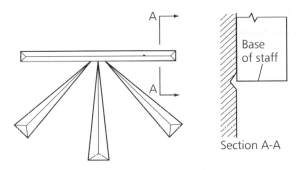

Ordnance Survey cut bench mark (OBM)

Fig 5.69 **OBM**

Work-based Evidence Required

■ **Interpretation of drawings, specifications, schedules, manufacturers' information, related to the work to be carried out**

To meet this requirement, obtain from your supervisor a witness testimony sheet stating that you have interpreted drawings, specifications and manufacturers information related to the work carried out.

When you have received the signed and dated witness testimony sheet from your supervisor, place it in your work-based evidence portfolio when next in college and map and record it against the syllabus.

Quick quiz Quick quiz Quick quiz Quick quiz Quick quiz

❶ List five types of information sources that may be used when planning work activities.

❷ On a scale drawing, if a written measurement differs from the scaled measurement, what action would you take?

❸ Briefly, explain what BS 1192 is.

❹ When using a scale of 1 : 20, what would a line drawn 150 mm represent?

❺ Why are graphical symbols used in drawings?

❻ What is a site datum?

❼ What do the abbreviations OBM and TBM stand for?

❽ What should you do once the datum peg has been positioned?

❾ How can levelling errors be minimized when transferring levels using a levelling board and spirit level?

❿ What does the term building line mean?

Information on Optical Levels

For more information about optical levels, why not contact the websites of the better known manufactuers and suppliers?

Information on Surveying Equipment

For more information about surveying equipment, why not visit the websites of the better known manufactuers and suppliers?.

Information on Construction Surveying

For more information on construction surveying, why not contact the websites of the better known manufactuers and suppliers? Or the following?

Ordnance Survey
www.ordnancesurvey.co.uk

Information on Optical Levels

For more information about optical levels, why not visit the websites of the better known manufactuers and suppliers?

Information on Building Control

For more information about building control, contact your local Town Hall, who will be happy to help you with your enquiries.

Information on the Setting Out of Buildings

For more information about the setting out of buildings why not visit the following websites.

CITB–ConstructionSkills
www.citb.co.uk

City and Guilds
www.city–and–guilds.co.uk

Information on Ordnance Survey Benchmarks

For more information about ordnance survey bench marks and datum points why not visit the following websites.

Ordnance Survey

www.ordnancesurvey.co.uk

Your local Building Control Department, the address of which will be in the phone book.

Information on Working Drawings

For more information about working drawings why not visit the following websites.

The Stationery Office

www.tso.co.uk

Ordnance Survey

www.ordnancesurvey.co.uk

As the national mapping agency, Ordnance Survey is responsible for the official surveying and topographic mapping of Great Britain. Ordnance Surveys customer information help line provides customers with details of products, services and general information related to mapping and the general environment.

Customer Information Help Line: 01703 792912.

Index